BRAVE THE WAVE

Discover and Fully Realize Your
Authentic Self

JOHNNY CAVAZOS MD

Contents

Introduction 1

Part I - It Starts with a Thought...9

  1 - We Think, We Become 11

  2 - A Spiritual Conviction.. 18

  3 - A Relationship of Riches.................................... 25

  4 - The Choice Is Personal.. 33

  5 - The Illusion of Easy 43

  6 - It Starts and Ends with Love 53

  7 - The Undeniable Prayer 60

  8 - An Embarrassment of Truth..................... 67

  9 - The Power of the Weird........................... 80

  10 - Near Death Can Bring New Life 91

  11 - A Spirit of Service.............................. 101

  12 - Making Your Life Fascinating........................ 108

Part II - What We Believe.. 119

  13 - The Bedrock of Belief...................................... 121

  14 - The Choice to Believe Is Ours 129

  15 - Chosen to Produce................................. 144

  16 - Apologize, Forgive, Love 151

  17 - The Path to the Well 165

  18 - When Everyone Loses........................... 180

  19 - The Hindrance of Guilt......................... 196

  20 - The Gift of Experience.......................... 208

Part III - E-valu-ate 217

  21 - Our Values, Our Vision...................... 219

  22 - Life's Biggest Obstacle........................... 233

  23 - Looking for WOTs............................... 243

24 - Climbing the Love Ladder...251

25 - Loving with Everything You Have...............................262

26 - Relationships over Opinions 278

27 - All Are Welcome..290

Part IV - Truth and Knowledge 299

28 - Roots of Truth...301

29 - Allowing an Experience 312

30 - The Will and the Word..319

31 - The Power of Obedience 330

32 - Experience Joy and Peace 339

33 -Personal Happiness...346

34 - The Power and Peace of Gratitude.....................................360

35 - Confidently Facing Goliath 373

Epilogue 384

Notes 388

INTRODUCTION

One hundred and thirty-four. That's how many ideas I came across that were unique to me before I wrote this book.

They're all in here.

Those ideas were the impetus for writing this book. Is there a possibility that you'll have heard of the majority of these? Absolutely. Is it possible you've been exposed to all of them? Less likely. When you look at reviews of nonfiction books, whenever there's a negative critique, a common word that's consistently used is "rehashing." People will criticize a book because the ideas it promotes are ones they've seen before.

In my decade-long research for this book, and in reading books on many topics, I've noticed how common it is to come across common ideas I'd seen or heard before. But by being patient, I found that there will also be unique or powerful ideas that are compelling, and that can change a person's life. Those are the ideas we're after.

Marketing guru Seth Godin and bestselling author Malcolm Gladwell both talk about the notion of ideas that spread and ideas that stick. When you reach for a book like this, it's usually to solve a problem or provide a solution to a crisis or to help you get through some issue or difficulty.

That's what happened to me.

Because of a series of repeated failures and missteps, I landed in a world of fear, frustration, and stress. This is where my own personal journey began. With a simple desire to learn how to deal and cope with anxiety, frustration, and the stress that comes with everyday life.

Two things happened that opened my eyes and changed my entire life for the better. First, Rick Warren's book *The Purpose Driven Life*. And second, I was introduced to near-death experiences through Howard Storm's book *My Descent into Death* and Dr. Kenneth Ring's book *Lessons from the Light*. This is where my journey began. It led to a decade-long search for purpose, truth, knowledge, and meaning. The best analogy is that it's like taking your car to a mechanic to replace a faulty fuel pump, and he hands you the keys to a new Mercedes Benz and says, "Take it, it's yours." (That's the way Elvis used to give away cars.)

But there's more value here than a new Mercedes.

From my own experience, it's very clear that when it comes to a change in personal behavior or some life-altering epiphany, there's an idea—or rather, a group of ideas—that will truly stick. They're kind of stuck in your head, and you can't seem to get them out, no matter how hard you try. Some are simple; some are more complex. What's interesting is that at first you don't know for certain if an idea you come across is going to grab you and not let go. You never really know which ideas will have the most impact.

A central idea that's a recurring theme in this book is simple and elementary, but it's also critical to understanding almost every other principle that's outlined here. It's the idea that no matter who you are, or how much money you make, or how smart you are, or what you believe, or what your race or ethnicity is—you're going to see trials, storms, and tribulations. They come like waves, one after another. Sometimes you can see them coming; sometimes you can't.

Picture yourself standing waist deep in ocean at the beach. The waves are coming one after another. Sometimes you get hit in the face, and you spit and choke on the salt water. Sometimes you turn and let the wave take you into shore. This book is like a boogie board. It will help you with the ideas and the confidence you need to brave the wave. Instead of looking at an oncoming wave as another trial or difficulty, we're going to learn to look at these troubles as opportunities for growth and for perseverance. They're the power and energy we need to get us through our daily lives.

This book will better prepare you to handle, understand, and grow from each wave. Remember, they keep coming no matter what, and we don't have the power to stop them. We may as well learn how to deal with them in a way that's practical and powerful.

By necessity, some of what you'll read in these pages is a description of what happened to me on my own particular ride. Or series of rides. From my own experience, I came to realize a kind of an enhanced vision. There was more clarity and understanding of why we're here and where our focus should be. It's like watching television in high-definition. You can see subtle details you couldn't see before on a tiny screen. The point is, they were already there.

I used to think I knew a lot about a variety of subjects. The thing that was the most startling and shocking to me was this:

I didn't know what I didn't know.

That's a common phrase that older people use when trying to put younger people in their place. "You don't know what you don't know."

I'm a physician with many and varied interests, and I'll never claim to be the smartest person in the room at a cocktail party. But I will bet money that I'm one of the most curious. One of the most shocking and life-changing ideas was the simple realization that I didn't know what I didn't know. I was looking for simple answers to help deal with stress and anxiety, and I ran across ideas that stuck. Those ideas led to many, many questions.

Ten years' worth of questions and answers. And those questions and answers led to the writing of this book.

This book is designed to open the mind and the "eyes of the heart." It's about reaching and fulfilling what we truly were meant to be. Our fully realized potential. Our authentic selves. If there's an authentic self, it stands to reason we may be pursuing a false self, a socially conditioned self.

If you're interested in taking this journey to authenticity, we should spend time preparing. We should begin by looking at where we are now.

Where are you?

If you're lost in the woods, you may want to look and see exactly where you are in order to figure out where you're going. Sometimes it helps to climb a big tree for a better view. Examining how we think, what we value, and what we believe at this moment in time helps us get a clear idea of where we are. Looking at ourselves closely helps us figure out if we're wasting time, energy, or effort on activities with very little value.

That was me. That's one of the most important things I came to realize and understand. Blown time, energy, and money. All wasted. *I didn't know what I didn't know.*

When you go on a journey, you take a backpack because you may need supplies. Sometimes that backpack is filled with things that hinder you, that slow you down as you go along. Some examples might be anxiety, low self-esteem, frustration, or anger and bitterness due to past hurts. And fear—that's a huge weight. Everyone's walking around with extra weight or unneeded baggage. This book will help you to lighten the load. We'll observe our past interactions with others to see if those relationships are having an impact that's weighing you down. You may not even be aware of them.

This book will help you get rid of some of the baggage that's just dead weight on your journey.

If you want to come along, we're probably going to need some supplies to ensure our survival. Real spiritual growth or maturation takes time. The needed supplies include confidence, guidance, love, spiritual vision, energy, and a sense of value and purpose. All these things are available to every single one of us as we strive to reach our individual potential. The most eye-opening and stunning revelation for me was that these assets are *always* available. They're already there for our use. Sometimes we just can't see them. *I couldn't see the obvious.*

Most adults value family life as one of the most important things in their lives. That attitude is helpful as we go along. Anyone who's interested in being a better husband, wife, sibling, child, parent, boss, or employee will benefit from this book. Relationships will be emphasized because the interactions we have as human beings are essential to our own sense of well-being and to our growth. Plus, relationships are essential in helping to elucidate and develop our unique authenticity.

I'm not a writer, pastor, or theologian. I'm more of a satisfied customer and an expert on one thing only: my own experience.

This book is about experience. One important truth is that *experience matters.* Experience makes a huge difference. Bought this car. Used this carpet cleaner. It's like telling others about a restaurant where you've really enjoyed the food and the ambiance. I'm not saying I'm better or smarter; I just want someone else to taste the great food I've tasted.

It's the same thing when you go on vacation. You went on an awesome cruise and visited cool Caribbean islands with beautiful, crystal clear water. First thing you do is tell your family and friends. "You should try this cruise! It's awesome." You just want to share something that would be beneficial to anyone or everyone. You share because you care. An honest testimony. You truly and genuinely want someone else to have the same experience.

That's exactly what I want. I want you to have the same *experience*. This book is about better relationships and unique experiences. It's about vision and clarity. It's about recognizing and fully realizing our authentic selves.

A Hall of Fame football player once said: "If you're the same person you were ten years ago, congratulations—you've just wasted the last ten years of your life." The way I think and what I believe and what I value are now totally different from what they were ten years ago. I've come to experience a peace, excitement, joy, love, confidence, and a sense of purpose that I'd never known before. There's no doubt in my mind that it's available to everyone. No matter where you are on your own path to discovering your authentic self, there's always room for growth. It's exhilarating, fulfilling, wonderful, and captivating, all at the same time. Personal, practical, powerful. That's the focus you'll see as you read on.

About seven years ago, I walked into a patient's room and saw a woman in her mid-fifties neatly dressed with her hair in a bun. She seemed upset about something more than her current illness. Tears rolled down her face.

I asked what was wrong. She told me she'd lost her husband about three months prior, and that she herself was given a diagnosis of cancer within the last two weeks. She was told there wasn't much anyone could do for her as far as treatment, and she probably had two to three months to live.

Normally, because of my feeling uncomfortable in such a conversation, I would have responded quickly, "I'm sorry to hear that. I'll be back in a minute." But this time, bending down, I put my arms around her and let her cry. She was sobbing and shaking for at least five minutes.

"It's okay, I'm here." That's all I said. That was all she needed. Not some scientific explanation or some complicated medical intervention or some cold, heartless test result. She needed love and someone to listen to her. Someone to comfort her.

That kind of interaction is exactly why we're on this planet. It's the crux of the matter. *That* is what we're here for.

I experienced feelings of fulfillment in that moment, but at the same time I felt distraught and empty because I wondered: How many opportunities like this to show love had I blown in the past twenty years?

Nothing can be done about the last twenty years, but something can be done about the next twenty. We can do a great deal to change our lives in the decades to come. That's the good news. We only have one life, but we can make changes right now that will have a major impact on those around us. We can make changes that lead to fulfillment and peace. Life becomes exciting, exhilarating, and fulfilling when we we're open to love, vision, and clarity. There's always something to do, learn, or try.

The truth is that we can see things we've never seen before. We can hear things we've never heard before. We can actually feel things we've never felt before.

I'm an expert on one thing: my own experience. I'm also an expert on the things that have been revealed to me. My experience with that one patient was eye-opening; you'll read about many more such experiences in this book.

This book is written and dedicated to one person: whoever wants to be in a different place from where they are now. The person who feels there's no light at the end of the tunnel. The one who's craving and thirsting for love, and not finding it in any relationships. The one who yearns for meaning, who feels an emptiness or drudgery in life. The one who's tired and has no energy, who struggles just to get up every morning. The one who feels like he's in a zombie walk, living through an episode of *The Walking Dead*. The one who feels cheated, resentful, or angry at people who've hurt her in the past. The one who feels helpless or hopeless to change his life for the better. The one who feels down about who she is.

This book can help anyone and everyone.

This is about sharing. This is a testimony about the great restaurant, the all-inclusive resort. The wonderful beach with sand like sugar and crystal clear blue water.

This is part of my own growth—and I hope and pray it will be a part of yours.

PART I - IT STARTS WITH A THOUGHT

1 - WE THINK, WE BECOME

E ven before my truck had come to a complete stop in the doctors' parking lot, the call rang out: "Code blue to ICU, code blue to ICU." It was easy to hear because my truck was only thirty feet from the ICU entrance.

"Looks like that's me," I thought. It was still dark outside. I hadn't even had a cup of coffee yet.

Walking quickly through the doors, I noticed the registration clerk behind the desk pointing to a room just inside the entrance. I got to the room and could see the patient lying on the floor with at least four nurses hovering around her. We struggled to get her up quickly to the bed while checking for a pulse and breathing. We started CPR, and the nurses began pulling out medications from our crash cart. We gave her a couple of rounds of medications to get her heart restarted, and we got a pulse and blood pressure back. Whew! She was lucky there were people around to start the resuscitation quickly.

As I was throwing my gloves into the trash can, I told the nurses, "Great job guys! You better get a chest CT. Bet you a hundred bucks she has a pulmonary embolism"—which is a blood clot in the lung. I spoke those words while walking out, strutting like a peacock, full of myself. Stupid me. I had no idea that this was the start of a new chapter in my life. Really it wasn't a new chapter; it was a whole new book. A very exciting one, and a very painful one.

Who are you? Who do you *think* you are?

What do you think about most?

We might want to quote the philosopher Rene Descartes: "I think, therefore I am." If it's more "I think, therefore I *become*," we're in business.

This book is about discovering our authentic selves. The self we were created to be. We begin by looking closely at where we are now. We look closely at our thoughts, our habits, and our values.

Most of us live in a world of busy-think. Errands to do. Tasks to complete. Bills to pay. Activities you need to be involved in. Noisy think. To-do thinking. We probably spend most of our time on that kind of thinking.

As we begin this journey, the practice of examining your thoughts and what dominates your thinking gives you a good idea of what's important to you. One goal of the early part of this book is to examine how we think and what we think about most.

Remember, this book is about discovering, developing, and fully realizing our authentic selves. Who we were created to be. I recently heard someone make this comment: "The self is not something you find, it's something you create." If that's true, it must also be true that we can create or build a false or inauthentic self totally influenced by our society or those around us.

Who decides who *you* were created to be? How you answer that question will have a major impact on your life and your eternity. How you think influences the process of discovering and realizing the authentic self. How you think about your relationships has a role to play in developing our authentic selves. We'll address relationships repeatedly, because not only are they important in themselves, but they also help us grow spiritually. They help us open our hearts.

Most people seeking to grow or looking for spiritual guidance have a specific need. It's hard to focus on the purpose of life when you're depressed. It's hard to focus on "Who am I?" when you're miserable in your marriage. It's very difficult to ask yourself, "Why am I here?" when you can't stand your job and you dread going to work.

I've been there. It's hard to look at the big picture if you're carrying around resentment, bitterness, or anger because of things people said or did to you in the past. Fear or anxiety may interfere with enjoying your life because you feel paralyzed. You may have questions that are spiritual in nature, and you want answers.

My journey started with fear, frustration, misery, and stress. I began to listen to tapes on meditation and tapes by Wayne Dyer on "The Power of Intention." I had no interest in spiritual growth or getting stronger in faith; I just needed a strategy to deal with my anxiety, and I just wanted to be happy. A game plan. That's all I was looking for. There were no big picture questions. There was no concern about asking what was important and what wasn't.

My own vision or idea of my authentic self was already decided by my choices. Or so I thought. The tapes were helping a little, but some of the ideas and suggestions seemed kind of made up. I was hearing things that didn't quite click or make sense to me.

After reading Rick Warren's book *The Purpose Driven Life*, I began to look at things differently. That began a ten-year journey of study and research and asking many questions. Reading and listening to speakers and searching began to change how I think.

What I've learned and come to know has impacted my relationships with my wife and children, family and friends, coworkers and business associates. It has opened a world that was already there. I just couldn't see it. In addition, I began to discover what I didn't know.

You may be having difficulty with fear and anxiety. You may feel empty or hopeless. You may not feel fulfilled, contented, or at peace. You may be having difficulty in your home with a parent or child or spouse. You may be having a tough time at work with a boss or coworker. If you can come along on this journey, you'll find answers. You'll begin to see and think about your relationships in a different way. You'll see improvement in your own home life and work life.

Once you begin to see more clearly, you'll learn which questions are the most important to find answers for, and which questions mean nothing. Sometimes we're asking the wrong questions, not the important ones. The reason they call them *important* is—well, they're important. A decade ago, those questions weren't important to me.

As I mentioned earlier, I'm not a philosopher or a biblical theologian or scholar, but I'm an expert on my own experience. We all are. All I know is that I've come to think totally differently about everything around me.

How you think influences and has an impact on everything around you. Sometimes we can be going down a path and not even understand what we're pursuing. How I think has had an impact on my marriage and made me a better husband. Not a perfect husband, but a better husband. It has had an impact on my work and how I think about it and the role work plays in my life. It has changed the way I think about being a parent, and has made me better at it. Not a perfect parent, but a better parent.

Coming to the knowledge of the truth changed the way I think about everything and has made a drastic difference in my values, my beliefs, my habits, and how I view this life and the next. As I discovered a clearer vision of my authentic self, my own goals became more easily discernible. I was discovering answers to life's biggest and most important questions—though I hadn't even been asking the questions. It's like the old Rolling Stones song, "You Can't Always Get What You Want." That's okay. Just focus on the need right now, whatever your personal need may be. This is a personal journey. It's specific to you *at this time* in your life. It's practical too. You can learn things you can use today, tomorrow, and for the rest of your life. Personal and practical.

If we stop to examine our thoughts and our mindset right now, we may be in survival mode: go to work, pay the bills. If you're a student, you're trying to get a degree or learn a trade so you can go to work, pay your bills. If you're married and have children, you go to work, pay your bills, and take your kids to their various activities—school, sports, music, dance, social, and the rest.

You're in survival mode. Life's coming at you wave after wave. We're going to look at waves differently as we go along. We can either cower in fear, or we can grab our boogie board and get ready for our ride. If you're in survival mode, you're kind of standing in the ocean up to your waist and taking every wave in the face. Sometimes you get a mouthful of salt water, and you cough and spit. You're taking life straight on, wave after wave, one problem after another. Spending your energy and determination just trying to keep standing. Does that sound familiar?

In this book, you'll see the following idea again and again (I repeat it for a reason): *No matter who you are, what you believe, how much money you make, how smart you are, or what you think you know—there will be waves, storms, trials, and troubles.*

While working on discovering our authentic selves, we're going to learn how to "brave the wave." If you say you haven't had any storms or troubles, we both know you're lying. Simple. You *will* encounter waves. If you aren't waiting to take the next wave in the face, you may be mindlessly pursuing things because you think they'll make you happy. I was doing that. *If I get this promotion, if I get this raise, I'll be happy.* Arms outstretched, grasping at air. Zombie mode. I was just surviving, taking waves in my face, sometimes walking like a zombie pursuing things that were a waste of precious time.

Here's where we introduce observation. Start honing your skills of observation. These will be important, because you need them to examine your own behavior. Is anyone around you pursuing activities that seem to be mindless? What about you?

There's a way to live that's more interesting, rewarding, exciting, and fulfilling. What I learned is that most of my frustration and fears and anxiety were due to my own way of thinking.

Most Americans are unhappy in their job. A survey reported by the national media found that "only forty-five percent of Americans are satisfied with their work"; for the research group, this represented "the lowest level ever recorded...in more than twenty-two years of studying the issue."[1]

Like "Lookin' for Love" in the Waylon Jennings song, we're looking for happiness in our pursuits. We may be chasing it and not getting the things *we think* will make us happy. Is it possible that therein lies one of our biggest problems? We may be angry and frustrated because we're not getting the things we expect at work or at home or in our relationships. Unmet expectations always lead to frustration and anger.

We should think differently. The only way to change the way we think is by coming to the knowledge of the truth.

Remember that ICU story I started telling you? Well, one of the nurses found me later to say, "You were right, doc; it was a pulmonary embolus." That was like the kiss of death for a prideful doc. Pride. *I was right.*

Well, over the next six weeks, I was never more wrong. Ever. I experienced a series of failures, slip-ups, and mistakes that reduced me to a big, soft, spineless ball of jelly. That was the beginning of my journey.

Next time you feel like tooting your own horn, put your lips together and make a fart sound.

2 -A Spiritual Conviction

Some of the frustration and anxiety we experience probably comes down to immature thinking. One basic idea that helped open my eyes is that looking to the world or to other people as a means or vehicle to happiness is a mistake. This is a difficult idea for some people to really grasp and get their minds around.

We're here for a reason. There's a purpose and a plan for every person on this planet. This is an important concept that we should all fully understand and embrace. You are a unique individual with unique gifts and talents. You have unique passions and a unique personality.

One of my favorite things to hear is when my kids or my wife tell me, "You're weird." I say, "Exactly right! You're finally beginning to understand!" Celebrate weird. Embrace your weirdness. Let's not ever be ashamed of who we are as unique individuals. *Weird* is defined as "unusual, otherworldly, supernatural, or mysterious." When we discuss near-death experiences (NDEs), you'll begin to realize that we all have an unusual, otherworldly, or supernatural component to who we are. Everyone. It's the essence of our authenticity. We'll get to the supernatural and the otherworldly later, but that's a compliment.

I already knew I was different. In medical school, we were offered free tickets to the ballet or the opera on the weekends to help us become more "cultural." I always thought, "Ballet? Opera? Where are the tickets for AC/DC or Tom Petty? That's culture, isn't it?" Looking at my own unique passions and gifts helped me realize that I wasn't living my own life to the fullest. Yeah, I got this medicine gig, but was there something else I should be considering?

Take some time to think about what you're most passionate about. Your passions are a gift from God.

We should remember that we're not defined by our work. It's something we do, but it doesn't define us. We're way more than our work.

As I was going through this exploration of purpose and meaning and looking at my own life, I stumbled onto the phenomenon of near-death experiences. I believe there's real value in studying these experiences and looking at what they can teach us.

As I grew spiritually, the study of NDEs reinforced what I was learning about our purpose in this life. They complemented each other. Looking at these experiences and understanding them has changed my life regarding how I see relationships. They've also brought the importance of relationships to the prominence they deserve. Wife and children, parents and siblings, friends and coworkers. All for the better.

As we go along, you'll see multiple references to NDEs in this book because they offer strong and powerful support and reinforce the principles I'm emphasizing. I'll selfishly admit that they're fascinating to me, but that doesn't negate the value of what they can teach us. There's true power that can help us strengthen our convictions.

A conviction is a belief, thought, or idea so strong that we're willing to live for it and to die for it. That's how we grow and learn to think differently.

Stop and consider that for a minute. Who or what are you willing to live for or die for? The patriots in the Revolutionary War were willing to die for freedom. The soldiers serving in our military are willing to die to protect and preserve that freedom. If we don't serve in the military or on a police force or in a fire department, there aren't many opportunities to put our convictions to the test when it comes to dying. But we can look closely at our own convictions. What are we willing to live for?

Some people have a conviction to get rich. The rapper known as 50 Cent had an album titled *Get Rich or Die Tryin'*. That's just an example of how much of a role money plays in our culture. Music, movies, television advertising, social media. How many people around you can you see living for that conviction? It's not difficult to see. This isn't judging, it's an observation. There are many people focused on materialism and on getting more money.

One little tidbit as we go along. Some of the principles we'll be going over have a unique side effect of opening our eyes and increasing our vision not only of our own behavior, which is what we're after, but also of other people's behavior. As I've learned more, and as I began to think differently, I could see more.

Resist the urge to point fingers and judge others around you. Make observations and mental notes, but don't judge. Our goal is to see our own behavior in an honest way. Remember, we're after authenticity. Our authentic selves. One important point is that no one gave me the authority to judge anyone. No one is in the judging business, unless you work in a court of law.

Another conviction we can have is to live for our families and make sure they're taken care of. We can make family and friends the thing we're most willing to live for and to die for. That's a good and valuable conviction. It's also the laboratory or classroom where much of the change in our thinking will come from—our relationships with others.

Some of us make a worthy cause a conviction we're willing to live or die for. Social causes or protecting the rights of people who can't speak for themselves. Those are worthwhile convictions.

Some of us think that our work, or our vocation, is our most important conviction. We live and breathe what we do in our jobs, and we see our work as the most valuable conviction in our lives.

There are no right or wrong answers here. The whole idea is an examination of the self. What's most important to you? What do you think about most? What are you willing to live for?

The most interesting and profound impact on my own way of thinking came about because I was discovering the phenomenon of near-death experiences while I was beginning to change the way I thought about my own faith. These basic principles of faith—looking at purpose and at what was the most important and valuable pursuit in life—were all pointing in the same direction.

I had a basic belief in the principles of Christianity, but I was more of a casual believer. My life was compartmentalized. Jesus was meant for Sundays, and for once a week asking for something in prayer while lying in bed. I wasn't even going to church services. The turning point came when I encountered an idea that stuck in my mind. There's the example of an idea that sticks; it's almost like when you're walking around with a small pebble in your shoe. This wasn't a pebble, it was a boulder. It's hard to walk around with a rock in your shoe. It's always there. You can't ignore it.

This idea came while I was reading a passage described in Raymond Moody's book *Life after Life,* where he documents how one person describes a near-death experience:

> I began to feel a sort of drifting, a movement of my real being in and out of my body, and to hear beautiful music. I floated on down the hall and out the door onto the screened-in porch. There, it almost seemed that clouds, a pink mist really, began to gather around me, and then I floated right straight on through the screen, just as though it weren't there, and up into this pure crystal-clear

light, an illuminating white light. It was so beautiful and so bright and so radiant, but it didn't hurt my eyes. It's not any kind of light you can describe on earth. I didn't actually see a person in this light, and yet it has a special identity, it definitely does. It's a light of perfect understanding and perfect love. Then the thought came to my mind, "Lovest thou me?"[2]

This account touches on many ideas I'll address in further chapters, but what I want to address here is that paragraph's closing question: *Do you love me?* This had a profound impact on me, because in Rick Warren's book *The Purpose Driven Life* I was reading how learning to love God and Jesus was one of the most important things we can do with our lives. The books I was reading on NDEs were more scientific and were making scientific observations about hundreds of NDEs. They didn't spend much time on spiritual issues. From one point of view, I was reading about people who, after death, had an encounter with a loving being whose first question to them was *Do you love me?*

At the exact same time, I was starting to read the Bible, and I was running across verses like this one:

> Yes, a person is a fool to store up earthly wealth but not have a rich relationship with God. (Luke 12:21 NLT)

Whoa there, Nelly. Those words were like a punch in the gut that knocked the wind out of me. Rich relationship *with God? Rich* relationship? That phrase became a broken record in my head, repeating over and over. I knew I didn't have that relationship. Jesus was only an acquaintance. Like the guy you see at the convenience store where you get a morning coffee, soda, or breakfast taco. You say "Hi" to him every morning. You're nice, cordial, and friendly. But do you know if the guy's married? Do you know if he has kids? Do you go to lunch with him? For me it was no, no, and no way.

Also I noticed how earthly wealth and "fool" were linked in that verse. That was me. I was the fool. I was collecting "things." Objects. I can see now that they had no real value. None. I started to think of things in terms of the "time machine test." If I'm going to buy something, I put it into a time machine and fast-forward twenty years. Most everything becomes junk. Really want that new laptop? Fast-forward twenty years. Junk. Really want that nice car? Fast-forward thirty years. Junk. Someone may say, "Doesn't my jewelry keep its value"? Okay, you buy that diamond necklace. Now flash forward two hundred years. Is there a huge demand right now for jewelry from the early 1800s?

What was really sobering to me was that I knew down to my bones that I didn't have a rich relationship with God. But the NDEs were talking about it, and looking at my purpose was pointing to the value of a relationship with Jesus, and the Bible was definitely emphasizing it. Those three lines of clear evidence were really starting to open my eyes. I started to think about my relationship with Jesus. What would I say, after I died, if a being clothed in light asked me, "Do you love me?" How would I respond?

How would *you* respond?

Did I have a rich relationship with God or Jesus? Did I love them?

I want to digress for a moment, because there'll always be skeptics and critics in this world who'll argue that maybe the near-death experience is a dream or altered level of consciousness. They'll also argue that the Bible is unreliable and full of discrepancies and inaccuracies. That's all okay. We have a brain for a reason, and I myself come from a medical background. We don't do anything in medicine until we have real proof.

All I can attest to is that I've done the hard work of reading and studying and researching both NDEs and the Bible. As I've mentioned, I'm not a biblical scholar. I'm also not an expert on the phenomenon of NDEs, nor have I had one. I'll argue that you don't have to die to get the benefits of NDEs. I myself am very satisfied with the validity of both the Bible and NDEs. What I'm arguing is that both are extremely useful in helping us grow spiritually. They can impact our lives in a tremendously positive way. They can help us reach the goal of what this book is about. Discovering and fully realizing our authentic selves. Getting us in position to brave the next wave for the ride of our life.

My own conviction is that it's obvious the Bible is primarily the Word of God. And NDEs help as an adjunct in our study and in our growth. I'm satisfied that both those sources are valid and both have tremendous value. The Bible especially is the kind of authority that invites study and effort to investigate its validity. It's okay to be skeptical and critical of the Bible and of the phenomenon of NDEs. It can be a good approach to be skeptical of people (even me) whose ideas or promises may seem exaggerated to you. I invite everyone to explore all the references I cite. They're fascinating reading. All skeptics and critics should invest the necessary time to investigate the Bible and NDEs. If done properly, it will take years. It has taken me about ten years so far, and I've just barely scratched the surface. Still got a long way to go.

The good news about the good news is that if you want to learn about it, there are probably millions of books and articles to explore. There are many books, articles, and websites to explore on NDEs. I'm fully satisfied regarding the validity of NDEs, and I'm fully convinced of the foundational truth of the Bible.

Knowledge and study are part of this journey. Like I tell my kids, there's no downside to acquiring knowledge or spending time in study. Knowledge is power. Knowledge is useful.

3 - A RELATIONSHIP OF RICHES

What does it mean to have a rich relationship with God? Jesus said we're fools to store up earthly wealth and not have a rich relationship with God.

How much time are we spending pursuing earthly wealth? When is enough going to be enough?

The value of that rich relationship with God and Jesus had never been a concern to me. As I think about it now, it kind of makes sense to me why I didn't value that type of a relationship. What I came to understand was that there was a barrier to recognizing the value of that relationship. Was it belief? No. Was it fear? No.

It was need.

Actually, for me it wasn't just need; it was also ignorance. I think that's what hinders many people from recognizing the value of a rich relationship with God and Jesus. They can't see the value or the need. That was me. Tons of knowledge, but I didn't know what I didn't know. Knowledge of the truth was lacking. I didn't know, see, or understand the underlying value of such a relationship. I didn't start looking at these issues until I was having difficulty with fear, frustration, and anxiety. I was looking for answers on how to deal with those issues. Instead, I began to see that I didn't have a rich relationship with Jesus.

As I started to delve deeper into the phenomenon of NDEs, I started to notice that the things shown to have the most value in those experiences were things I didn't spend much time on.

In his book (4) *Life after Life*, Dr. Raymond Moody reports this:

Some of those I interviewed claim that, while they cannot adequately explain it, everything they had ever done was there in this review (what has been described as a life review), from the most insignificant to the most meaningful. Others explain that what they saw were mainly highlights of their lives. Some people characterize this as an educational effort on the part of the being of light. As they witness the display (of their life review), the beings seem to stress the importance of two things in life: learning to love other people and acquiring knowledge.[3]

This was consistent with what I was learning about our unique purpose in this life based on our gifts and talents. What those talents are and how they're to be used.

The teachings of Jesus were saying essentially the exact same thing:

As the Father has loved me, so have I loved you. Now remain in my love. If you keep my commands, you will remain in my love, just as I have kept my Father's commands and remain in his love. I have told you this so that my joy may be in you and that your joy may be complete. My command is this: Love each other as I have loved you. (John 15:9-12 NLT)

The reality is that we're on this planet to learn to love others. Another common question people report being asked by the "being of light" was this: "What do you have to show me that you've done with your life?" In *Lessons from the Light*, Dr. Kenneth Ring writes,

The Light seems to be telling us, each of us, that we have a unique gift, an offering to make to the world, and that our happiness and the world's are both served when we live in such a way as to realize that gift, which is no less than our purpose in life.[4]

Boom. There it is. *"Our* happiness and the *world's* are both served."

Those are the ideas I began to think about most: Did I love God or Jesus? Was I learning to love others? What have I done with this life?

The way you look at those questions, and how much you value the answers, will determine how you plan to live your life. These are the most important questions to ask and answer. Those answers determine where you spend eternity and what you do in eternity.

I became consumed with those questions. How would I answer them—both now and when I finally stood before God? How would *you* answer those questions? Our answers will shape the process of discovering and fully realizing our authentic selves. We know the test questions. They've been revealed to us.

As I was studying many books on NDEs, there was one that described a unique and unusual experience. In an interview about his book *My Descent into Death: A Second Chance at Life,* author Howard Storm[5] describes where he's sitting down in his NDE and talking to Jesus. He'd already been in a dark and disturbing place. Jesus reached down and rescued him from that harrowing and terrifying experience. Howard's NDE is one of the most graphic descriptions of a hellish NDE that you'll find. Howard's NDE is unique because it goes far deeper and is more involved than what many people have described.

In his interview, Howard tells us that he asked Jesus, "Why are we here? Why did you create us?" And Jesus answered that the world is like God's garden, where God made everyone to bloom and to be beautiful—with each person unique and special, to be beautiful in their own way.

Now stop and read that again. This book is about discovering and fully realizing our unique and authentic selves.

In all this searching and learning, I kept running across Bible verses that reinforced what these experiences were telling or revealing to *us*, not just me. Like these words from Jesus:

> Not everyone who calls out to me, "Lord! Lord!" will enter the Kingdom of Heaven. Only those who actually do the will of my Father in heaven will enter. On judgment day, many will say to me, "Lord! Lord! We prophesied in your name and cast out demons in your name and performed many miracles in your name." But I will reply, "I never knew you. Get away from me, you who break God's laws." (Matthew 7:21-23 NLT)

I like this translation because it doesn't really sugar-coat anything. The phrase "I never knew you" really made me stop and think. So did my sense that it's like Jesus doesn't want us around him if we break God's laws. We'll discuss that in coming chapters, but from this verse there's clear value in knowing Jesus. There's a difference between knowing *about* Jesus and *knowing Jesus*. I didn't really know him. Kind of like a salesperson at a store, or the person who cuts your hair. We can all pray to God and Jesus, but can we say we love them the way we love a wife or husband or our own children? That wasn't me. Learning to love others wasn't high on my list of things to do. Discovering my authentic self and my purpose were not high priorities.

Looking for answers to help with fear, anxiety, and frustration began to reveal questions that were clearly more important. Where does my authentic self lie? Am I fulfilling the purpose God has in mind for me? Am I spending time and effort learning to love? Is my relationship with Jesus high on my priority list? The hard questions require a hard look at ourselves. That's what this whole book is about.

One of the mirrors we can use to look at ourselves is the Bible:

> But don't just listen to God's word. You must do what it says. Otherwise, you are only fooling yourselves. For if you listen to the word and don't obey, it is like glancing at your face in a mirror. You see yourself, walk away, and forget what you look like. But if you look carefully into the perfect law that sets you free, and if you do what it says and don't forget what you heard, then God will bless you for doing it. (James 1:22-25 NLT)

Being willing to look at our own flaws and imperfections and being willing to learn and be humble will help change your life.

But honestly, nothing changes until we can accept responsibility for our own behavior. You can see people around you who have a total lack of self-awareness. Unwilling to see their own behavior and too immature to accept that they can improve. Observing people is helpful because we can learn from their behavior. There are plenty of examples of people who say or do things that are so outside the norm, it's shocking. We can see politicians and celebrities act in this way. There's a category for them. Jaw-droppers. There's nothing we can do but drop our jaws at their behavior.

Sometimes we ourselves may have acted like a jaw-dropper. Can you think of times when you did? Hopefully there aren't many. We'll get to that a little later.

In my own experience, and from observing people around me, there's no improvement or change for the better until we can look directly in the mirror and take responsibility for our behavior. We want to avoid being in the jaw-dropper category. Sometimes it's tough, but it's worth it. That's why there are so many critics, bullies, and body-shamers on the internet. It's much easier to point out flaws in others than ourselves. We can see the propensity in our society and culture to blame and criticize others for our problems or our mistakes. That's what five-year-olds do. "You made me do it!" It takes maturity to look at ourselves and find things we can improve. When we can do that, we grow closer to our authentic selves.

As we go over how we think, there are specific needs we may have as we come to this journey. That's important, because we all have a backpack with us, and we each must figure out what we're bringing on this road trip. You may be bringing three or four bags of anger, resentment, or bitterness because of past hurts. You may have a box or two of marriage or relational problems. You may be carrying a carton or two of fear, anxiety, and frustration. You may have a case of habits that are self-destructive like alcohol or drug abuse or an addiction to pornography.

Some backpacks are heavier than others. Everyone has a backpack though. Hopefully that backpack may get lighter as we move along.

Just a little warning. The road isn't easy, and it's a long one. The only guarantee is that the journey is worth it because of the profound impact it can have on this life and the next. Plus, we benefit—and everyone around us benefits—in a powerful and positive way.

The more we know and understand about the truth, the less fear, frustration, and anxiety we'll feel. For me personally, there was one question that was always in the back of my mind. Why didn't anyone point all these things out to me before? These important principles and ideas seemed to be hidden, or at the very least, not emphasized. Why? High school, college, medical school: no one talked about loving others much. Or if they did, why didn't that message hit home?

There wasn't any instruction in medical school about how sometimes a person who's dying, or their family member, just needs a touch on the shoulder, or a warm, caring hug. Sometimes that's more important than knowledge or skill. Not one lecture on that. I learned that lesson on my own much later in my career.

Why didn't anyone tell me that the Bible was the most important way that God spoke to me? For sure there was no emphasis on Bible reading in my home. Why didn't anyone tell me that the best way to get to know and love Jesus was in prayer and reading the Bible? Again, if that was taught, why didn't the message have an impact on me?

Honestly my memory is good, and I can remember rules and principles and regulations being pounded into my head when it came to faith. What other ideas and important principles was I missing out on? I knew I believed in Jesus and in God, but I came to realize that I wasn't paying any attention to what Jesus and God were saying because I wasn't reading the Bible. I felt stupid. I believed God was all-knowing and all-powerful, but I'd chosen to ignore him on some of the most important decisions of my life.

Faith and church services were compartmentalized for Sunday. I wasn't even going to church services. It was kind of over here in a box. It was also kind of like a law, and there was more emphasis on the consequences of missing church. Rules, laws, and regulations—but no emphasis on Bible reading. No emphasis on knowing and loving Jesus. The Bible was just more rules and regulations.

I'm kind of embarrassed to admit that I went decades without reading the Bible, but I know now that I was a member of the majority. We know from survey statistics that the majority of believers in this country don't spend much time reading the Bible.[6] Three out of four people in this country don't read the Bible regularly. I'm not surprised by that number. That was me. But I came to realize that the Bible is the main vehicle God uses, among many others, to speak to us. Jesus wants us to get to know him. Spending time with Jesus in prayer and in Bible reading and meditation is the primary way. When this idea became crystal clear in my mind and heart, I began to take my spiritual growth seriously.

Here's an illustration of the principle of a rich relationship. Let's go back in time to your junior high or high school days. Remember when you had a crush on a girl or a boy? You thought about that person all the time. He or she liked you. Everything was clicking. You were holding hands going to class. Oh, how sweet. You were spending time together after school. You were in the bliss of a crush. You got closer and closer.

If you're a guy, you thought about her all the time. You were at a movie and now dropping her off from a date, and there you are; you want a kiss. Get ready, hot lips. You go in with both lips blazing. But wait, here it comes. She says, "Hold on, I have to get to know you better." Waa, waa. The Debbie Downer sound. But you don't give up. You have a crush. So you spend time with this person, while your lips cool down. You talk on the phone. You get to know each other, and each other's cute little habits (which will turn into those annoying big habits after you're married).

It's the same thing with Jesus. We spend *time* with him. We spend time reading the Bible. We spend time in prayer, and we listen for the voice of the Holy Spirit and of Jesus. We read what he has spoken to us. As we read the Bible, it begins to come alive. When we read what Jesus says, his personality comes through. We begin to know how he thinks. We begin to see what he values and what he thinks is important.

We get to *know* him.

4 - THE CHOICE IS PERSONAL

One principle that really opened my eyes in all this study and learning was the idea of choice and free will. How we think about our own choices will help us grow in our relationship with Jesus and with each other. It's our choice. We're as close to Jesus as we choose to be. In my humble, non-biblical-scholar opinion, going to heaven is our choice.

How do I know this? Well, if we think about hell in terms of defining it, it means total separation from God, because we chose to reject Jesus in this life. That's a simple definition. If it's true, the opposite must be true. If we choose to accept and believe Jesus, and learn to love Jesus with everything we have, then that by itself is the definition of heaven. If hell is total separation from God, heaven must be a loving, thriving, growing, intimate relationship with Jesus, and by extension, God.

In addition, we're each given unique gifts and talents. How we use those unique gifts in this life determines the nature of our responsibilities in the next life. We'll be going over that in later chapters.

Here's another idea that got my attention. What you do in the next twenty or thirty years will have a major direct impact on what you'll be doing in the next twenty or thirty *billion* years. Try wrapping your head around that idea! If you can believe that's a true statement, we can move on.

Love is a choice. As our little trip to high school tells us, spending time with someone in a relationship is a choice.

Feeling guilty is a choice also. I remember watching a YouTube video, and there was a pastor speaking to some college students. At the end of his talk there was an opportunity to ask questions.

One young woman stood up and asked the speaker, "If I don't believe in God, then I'm going straight to hell after I die, right"? There was kind of an angry tone in her voice. I like to watch debates between believers and nonbelievers because I learn something every time. But my personal observation is that nonbelievers seem to be angry. Sometimes very angry. There's a kind of aura of anger surrounding them. It's palpable. That's just my observation. Anyway, the speaker responded quite calmly, "Well I don't think that God is going to force you into heaven." That response speaks volumes. Jesus wants us to come to know him voluntarily. He wants us to spend time with him because it's our idea, not because of some rule, regulation, or law. God isn't going to force us into heaven. He's trying to guide us there.

Ask yourself: Could it be possible that God and Jesus want me to be in heaven more than my own very desire to be there? Why else would God create us? How you think about the answer to that question will influence this life in a very positive and powerful way.

On that YouTube video, what was interesting to me was that this young student responded, "Well, what if I want to go?" The speaker answered, "Why would you want to go to heaven? If you don't believe in God, you don't believe in heaven."

We can get a good idea of how important getting to know Jesus is to us by looking at our actions. How much time do we spend with him? How much time do we spend reading his words in the New Testament?

One very important idea regarding our freedom to choose is that I can choose to ignore my relationship with Jesus, but I'm not free of the consequences of that choice. The way we think about that relationship and the value we place on that relationship will have the most power and influence on our actions. If we don't see value in our relationship with Jesus, we won't spend any time, effort, or energy in developing it. It's very simple.

Here's a quote from Greg Behrendt, author of the book *He's Just Not That Into You: The No-Excuses Truth to Understanding Guys*: "A man who wants to make a relationship work will move mountains to keep the woman he loves."[7] That's probably true for women too. She'll move mountains to keep the man she loves. I reference that book because it's about relationships. It's not heavy reading, but it's still about relationships. The Bible is also about relationships. How much time do we spend with Jesus? Are we just "not that into" Jesus? Are we willing to move mountains for Jesus?

As we go along, we'll go over why ignoring our relationship with Jesus may be a huge mistake. We don't have to worry about his love; he promises to never leave us:

> And be sure of this: I am with you always, even to the end of the age. (Matthew 28:20 NLT)

We can say that we value the relationship and think it's important, but if our actions don't line up, we know what the truth is. Talk is cheap.

That's what we're trying to develop. Self-awareness. We should be able to look honestly at ourselves to know where we are at this point in time. What do we think about? Where do we spend most of our free time? How about our money? What do we talk about the most?

Here's a fun experiment. Next time you're having a meal with friends or family, observe and take note of what each person around you is talking about. More than likely you'll notice that someone will mention a topic more than once. By the third repetition, you know that whatever that topic is, it's currently important to that person *at that time*. Critics and cynics will say,

"Oh, that's so obvious." Yes, but what you need to understand is that the person can't help talking about it. It's subconscious, and most of the time people aren't even aware of it.

Be an observer. Being an observer is difficult because we're too busy talking about the things that are important and personal to us. Observation is powerful. If you're sitting at a table with four stay-at-home moms, you'll hear kid and husband talk. But pay attention, and you may hear some things that are deeper, or that are bothering someone. Also, you can start to observe your own thoughts and what's important to you.

Practice observation. Not to judge or point fingers, but to help you develop your own skills and notice things around you. Write down what your spouse talks about over a week-long period, and you'll have a good idea what's really important to him or her. (Don't tell them it was me who suggested it.) Listen also to what your own speech tends to focus on.

As we go along, you'll see more, hear more, and understand more. Jesus said this two thousand years ago:

> Do you not see that whatever goes into the mouth passes into the stomach and is expelled? But what comes out of the mouth proceeds from the heart, and this defiles a person. For out of the heart come evil thoughts, murder, adultery, sexual immorality, theft, false witness. (Matthew 15:18 ESV)

Jesus is talking about sin here, but this also tells us that what's in your heart comes out of your mouth. It could be kindness, goodness, and love. My point is that it's impossible for anyone to keep from talking about what's important to them. It's impossible to not think about what's important to you. What do you think about most? If you're around people you're comfortable with, you'll talk about what's in your heart. Every time.

So there's talk, and then there's action. Both are very important to be able to see ourselves and those around us. One of my favorite quotes is this: "I'm sorry, I can't hear what you're saying; your actions are screaming too loudly."

Listen again to Jesus:

Don't store up treasures here on earth, where moths eat them and rust destroys them, and where thieves break in and steal. Store your treasures in heaven, where moths and rust cannot destroy, and thieves do not break in and steal. Wherever your treasure is, there the desires of your heart will also be. (Matthew 6:19-21 NLT)

There again, he's telling us that whatever's important to us, or whatever we value—that's what we'll be spending our time and energy on, fueled by the desire of our heart. These are all clues to the real focus of our lives at this time. But do these pursuits or projects line up with our authentic selves? The selves that we were created to be? The way I came to think about this is that if I die today, the only thing I'll own when I stand before God is my relationship with Jesus. I won't have any pockets for objects or money.

In *Lessons from the Light*, Kenneth Ring documents one person's description of the time right after death:

I found that among the few things that people can take with them when they die, love is probably the most important. The only things left after one leaves his or her body are energy, love, personality, and knowledge.[8]

Love and knowledge. It's clear that we can do something about love and knowledge. It's interesting that Dr. Ring also mentions personality. Our authentic selves, maybe?

We have the power and ability to do something about love and knowledge. You may ask yourself, what are my talents? What's my purpose? How should I be spending my time? Well we can start with love and knowledge. Knowing and loving Jesus is a great place to start because our relationship with Jesus is the most valuable thing we own. It's the most valuable diamond in the world. Ask yourself if there's anything more valuable. It's valuable because it has the most influence on our ability to love others. God may ask us, "Do you love me?" but only he can see what's in my heart or in your heart. He already knows the answer to that question.

Jesus talked about that also when he mentioned the "fruit" of our lives:

> Watch out for false prophets. They come to you in sheep's clothing, but inwardly they are ferocious wolves. By their fruit, you will recognize them. Do people pick grapes from thorn bushes, or figs from thistles? Likewise, every good tree bears good fruit, but a bad tree bears bad fruit. A good tree cannot bear bad fruit, and a bad tree cannot bear good fruit. Every tree that does not bear good fruit is cut down and thrown into the fire. Thus, by their fruit you will recognize them. (Matthew 7:15-20 NIV)

Here Jesus is telling us about observing behavior. He says "Watch out." People's actions speak way louder than words.

I'm always trying to get my kids to look at the motivation behind the behavior of other people, such as their friends. People's actions reveal their hearts. You're in a relationship, let's say, and the other person is telling you, "Oh, I love you and I miss you." Then the weekend comes around, when you're ready to spend extended time with this person, but they go off with their friends. Waa, waa. Their talk was a cheap whisper; actions scream louder.

The same thing applies to us. How much time do we spend with Jesus?

As I was beginning to understand that having a relationship with Jesus was a central part of my life on earth, it became clear that the closer we get to Jesus, the more we can see of him (and also understand more of the world around us):

> Those who accept my commandments and obey them are the ones who love me. And because they love me, my Father will love them. And I will love them and reveal myself to each of them. (John 14:21 NLT)

Read that again and look at the last six words: *reveal myself to each of them.* Here's another example of an idea that sticks, with enormous implications for our lives. This verse had a huge effect on me because it clearly explained the idea of a personal relationship with Jesus. He reveals himself to each of us in a very personal and unique way. These are private revelations.

God revealed himself through Jesus two thousand years ago. Jesus reveals himself personally in our lives *now.* He uses his Word or other people or difficult circumstances. This is another idea that's helpful and useful. When we learn to look at the next wave as an opportunity to get closer to Jesus, then we're growing.

Here's where experience is powerful. From my own experience, all my spiritual revelations and growth in my personal relationship with Jesus came about because of big, tough, painful, difficult waves. I'm sure you can learn lessons on a beach drinking a margarita, but from my experience, most of the valuable lessons came through pain, trials, and difficult circumstances. Waves.

Think about the vacations you've been on. From my own experience, our family tends to laugh and recall vacations that took an unexpected or unusual turn, when we faced a trial of some kind, or some event happened that made our experience uncomfortable, and we had to adapt on the fly. Missing luggage. Unexpected two-day layover in a city we never planned to visit (this actually happened). Something went wrong. We never talk about vacations where everything turned out exactly as we planned, without a hitch. I think that's interesting.

Here's another idea that we'll develop. Jesus not only gives us truth and love, but he'll allow an *experience* of his love. We'll get to this later, but that's one unique aspect of our relationship with Jesus. It's part of the Christian worldview. He reveals himself consistently as we take this journey seriously and grow spiritually. From a practical viewpoint, you'll see how your relationship with Jesus plays an important role in every single problem that you encounter while dealing with everyday life.

Matthew Kelly summed it up very well in his book *Rediscover Jesus*:

> The more we discover who Jesus truly is, the more we will place him at the center of our lives. It is the only sane response to knowing him. The more we place Jesus at the center of our lives, the more life begins to make sense. It is simply impossible to make sense of life without the clarity that comes from placing Jesus at the center. I have tried this foolishness and I have failed. You can try if you wish, but you will fail too.[9]

This description is consistent with my own experience. The most exciting parts of this journey are the revelations and clarity that come from placing Jesus at the center of our lives. A whole world of clarity opens up when you begin to know Jesus in a more intimate way. There's no exaggeration in claiming that every single fear, problem, or need we have can be influenced and affected in a personal, powerful, and practical way by our relationship with Jesus.

This is my testimony and personal experience that I highly recommend. It's the delicious food at the awesome restaurant. It's the wonderful vacation at the beautiful resort. In my humble, non-biblical-scholar opinion, the value and positive consequences we gain in this life and the next by our relationship with Jesus are too important and valuable to ignore.

Jesus guides us in his words. He helps us with the practical and useful in our daily lives. It's the kind of help we absolutely require:

> I am the vine; you are the branches. If you remain in me and I in you, you will bear much fruit; apart from me you can do nothing. (John 15:5 NIV)

Here's another idea that can be of tremendous value in your own spiritual growth. It's the idea of repetition. We'll look at this verse again, because *it's that important.* When there's repetition in a Bible verse, pay attention. When you repeatedly receive a certain impression or hear a certain whisper about an idea—pay attention.

Notice that there in John 15:5, Jesus doesn't say, "Apart from me, you may have to work a little harder to get to your goals." He doesn't say "Apart from me, it may take you a little longer to get where you want to be." He says, "Apart from me, you can do *nothing.*" No thing. What's more practical than that?

Getting back to choice, we can choose to ignore loving God and learning to love others, but again, we aren't free of the consequences of that choice. Jesus said,

> Love the Lord your God with all your heart and with all your soul and with all your mind. This is the first and greatest commandment. And the second is like it: Love your neighbor as yourself. All the Law and the Prophets hang on these two commandments. (Matthew 22:37-40 NLT)

As I was mentioning earlier about important principles, I was aware of these two commandments, I just didn't really understand their depth. *All* your heart, mind, and soul—that's deep! Loving my neighbor is also a little more involved than anyone might imagine at first.

We'll go into depth regarding those principles. Both these commands were a lot more difficult than I previously thought. Both require effort, energy, and desire. Just like any relationship in our lives: marriage, being a parent, being a friend, or any other important relationship.

5 - THE ILLUSION OF EASY

In terms of practical and powerful—it's time to digress for a second. I'm going to suggest something as you go along, because there's real value in doing this. If I didn't think it had value or wouldn't help you, it wouldn't be mentioned.

If you're going along reading and something strikes you in a powerful or unusual way, stop. Underline it. Write it down—I suggest getting a small notebook for taking notes as you're going along, or keep a digital journal that can be backed up. This is even more important when you come across Bible verses that are screaming out at you. I'm going to talk more about the Bible, but I want to mention again that it's a *personal experience*. As you read the Bible and come across verses that strike you, stop. The Bible is the primary way God speaks to us.

It's just like cell phone reception. When a voice is breaking up, and then it improves in a certain place as you're walking along, do you keep moving, or do you stay in that spot so you can keep hearing the voice clearly? If you're reading the Bible and something really jumps out at you, that may be a message from God that you need *at that time*. Purely personal.

Remember that principle of repetition. What's weird is that you may see the same idea later that afternoon on a *Happy Days* rerun. Sometimes the Fonz will repeat the same thing you read in the Bible. (Or does that happen only to me?)

Also, when you write down or type out your notes, you're engaging other parts of your brain. It's an action. I'm a witness to the fact that as you go along in this spiritual journey, your eyes, ears, and heart are more in tune with your spirit. We'll go over how we think about our spirits a little later. You'll see, hear, and feel more of what's going on around you. An important thought or idea disappears from the front part of your mind within a few hours. If you write it down, it lasts much longer. Ask questions. Write them down and look for answers. Much of what's being shared here is from the hundreds of questions I asked. The answers came through many sources. People, events, the Bible, or circumstances. We have many resources at our fingertips. In prayer, ask God and the Holy Spirit to help you see.

Writing things down in a notebook changes everything. It engages other parts of your brain and turns you from a passive listener to an active, engaged participant. That's one guarantee I fully stand behind. You'll forget important lessons. That's why you should write them down and review them.

Historians and researchers are always looking for events in history. They don't become real or factual until someone writes the event down. The historical proof or factual strength of an event is related to how much time has passed from the event and when it was written down. It's this basic premise that we use to authenticate the Bible itself and the historicity of Jesus. Very strong historical evidence.

When you write something down in a journal, you're taking down a history of your spiritual life and hopefully your spiritual growth. You're recording the progress of your spiritual journey. What's even more valuable is when you go back and relearn things you most likely forgot about. In the margins of your Bible, you can write down ideas that you learned. Put a date and a time next to it. Writing something down uses different areas of your brain and burns a value idea into your mind. Like a tattoo.

Stopping and thinking engages your mind. When you hear an idea that really gets your attention, and then apply it to your own life, it becomes personal. That's important, because your relationship with Jesus is personal. What's even more interesting is that over time, as you begin to see and understand more, you begin to see his hand on past events that you weren't even aware of. That's when things evolve from personal to practical. He'll open your eyes to events in your past when you may not have been so spiritual. I can think of at least three events in my own life where I should have died. He showed me how he was there and helped me to live through each situation. Why? Because there was a bigger plan. One that I wasn't even aware of. Then the practical becomes powerful. In this instance, I didn't know what I didn't know.

Let's stop for a second so I can spell out my disclaimer about "easy" in this chapter's title. Regarding the "rich relationship" we talked about earlier, I feel compelled to mention that none of this is easy. Honesty and truth are extremely important, and I don't want you to be misled. We're interested in discovering and developing our authentic selves. Most people who've reached adulthood already understand how relationships can be difficult and require effort. I just want to reinforce that idea. There's no magical, quick way to spiritual growth and better relationships. It takes time and effort to develop self-awareness and to come to the knowledge of the truth. It takes maturity and humility and a willingness to look at ourselves and be open to the idea that I'm playing a role in my own problems.

The root of many of my own problems was one thing: me.

I emphasize this because we live in a world that uses catch phrases or words to sell products. They grab people's attention. The most commonly used words in advertising are *free, now, you, save, money, easy, proven,* and *guarantee*.[10] We're bombarded with ads using these words all the time. People are preprogrammed to look for free and easy.

Embrace the mindset that there is no free, there is no easy, there is no guarantee, and there's not much proven out there.

There are no quick and easy steps to *anything*. If you're an adult who has been through any difficulty, you already know that anything of real value is difficult and requires time, effort, and energy. We don't teach our kids about free, easy, or quick results when trying to get an education, open a business, or raise a family. It's probably more effective to go into a task focusing on how hard that task will be and how much you're going to have to work at it before you start. "If the road you are on is easy," Terry Goodkind says, "it's likely you're going the wrong way." That mental attitude is probably most effective.

I probably am guilty of over-emphasizing hard work, discipline, sacrifice, effort, and focus to my kids when it comes to reaching goals. Everyone knows that these are needed in most of the large important goals we aspire to achieve. Want a good education? Effort, energy, sacrifice, and discipline. Opening a business requires sacrifice, hard work, energy, and discipline. Being a good husband, wife, or parent requires self-sacrifice, hard work, effort, energy, and patience. Humility is in there too.

Is marriage easy? Is parenting easy? Is going to college or getting a degree easy? Is work easy? There may be a few lucky people out there who say their marriage is easy and their spouse is perfect. Or that all their kids are well behaved and easy to parent. If you can say that, you're in a very rare group of people (or you're lying). The rest of us have to work at our marriages. We have to work at raising our kids, and we have to work at trying to be better parents.

Our relationship with Jesus deserves our best effort, a sacrifice of our time, and a determination to move that relationship to the center of our lives. He gives us a gift that's infinitely more valuable than any person or thing can offer. Salvation.

Whatever goal we're after—whatever dream we aspire to—will be hard to reach. Most people are looking for quick and easy. Jesus spoke about this:

> Enter by the narrow gate. For the gate is wide and the way is easy that leads to destruction, and those who enter by it are many. For the gate is narrow and the way is hard that leads to life, and those who find it are few. (Matthew 7:13-14 ESV)

If we're willing to go through the narrow gate and follow the path that's more difficult, it leads to life and reward. We already have an intuitive, instinctual, built-in mindset that choosing to do what's right usually means choosing to do what's hard.

One of the most important principles I learned is that Christianity is not a religion, it's a relationship. Grab onto that idea and don't let go. Christianity is about our relationship with Jesus. The Christian life is a tough road. It's a tough gig. It isn't easy. Rock musician Alice Cooper, who's a born-again Christian, summed it up:

> What people don't realize is that when you become a Christian it doesn't make things easier, it makes them harder. It makes your life harder. It makes your soul at ease with God because you know where you are with Him. It doesn't make your social life or your normal life in America any easier. In fact, it puts you under the microscope.[11]

Now that rings very true.

Jesus warned us. Yes, it's tough, but it's also exciting, rewarding, exhilarating, challenging, fascinating, terrifying, and fulfilling all at the same time. To me, there's no better way to live. As Rick Warren says, the deal that Jesus offers can't be found anywhere else and can't be beaten: "Since my past has been forgiven and I have a purpose for living, and a home awaiting me in heaven, I refuse to waste any more time on shallow living, petty thinking, trivial talking, thoughtless doing, useless regretting, hurtful resenting or faithless worrying."[12]

When I list "terrifying," I mean that sometimes God is going to ask you to do something outside your comfort zone. It's a test. Like writing a book when you've never written one before. We reach that goal with his help, and we grow in faith and love. We grow in our relationship with Jesus. But it's never easy. Never.

Think about your own life and the difficulty you've faced in reaching your goals, or in your relationships. Now think about things in your own life that are easy for you. Talk about a valuable and useful idea! Some things are easy for you but not for people around you. Can you draw or paint a picture? I can't. Can you sing? I can't. Were you a good athlete in school? I wasn't. Things you can do that others around you can't do are a clue to your unique gifts. They also give us a glimpse into our authentic selves. I bring this up now because we can also learn from what's easy.

There are also things that are easy for every person on the planet, and all you need do is look around and see that this is true. One thing that's true for everyone is that it's easy to sin. What about being selfish? That's one of the easiest things in the world. It's much more difficult to think about others than ourselves. Sin and self-centeredness are totally related, because when we choose to sin, we're thinking only about ourselves.

Another thing that's easy for everyone is criticizing other people. Just get on the internet and look for people bullying or body-shaming or critiquing other people. The trolls. It's easy to criticize other people but way more difficult to look in the mirror and try to improve our own faults and flaws. There'll never be a shortage of critics, because criticizing requires minimal effort. It's also easier to blame other people for our mistakes or bad behavior than it is to accept responsibility ourselves. It requires maturity to take responsibility for our own actions when we've hurt someone else. Being critical of others is way easier than taking a hard look at ourselves.

Remember, there can be no significant change for the better until we're able to look at ourselves and see where we can improve. There's no reason to be afraid of this, because no one's perfect. No one. We're all flawed.

That's why spending too much time worrying about people's opinions of us is not a good investment of our time. Those people who are so generous with their opinions are also flawed. We need to commit to the principle that *what others think about us is none of our business*. If it was supposed to be our business, we would be able to read other people's minds. But the value of those opinions is very limited. We'll go over that extensively. Also, we can waste time being critical of others and judging or comparing ourselves to others. That's a big trap. It's why Jesus said,

> Why do you see the speck that is in your brother's eye, but do not notice the log that is in your own eye? Or how can you say to your brother, 'Let me take the speck out of your eye,' when there is the log in your own eye? You hypocrite, first take the log out of your own eye, and then you will see clearly to take the speck out of your brother's eye. (Matthew 7:3-5 ESV)

Notice here that Jesus says we can see more clearly if we take the log out of our own eye. If we can look at our own behavior and flaws, it allows us to see more clearly. That's what we're after. Clear vision. We want to try to develop the "eyes of Christ." But we can still help our brother take the speck out of his eye. We should be gentle. When you take a speck out of someone's eye, you don't use a shovel.

Let's come back to the concept of choice for one last idea, because it's very important. We can choose to pursue our own pleasure and our own plan for our lives, or we can pursue God's plan for our lives. We can also choose to totally forget about trying to discover and fully realize the authentic self that God created us to be. We're all free to do that. We can ignore his idea for our lives, but we'll face repercussions.

We should remember that we existed in God's mind in a unique and individual way even before the world was created:

> For he chose us in him before the creation of the world to be holy and blameless in his sight. In love, he predestined us for adoption to sonship through Jesus Christ, in accordance with his pleasure and will—to the praise of his glorious grace, which he has freely given us in the One he loves. (Ephesians 1:4-6 NLT)

That reminds me of a story when I was in residency training. I remember I was assisting a pulmonary specialist doing a bronchoscopy on a gentleman in his fifties. The pulmonologist was doing the procedure and every so often would stop and hand the eyepiece to me to point out different areas of interest. The patient was a smoker with a history of a nagging cough and spitting up blood. I was really taken by the glistening almost pristine look of his bronchial passages that resembled pink tunnels, so perfect and clean. The pulmonologist slowly advanced the scope and then he suddenly stopped looked at me and then showed me what he was looking at. A dark, irregular, ugly looking tumor. We both kind of shook our heads. We knew. He didn't have many months left to live.

The thing that struck me was the comment the patient made after the procedure. He was awake and lightly sedated, and as we were finishing up, he said, "Yup, I made a decision. Doc, I'm giving up smoking. That's it. I'm done."

Remembering that event made me realize that doing something about my purpose is not something I can put off until I'm standing before God after I die. I'm uniquely responsible to discover, develop, and realize my authentic self. I'm to use my unique gifts in a way that benefits others. When I serve God and others using my gifts, I'm closer to true authenticity.

We're each personally and uniquely responsible for our own eternity also. It's no one else's responsibility. Our eternity? It's on us.

Our relationship with Jesus is personal. Our pursuit of the realization of our authentic selves is personal. If you think you can figure out God's plan for someone else's life, get rid of that idea immediately. Figuring out God's plan for another person is impossible. More importantly, it's none of our business. Although we do have a responsibility to share with our children, family, and friends that God has a plan for their lives as well. My kids are sick of hearing about it from me. God's plan and purpose for my life is unique, and it involves discovering my gifts, talents, and passions. It involves fully realizing his vision for me. My unique talent, gifts, and passions are not there by accident, and if I don't spend any time carrying out God's plan for my life, it won't get done.

Part of his vision for me is developing a relationship with Jesus. That's a vision he has for everyone on the planet. We're adopted through sonship (or daughtership) through Jesus Christ. But there's a unique plan for us as individuals that's totally left up to you and me to personally execute or implement.

That idea is always in the back of my mind: No one else can really know, understand, and execute God's plan for my life except me. And no one else can really know, understand, and execute God's plan for *your* life except *you*. If you and I don't execute our individual plan or purpose, it won't get done.

The scariest idea to me is the idea of regret. We all have regrets we can think about and wish we could have done something differently, or gone in a different direction at a fork in the road. Personally, I don't have any huge regrets that I think about every day, or that dominate my thinking. I just don't want to get to the end of my life feeling like it was wasted. I see people around me spending so much time, energy, and effort on things of questionable value. You know how people say, "I have bigger fish to fry"? It suggests that what they're working on now is more important. What I found out from my own life was that all those "bigger fish" I was frying were really minnows on matchsticks.

I really hope that this book will help open your own eyes and help you examine your own life. Any minnows frying on matchsticks?

6 - It Starts and Ends with Love

You were created because of love. The only thing you'll take from this life is love. It starts and ends with love.

We can probably finish the whole book right here by summing it up: *It's all about love.* If you took my advice and started a notebook or a journal, you can write in the center of the page: *It's all about love.* The end.

It's truly the beginning. One thing I like about studying NDEs is the kind of bridge they can build to the past. We see and hear about these experiences, and they reinforce what Jesus and the Bible were saying two thousand years ago. It's the modern world and the present showing us how valid and useful those teachings from the past really are. The message is as relevant today as it was then. The principles haven't changed.

It should be obvious to anyone that love is the overwhelming message of NDEs and the Bible. The one consistent observation from scientists and researchers who've taken accounts of these NDEs is the striking inability of the people going through these experiences to describe the total love, acceptance, and warmth of the "being of light."

Below are some quotes from the books *Life after Life* by Raymond Moody, *Lessons from the Light: What We Can Learn from the Near-Death Experience* by Dr. Kenneth Ring, and *Imagine Heaven* by John Burke. (I've also included representative NDE accounts from the Near-Death Experience Research Foundation website, which is an excellent source if you're interested in furthering your knowledge regarding NDEs.)

> The Light told me everything was Love, and I mean everything![13]

> I was shown how much all people are loved. It was overwhelmingly evident that the Light loved everyone equally without any conditions.[14]

> The Light was extremely concerned and loving toward all people. I can remember looking at the people together and the Light asking me to "love the people." I thought, "If they could only know how much they're loved, maybe they wouldn't feel so scared or lonely anymore."[15]

That last sentence is key. The actual ability to feel or recognize the vastness of the love of God and Jesus for each of us changes everything. Again, this is about *experiencing* his love. I would argue that you don't have to nearly die to feel or experience that very love.

Here are more examples to consider:

> This is the hardest thing to try and explain.... Words will not come close to capturing the feelings, but I'll try: total, unconditional, all-encompassing love; compassion, peace, warmth, safety, belonging, understanding; overwhelming sense of being home, and joy.[16]

> When we got to the light, the totality of life was love and happiness. There was nothing else. And it was intense. Very intense and endless in scope. I felt an extreme sense of love and peace and beauty that I cannot describe in words.[17]

Here we see a common theme of the inability to describe in our own limited words the sense of love and acceptance coming out of the light.

Here's a Bible passage about light:

This is the message we have heard from him and proclaim to you, that God is light, and in him is no darkness at all. (1 John 1:5 ESV)

We go on with NDE quotes:

From the moment the light spoke to me, I felt really good—secure and loved. The love which came from it is just unimaginable, indescribable. It was a fun person to be with! And it had a sense of humor too—definitely![18]

Here's a nice summary of NDE experiences from the same book, *Life after Life*:

Almost everyone has stressed the importance in this life of trying to cultivate love for others, a love of a unique and profound kind. One man who met the being of light felt totally loved and accepted, even while his whole life was displayed in a panorama for the being to see. He felt that the question that the being was asking him was whether he was able to love others in the same way. He now feels that it is his commission while on earth to try to learn to be able to do so.[19]

These experiences are remarkably similar when it comes to the love that's felt by these people who were near death. It appears that God and Jesus are trying to get us to understand the depth and vastness of their love. Jesus offers us truth, but he also offers us an experience of his love. He wants us to truly feel the magnitude of his love. But we don't seek an experience first, we seek a relationship, and we get to know him by spending time with him. If we're believers, it's incumbent on us to try to comprehend and experience this. When we get a minor grasp of this, it changes the way we think and changes our lives.

As Christians, we're in the love business. Are you open for business? Because business should be booming.

In life, "the main thing is to keep the main thing the main thing" says Stephen Covey. Jesus would argue that love is the main thing. Grasping and really understanding and feeling the love of God, and being able to open our hearts so that there's room for its magnitude, is his desire for our lives. Then we allow that love to emanate from us. We're conduits for the love of Jesus.

> Dear friends, let us continue to love one another, for love comes from God. Anyone who loves is a child of God and knows God. But anyone who does not love does not know God, for God is love. God showed how much he loved us by sending his one and only Son into the world so that we might have eternal life through him. This is real love—not that we loved God, but that he loved us and sent his Son as a sacrifice to take away our sins. Dear friends, since God loved us that much, we surely ought to love each other. No one has ever seen God. But if we love each other, God lives in us, and his love is brought to full expression in us. (1 John 4:7-12 NLT)

This is one of those stop-and-read-again verses. Probably good to memorize too. It's so encompassing and important. It's the kind of passage that spells out truth so clearly that I really don't have an excuse for not taking it seriously. Personally, I feel that if I didn't pay attention, and then stood before God and Jesus, I think they would both look at me and say, "Seriously? Dude, how much more clear do we have to make it?" Then I kind of imagine an upward smack on the back of my head.

That's one of the reasons NDEs carry so much power for me. It's like Jesus is grabbing us by our shirts and shaking us: "Hey guys, pay attention! This is really important!"

Here's more biblical support from two thousand years ago describing and outlining how important love is:

And may you have the power to understand, *as all God's people should,* how wide, how long, how high, and how deep his love is. May you experience the love of Christ, though it is too great to understand fully. Then you will be made complete with all the fullness of life and power that comes from God. (Ephesians 3:18-19 NLT)

So now we have the apostle Paul telling us the exact same thing. That's what Jesus wants for every single one of us. He wants it more than you do.

I finally understand what Paul is talking about, but it took time for me to gain an experience of his love. What's unique here is that he describes this as if it's our responsibility, and within our ability. He says "as all God's people should." It's part of our job. We make an effort to try and understand how wide, long, high, and deep the love of Jesus truly is. Remember that the apostle Paul, who wrote that statement, had a personal intimate experience with Jesus on the Damascus road (Acts 9:3-19).

In my humble, non-biblical-scholar opinion, there's value in studying the Bible and the near-death experience. If you can glimpse or experience the love of Jesus, it's life-changing. If you look at the life of Paul and the lives of people who've had a near-death experience, one thing is certain: there are many changes in people's lives after they have an NDE. Paul changed from a murderer of Christians to someone willing to die for Jesus.

These types of experiences change people's lives now just as they did two thousand years ago. Most importantly, what we learn from these experiences can change our lives too. We don't have to be near death to experience the love of Jesus. It's freely available to us at any time.

It's like children who grow up in a loving family, getting plenty of love and support from both parents. Children like that grow up knowing they have the love, support, and affirmation of both parents, and they feel safe, secure, and confident. They have the idea that they can do anything or pursue any goal they're interested in. If someone criticizes them or tries to put them down, it has minimal impact. They know they're loved and have value, and that they're special and unique.

That's exactly how Jesus wants you to feel: you know you're loved and unique. If someone tries to put us down, we can respond, "It doesn't really matter what you say, Jesus loves me more than you can possibly imagine, and he made me this way for a reason. I may be weird to you, but I'm beautiful and lovable to him. He created me this way, and he doesn't make mistakes. That's all that matters to me." When you think that way, things change.

This brings me to an important idea that you'll see again in this book: humans are human. If we can keep in mind and remember that people say stupid things all the time, we won't be slaves to the opinion of others. We won't be so upset if someone is mean or rude or says ugly or mean things about us, and we'll be more free to develop confidence, self-esteem, and a sense of self-worth.

People do stupid things all the time. Let me be clear. I'm not saying people are stupid. I'm saying that *we all say and do stupid things*.

You may be walking around with hurt or pain because of things someone said to you. Some of those things are straight-up lies.

Remember what we said about critics. And try to remember also that it's the opinion of God and Jesus that matter. Some people who are closest to you may criticize you. Maybe a parent or a spouse. Someone you love dearly. Those are the criticisms that hurt the most. I've been on that roller-coaster ride.

But remember, *humans are human*. They make mistakes. Don't let what someone said about you five, ten, or twenty years ago have any bearing on your opinion of yourself. Begin to realize that Jesus says we're valuable.

You should remember what all these people who've had NDEs are saying, and what the apostle Paul said—and what Jesus said:

> My sheep listen to my voice; I know them, and they follow me. I give them eternal life, and they shall never perish; no one will snatch them out of my hand. My Father, who has given them to me, is greater than all; no one can snatch them out of my Father's hand. I and the Father are one. (John 10:27-30 NIV)

This is a promise. We're safe. We have value. Every one of us.

That's part of our journey in these first few chapters. Not only seeing where we can improve, but trying to develop the "eyes of Christ." Jesus sees every person, including each of us, as lovable, valuable, acceptable, and forgivable. Every one of us.

This brings us to our backpack for the journey. Is there any fear, anxiety, or low self-esteem buried in that backpack? We know from the Bible that God doesn't want us walking around with any of those burdens.

As we begin to grow in our understanding of the love of Jesus, our confidence expands and our fear contracts. It takes time, but we're beginning to travel in the way God intended. Boldly.

So look around in that backpack. Any low self-esteem? Get rid of it. Begin to change the way you think.

> For the Spirit God gave us does not make us timid, but gives us power, love and self-discipline. (2 Timothy 1:7 NIV)

7 - THE UNDENIABLE PRAYER

S o here's the introduction of the idea of the undeniable prayer. Some of us aren't as spiritual, or we haven't been taught some of these ideas of faith. I myself didn't learn about the importance of the Bible until much later in life. We're all from different backgrounds and faiths and experiences.

In my humble, non-biblical-scholar opinion, there are some prayers that God will not deny. They're answered every single time. In some situations, like coming to the knowledge of the truth, God has a desire for us to pray for something more than we want that prayer answered. He has been waiting.

Accepting what Jesus has done for us on the cross is another example. It's the undeniable prayer. It's answered every time. Sometimes we pray for something, and that prayer isn't answered because God knows what's best for us at that moment. But if you haven't yet turned your life over to Jesus, and you're willing to make this commitment and truly believe it in your heart, it will be answered every time. We know this because there's never a time when accepting Jesus is not the best thing for us. Ever. Life's always better with him than without him. He's dying to know us, and he already died and rose again so that every one of us has the opportunity for salvation.

Below is a good prayer that sums up everything. If you feel compelled to pray this now, that's good. If you aren't ready for this type of commitment, that's fine also. It's a big step, if you haven't already turned your life over to Jesus. It isn't something to be taken lightly.

This is the one prayer that will be answered. Every time:

God, I recognize that I haven't lived my life for you up until now. I've been living for myself, and that's wrong. I need you in my life; I want you in my life. I acknowledge the completed work of your Son Jesus Christ in giving his life for me on the cross at Calvary, and I long to receive the forgiveness you've made freely available to me through this sacrifice. Come into my life now, Lord. Take up residence in my heart and be my King, my Lord, and my Savior. From this day forward, I will no longer be controlled by sin, or the desire to please myself, but I will follow you all the days of my life. Those days are in your hands. I ask this in Jesus's precious and holy name. Amen.

I put this prayer in here early so that it's accessible. There's zero pressure. Every time we do something spiritual, like spend time with Jesus, or read the Bible, or go to church services, God wants us to do so under our own volition. Our choice.

We just went over the idea of choice. Let's be honest, it's kind of intimidating. The "desire to please myself" isn't going to go away in one day because of the nature of who we are as humans. (We'll go over the self, sin, and our spirit in coming chapters.)

When we say a prayer like this, Jesus doesn't expect perfect. He never did. We're going to stumble. Everyone does. Really the prayer is saying, "I didn't understand before what it meant to have a relationship with Jesus, and now I do." It's about the desire to change and wanting to get to know Jesus.

The come-into-my-heart part is what has power. Remember that you won't make this kind of a commitment until you realize you have a personal need for Jesus. Everyone needs Jesus. They just don't realize it.

Sometimes we don't know what we need most. Jesus paid the debt he didn't owe, because we owe a debt we'll never be able to pay. Love is not a feeling. Love is giving someone what they need most when they deserve it the least. We all need that type of love. That's the type of love Jesus gives. You ask him to come to you and reveal himself, and he will. That's his promise:

> Those who accept my commandments and obey them are the ones who love me. And because they love me, my Father will love them. And I will love them and reveal myself to each of them. (John 14:21 NLT)

We've just gone over the importance of the recognition of the love of Jesus. What you may not see is that when you ask Jesus to come into your heart, he has been waiting for you to ask and aching for you to ask for so very long. He will come. Open your heart and your eyes and your ears. You better be ready and work on your awareness, because he'll reveal himself in many, many ways. Surprising, wonderful ways that will make you smile and laugh out loud. You'll ask yourself, "Why didn't I see this before?"

When you pray this prayer, and begin to spend time with Jesus and get to know him, he will show himself. But you must pay attention. You should look, listen, and seek. Start with the New Testament. Jesus reveals himself first in the Word. Remember the idea of a "rich relationship with God." Any rich relationship requires communication. It's a two-way street. We get to know him by spending time with him in prayer. Both God and Jesus speak to us through meditation and the Word. He also reveals himself in your daily life and in circumstances. It's wonderful and incredible. But it's very personal: "I will reveal myself to each of them."

So after I said the undeniable prayer and recommitted myself to knowing Jesus, my way of thinking about God and Jesus totally changed. This is consistent with many of the ideas coming in the next chapters of this book. God doesn't change, and neither does Jesus. The way we see things and think about things are what really change. The change begins within you. This is a very personal experience.

Here's more proof that he's waiting for us:

> This is good, and it is pleasing in the sight of God our Savior, who desires all people to be saved and to come to the knowledge of the truth. (1 Timothy 2:3-4 ESV)

Things change inside us that allow us to see and understand and recognize what's important, but also what's already there. If you pray the undeniable prayer, the change happens in *you*. How you think now about God or Jesus has already been established by upbringing, family life, and your own personal study and experiences. It has been established, and it's where it is right now based on all those factors.

Remember, the basic story I'm telling in this book is just my own testimony. It's what happened to me. That's all. I'm the only expert on my own experience; you're the only expert on your own experience. I share because I care. My very strong desire is for you to have the same experience. Jesus knows what's in my heart. It's eating at the restaurant that had great food, and I'm suggesting it for you on your next date night. I'm confident you'll love it. It's going on the cruise and the great vacation; I truly believe you'll have a great time on the cruise and will want to go again.

The most important and significant change for me was a transition of my vision, belief, and understanding of who God and Jesus really are. In my youth and teenage years, my image of God was more of a judge. He was waiting to catch me in some kind of sin so he could zap me. There were rules and laws and regulations, and he was up on a bench looking down on me, and I was just trying to be good. I didn't want to end up in hell.

Remember we defined hell as total separation from God, as caused by the rejection of Jesus through our free will and choice.

It's total separation from God—and rejection of God—by choice.

In my college and medical school years, God was more like a genie in a bottle. I left him in the closet and prayed to him on occasion in the evenings, but I fished around for the bottle in the corner behind the shoes only when I needed something. Then I came to the knowledge of the truth. I began to see Jesus the way he truly is. He showed me the role he wants to play in our lives. Jesus wants to be our best friend. God is our loving Father.

It's very hard to grasp and conclude that an all-powerful, loving God and Savior desires a relationship with us more than we do. That's who he is.

Everything comes down to a very simple idea. The most valuable thing we can own is our relationship with Jesus. He's the only way to God. That was the idea that changed my life for the better. That relationship is the source of change for every other relationship. I came to that realization, understanding, and true conviction. (Remember, a conviction is a faith, belief, or idea so strong that I'm willing to live for it as well as die for it.)

So this is really a nitty-gritty type of decision. It's cut-down-to-the-bone important. But the reality is that everyone must decide what to do with Jesus. Even if you choose to ignore the ideas or teachings of Jesus, that's still a choice. Even if you choose to continue with your own plan or continue with your own pursuits, you're still making your decision.

I've always liked the lunatic, liar, or Lord argument by C. S. Lewis in his book *Mere Christianity*:

> I am trying here to prevent anyone saying the really foolish thing that people often say about Him: I'm ready to accept Jesus as a great moral teacher, but I don't accept his claim to be God. That is the one thing we must not

say. A man who was merely a man and said the sort of things Jesus said would not be a great moral teacher. He would either be a lunatic—on the level with the man who says he is a poached egg—or else he would be the Devil of Hell. You must make your choice. Either this man was, and is, the Son of God, or else a madman or something worse. You can shut him up for a fool, you can spit at him and kill him as a demon or you can fall at his feet and call him Lord and God, but let us not come with any patronizing nonsense about his being a great human teacher. He has not left that open to us.[20]

Wow. That's heavy stuff. But if you stop and think about it, it just rings true. What he's saying is that there's no middle-of-the-road approach to Jesus. Other faiths will describe him as a good teacher or a great philosopher or even a prophet. Either we believe what Jesus said in the New Testament, or we think he's a liar. He's not just a "good guy." Sorry. He's the Son of God. The thing that we must remember is that everyone on this planet must choose. Everyone. He's either telling the truth or he's lying.

Personally, I'm betting my entire life that Jesus is telling the truth. I've gone all in. Well, maybe not all in; I may have a few chips left in my pile that I'm trying to push into the center pot. Some of those stubborn habits or hang-ups are tough to get rid of.

Every person on this planet must decide. You too. Some people are always cynical, no matter how much evidence is presented to them. They keep asking for more proof. There were no video recorders or smart phones two thousand years ago, but there's a ton of historical evidence to support the reality of the life, miracles, and resurrection of Jesus. I've studied the historical evidence and I've read books, just because it's fascinating to me. The more I learned, the stronger my faith became.

If you have questions, that's good. Questions invite the engagement of our mind. Jesus said that we're to love God with all our heart, soul, and *mind*. You have questions for a reason. I would pursue those questions and do some digging for yourself.

Remember that Jesus is the most valuable diamond in the world. It takes some effort to learn about him and grow in our relationship with him. I would start by finishing this book while starting to read the Bible. The one thing that I've learned and experienced is that getting closer to Jesus, it's not like you *know* truth; you *feel* truth.

Let me digress for just a second. One of the goals of this book is a renewing of the mind. *Metanoia* is the Bible's original word for it (in Greek). *Meta* means change; *noia* means mind. The word *repent* means to turn from sin; it's also an English translation of that Greek word *metanoia*. When we begin to think differently about Jesus and about our spirits and about our purpose, then we'll change our behavior for the better.

How we think is one of the starting points on this journey. We must learn and understand how we think. We must measure or test that way of thinking to see if it lines up with truth—if it lines up with Jesus.

8 - AN EMBARRASSMENT OF TRUTH

So now we come to story time. This is going to be difficult for me because it's so embarrassing. The only reason I'm willing to fall on the sword and tell you about this is that I truly believe it happened so that I can share it with you. This is an illustration of the value of truth. We can all learn from it. So please learn from it. We'll talk about truth in detail later, but if you don't look at how you think about truth and seek truth, then you could be harming yourself or someone you love. Most of the changes I've experienced have happened to me because I came to the knowledge of the truth. The value of truth can't be underestimated. You won't find claims in this book about my being the smartest person in the world or even in the room, but I'm not stupid either. We can talk about what my class rank was or summa cum laude this. Whatever. Who cares. I share because I care.

Picture in your mind someone driving around in a black sports car that someone has keyed. The scratches are on the driver and rear passenger doors. Long scratches, five or six feet long. Ugly scratches, down to the metal. More obvious because the car is black.

That was me. Don't ask what kind of car it was, because that's not important. Let's just say it wasn't a piece of junk.

I drove around in that keyed car for months, mainly because of the cost of a huge deductible to get the car repainted. Here's the embarrassing part. One beautiful afternoon, as I'm pulling up to a convenience store parking lot, a guy comes up to me and tells me he can fix the scratches for three hundred dollars. "Wow," I think to myself, "that's a good deal." What a dummy. He shows me a business card that says he works for an auto body shop, and he says he does side jobs part-time to make extra money. (Is that snickering that I hear from you?) Let me mention that usually I'm Mr. Skeptic. Usually, I assume "rip-off."

Sometimes your vision becomes blurry if you aren't walking on the right path, and I can tell you that when it came to my spiritual journey, I was off the path. No "eyes of Christ"; just Ray-Bans.

Anyway, after I agree to have my car "fixed," this guy pulls out an electric sander and sands down to the metal. Then after going to a shop to get the "right paint," he brings a spray paint can and spray paints the large defects he created with the sander.

In my defense, I'm saying to myself, "This just doesn't seem right." Well, it didn't dry the right way, and after one pass at the car wash, the paint just came off under the jet sprays of water.

Okay. That was an embarrassing story. Done laughing?

I came to understand truth and knowledge when I went to the dealer body shop, and the manager took me to the back. He showed me all the steps it takes to fix scratches on a car door. You take the door off, remove all the paint, and more steps that I don't remember because I was too angry with myself to keep listening. I felt so foolish, and there was no way I was going to tell the manager that story.

We all do dumb things. People say and do dumb things because we're human.

The moral of this whole story is the value of truth. If I'd known what was involved in fixing car scratches properly, I would have told the con artist he was crazy. Well, who's crazy? People who don't seek truth. Yeah, I lost a little money, but it didn't have an impact on my life or my eternity. Plus, maybe you're starting to see the value of truth.

Here's another illustration. A true story. One bright Monday morning, I walked into an exam room to see a patient. "Good morning, Mrs. Johnson. How can I help you today?"

This was her response: "Doctor, I came in to see you because I have this enormous headache. It started yesterday, and it's getting worse. This morning I felt like my head was going to explode. You have to help me! This pain is unbearable, and I feel like my eyes are going to pop out of my head. I've had headaches before, but this is without a doubt the worst headache of my entire life!"

My response: "Mrs. Johnson, this is quite concerning. The thing that's most alarming is that this is the worst headache of your life. I believe the best thing for you to do is get in your car and go directly to the emergency room, because it's my opinion that you need a CAT scan of your head right now. I'm worried that you may have something called a sub-arachnoid hemorrhage, or a ruptured blood vessel in your brain. I think you should go now."

Her response: "Oh, wait. Hold on a second, doctor. It's not really *that* bad."

So why this story? As you can see, there's a quandary here. I'm stuck. Where's the truth? Is the headache really bad? So now she's going to tell me a different story. Which one is true? Was the first one a lie?

It's hard to know where you're going without the truth. Truth is what is in accordance with fact or reality. It's the way things really are. To find truth, we need a roadmap for our lives. We need a guidebook to help us find our way. We're on this journey, but we need a map or GPS or something.

That's where the Bible comes into play. We've already talked about how the Bible is the primary way God communicates with us. It's also the way we get to know Jesus. It's one of the primary ways we spend time with him, besides prayer and meditation. The Bible is the instruction manual for life. It's our GPS for guidance through the maze. There's no question or situation you can think of that can't be addressed or answered by the Bible.

There's also power in the Word. If we go back to the personal and practical, the Bible is meant to guide us in a very personal and practical way. Everyone should have their own Bible. It's critical for getting an idea of how Jesus really thinks. We read the Scriptures and we understand how God thinks in any kind of situation. Once we begin to think the way God thinks, we're on solid ground.

My favorite definition of wisdom is that it's thinking the way God thinks. Another good one: wisdom is the combination of knowledge and obedience. We become wise if we act on what we know.

The Bible is a gift for all of us and each of us. If you've never really read the Bible, that's okay. I'd never read the Bible until about ten years ago. It's never too late to start. Just start. My recommendation would be to start in the New Testament, if you have limited experience with Bible study. I say that because we've been emphasizing a relationship with Jesus, and that relationship begins by reading and studying his words.

We're told to love God with all our mind, soul, heart, and strength. How can we begin to love Jesus when we don't really know him? We get to know him by spending time with him and understanding how he thinks. We do this by getting in his Word and spending time in prayer. Talking to him and being quiet. We also listen to him.

We've discussed writing down your thoughts and ideas in a journal. I recommend writing down notes with dates and times in the margins of your Bible. When you're going through it, write down your thoughts, and put a date and time next to a notation. It's a guidebook for you.

As you read, ask questions. There are numerous resources out there to find answers to your questions.

One thing that's quite interesting and magical about the Bible is that you can read a verse seven times, and then on the eighth time, something will strike deep in your heart. It's almost like somebody snuck in in the middle of the night and wrote something new in the Bible. You often say to yourself, "Why didn't I see that verse before?" The reason is that you didn't need that verse before; you need it *now*.

You may already know what I'm talking about. This is where Bible study and reading is personal. It's that unique message that's meant for you and you alone *at that time*. It's very personal.

Remember the cell phone and losing reception? You start walking around like an idiot: "Can you hear me now?" When you get the "Yes, I can hear you," what do you do? You stop. You stop so you can keep that clear communication. That's exactly like the Bible. When you read something that strikes you, God (through the Holy Spirit) is speaking directly to your heart. So *stop*. Write notes in the margin. Ask God, "What are you trying to teach me here?" Stop and think about the verse; keep going over it.

Hearing and recognizing the voice of God is worth another book itself. The one thing to remember is that it takes time and practice. Also, there will be passages you don't understand. Count on it. There are many gifted teachers who have a unique talent to explain and clarify biblical principles. Begin to study and choose someone who explains difficult passages in a way that you understand and can clearly identify with. There are many pastors and church leaders who have a gift for explaining biblical principles.

One thing I learned that's of great value is that we should also read and interpret the Bible ourselves. If you're not reading the Bible, it's like not reading your texts for a week, and Jesus has been texting you over and over. "Are you there? *Hello?*"

How do you view the Bible? If you think of it as just another book of rules and regulations (like I did), you aren't going to be motivated to pick it up.

But the Bible is serving way more than one purpose. What if it's like our cell phone to hear directly from God? What if it's the primary way that an all-powerful and all-knowing God speaks to us and guides us?

It probably doesn't really matter much which idea or thought motivates you to pick up the Bible; what matters is that you pick it up. There's real value in learning the teachings of Jesus and spending time with him. If you begin to read the Bible, the person who benefits the most is you. Then by extension, your family benefits as you begin living out biblical principles.

It's interesting that ninety percent of the population believes in a God who is all-knowing and all-powerful, but we don't ask his advice on the most important questions of our lives. That was me. Decades of totally ignoring the Word of God. What changed for me is that I came to see there's not much in this world we can rely on for truth.

We must be honest and realistic with ourselves. I know from personal experience that we can't rely on science. I call it the tap-on-the-shoulder test. We do things for years in medicine because of what we consider to be "standard practice" in individual disease states. Then comes the inevitable tap on the shoulder: "Uh, we were wrong about that treatment; you may want to stop doing that." Happens all the time. Don't get me wrong; I believe in what we do. Medicine in the United States is something I'm proud to be a part of. The truth is that we sometimes make mistakes, as far as medical science goes. We get it wrong sometimes. Remember, scientists and doctors make mistakes too, even if they mean well. George Washington's doctors were removing blood from him on his deathbed. Probably not a great idea. "Bloodletting was the literal bleeding of a patient with the idea that in order to rid the patient's body of any disease-causing pathogens, their 'bad blood' must be drained off. However, all this medical procedure did for Washington was cause him to go into shock from loss of blood."[21]

Where can we go to find truth? Science? Scientists make mistakes all the time. The world? Culture? None of those are satisfactory.

The problem with science, the world and culture is that they're all run by people. You remember what I said about humans? They have this nagging problem of being human. They make mistakes. Albert Einstein once said: "Two things are infinite: the universe and human stupidity, and I'm not sure about the universe."

Can we look to governments or ideologies to find truth? Communism has been given credit for at least a hundred million deaths over the past century.[22]

If you can come up with truth that's better or more reliable than the Bible, I'm all ears. Why do I trust the Bible? It's the inspired Word of God. God never lies. Also, the Bible never changes. No one comes tapping us on the shoulder pointing out that the Bible was wrong on this principle or that principle.

Governments, ideologies, science (medical or otherwise), culture, and the world—all are run by humans. There are some "mistakes" or discrepancies in the Bible, because it was written by people. It's kind of like churches or faiths. They're easy targets because they make mistakes and aren't perfect. Why? Because they're run by people. Don't waste your time looking for a perfect church. But God's biblical principles are never wrong and never change.

If you can come up with a better standard for truth than the Bible, you're free to follow that decision. But if you choose to start reading the words of Jesus and spend time in his Word, it's a choice that will impact your life in a very powerful, practical, and personal way, now and for eternity.

Our Bible study is personal. It reveals truth to us as unique individuals. It's a guidebook for each of us. As I mentioned, there are many gifted teachers who have a unique talent and are able to explain or clarify biblical passages. I have my go-to people who explain biblical verses. I also have my go-to people who really move me with their sermons on biblical principles. I won't mention those, because everyone's different; someone who moves me and can speak to my heart may put you to sleep.

You may remember Siskel and Ebert. I used to watch their show about which movies were good and worth the effort to see. I realized that my tastes always lined up more with Gene Siskel. I also used to look at the newspaper and figured out which movie critics I tended to agree with. When Gene Siskel and the movie critics from *Rolling Stone*, *USA Today*, and the *Wall Street Journal* all agreed that a movie was great, it was close to 99 percent accurate that I wouldn't be disappointed when I saw it. Now we have Rotten Tomatoes. I don't always agree with Rotten Tomatoes.

It's kind of the same with biblical teachers or scholars. They may be able to say things to you in a way that's deeper than your own mental reasoning or understanding. Just like figuring out movie critics, it takes time to find gifted Christian teachers who explain things in ways that make sense to you personally. Someone who you like, who really clarifies biblical passages for you, may totally confuse me.

We should also read and interpret the Bible ourselves. Believe it or not, that may be one of your gifts: the ability to discern Scripture. There are probably people out there who've never read the Bible but are gifted at scriptural interpretation. That's amazing. You may be one of them. You'll never know until you start reading and studying the Word. And as you do, you'll come across passages that will really have an impact on you and open your eyes.

I prefer Bibles with the words of Jesus highlighted in red. They really kind of zero in on what's important. We should remember that when Jesus is speaking, he's really telling us what God wants us to know and what God thinks is important. Just as he says:

> I don't speak on my own authority. The Father who sent me has commanded me what to say and how to say it. (John 12:49 NLT)

Something that's fascinating is *how* Jesus says what he says. Sometimes Jesus gets emotional, animated, and excited. When he does, pay attention. Those are clues.

So read the red, know the red, live the red.

A crucial part of Bible study is going over a verse and meditating on it, then being quiet and listening for the voice of Jesus. It's a skill that takes time to develop. The ability to decipher his voice from the noise in our head requires effort. Those voices should be tested against the words of Jesus. The red.

Jesus speaks to everyone. Write down what he's saying to you in your journal, and put a date and time by it.

As I mentioned, starting in the Gospels and the New Testament was helpful for me. Starting with the Old Testament was a little too tough. It's like when you're four months old and someone sticks a piece of filet mignon in your mouth. You don't have the teeth to chew on it. In my humble, non-biblical-scholar opinion, starting in the New Testament and growing in your relationship with Jesus helps us to understand and appreciate the Old Testament more, though it's all about Jesus anyway. Don't get me wrong; we can't ignore the Old Testament, because those books contain so much wisdom, and offer so much potential to learn the mind of God. Proverbs, Psalms, Isaiah, Daniel, Jeremiah, Genesis—all those books are loaded with important wisdom.

My experience was that I first developed a relationship with Jesus by Bible study, quiet time, and reading the New Testament. I got to know him well. I learned how he thinks and how he speaks, and I got a feel for what he thinks is important. In doing that, if someone starts to tell you something about what Jesus said, and it doesn't jibe with your own perception, you have a sensor or truth alarm. "Yup, that sounds like Jesus," or, "Nope, that doesn't fit with what Jesus said or did."

For example, suppose I tell you that life becomes easy once you start following Jesus and begin to live your life in the way he wants; you pray for something and it's yours, because God wants us all happy and wealthy, with no trouble or suffering in our lives. If you're well acquainted with the teachings of Jesus, then you would know that I'm trying to sell you something that's not the truth. Jesus didn't promise wealth, comfort, or an easy life. As a matter of fact, he talked about trouble, trials, persecution, and the cross. He said the world would hate his followers:

> If the world hates you, remember that it hated me first. The world would love you as one of its own if you belonged to it, but you are no longer part of the world. I chose you to come out of the world, so it hates you. Do you remember what I told you? 'A slave is not greater than the master.' Since they persecuted me, naturally they will persecute you. And if they had listened to me, they would listen to you. They will do all this to you because

of me, for they have rejected the one who sent me. (John 15:18-21 NLT)

I've read Christian books that will say, "Separate yourself from the world as radically as you can." That agrees exactly with what Jesus is telling us in those verses: "I chose you to come out of the world." It's kind of a perplexing idea, because we're to love and serve others and be in the midst of them, but at the same time we're to separate ourselves from the things of this world. My approach is to not get caught up in the way the world thinks and acts or what the world values. One of my favorite things that Rick Warren talks about is how the world cares about "looking good, feeling good, and having the goods," but Jesus tells us to live above the world and what it values.

Sometimes when I share with someone about what Jesus has told me, people are shocked. "What do you mean?" they often say. Or I get an eye roll: "Yeah, right." They don't believe that Jesus would speak to us. But God created us to love us—isn't that true? The Bible says,

> For God so loved the world, that He gave His only begotten Son, that whoever believes in Him shall not perish, but have eternal life. For God did not send the Son into the world to judge the world, but that the world might be saved through Him. He who believes in Him is not judged; he who does not believe has been judged already, because he has not believed in the name of the only begotten Son of God. (John 3:16-18 NASB)

That's the verse you see on signs at football games, right? God sent Jesus because of his *love*. He sent Jesus to live among us and die for us. Jesus proved his divinity by all the miracles and the resurrection. Is he now going to ignore us and never speak to us? Really?

> But if any of you lacks wisdom, let him ask of God, who gives to all generously and without reproach, and it will be given to him. But he must ask in faith without any doubting, for the one who doubts is like the surf of the sea, driven and tossed by the wind. For that man ought not to expect that he will receive anything from the Lord, being a double-minded man, unstable in all his ways. (James 1:5-8 NASB)

Let me tell you something I learned that has real value. The thing that shocked me the most was not that Jesus speaks to us, but in how many ways he communicates with us. He's communicating with us in so many ways that we aren't even aware of.

We should put time and effort in developing our relationship with Jesus. It takes time and effort, but it's well worth it. The whole world begins to open up. It's kind of like the movie *The Matrix*. At the end, Keanu Reeves becomes "Neo" because he can see all the digital information around him. He can see the things he couldn't see before, and that's when he had access to his power. Likewise, we begin to see the presence of Jesus around us—his love, his power, his influence.

The best example I can give is the contrast in statements made by the Soviet cosmonaut Yuri Gagarin and the American astronaut John Glenn, the first Russian and the first American to orbit the earth in outer space. Gagarin told his Soviet leaders, "I looked and looked, but didn't see God anywhere." John Glenn said, "To look out at this kind of creation and not believe in God is to me impossible. I saw God everywhere. I saw his splendor in the universe."

So what do we learn from all this? The point is that God is everywhere, and the spiritual world surrounds us. As we begin to grow and learn to align with our spiritual selves, our authentic selves, we develop a new set of eyes. But the change begins in us. We have the eyes of our body to see the physical world, but we use the "eyes of our hearts" to see with our spirits. This is the next idea: the weird.

9 - THE POWER OF THE WEIRD

So many of the most important changes occur in us when we begin to see ourselves the way we truly are.

You and I are *spirits*. As C. S. Lewis expressed it, you don't *have* a soul; you *are* a soul that has a body. We aren't bodies who happen to have a spirit, but spirits who happen to have a body. How you think and what you believe about this basic principle has a major impact on your ability to reach your authentic self.

This is spelled out again clearly in both NDEs and in the Bible. Remember, *weird* is defined as "supernatural, otherworldly, unearthly, mysterious, unusual." That means you. I'm weirder than you. Just kidding.

I do like the idea of being mysterious. The body is natural, the spirit is supernatural. The body is earthly, the spirit is unearthly. We know much about the human body, but the spirit is mysterious. That means being weird is something we need to think about—something we should embrace, be proud of, and (most importantly) explore.

This is also directly related to our authentic selves. The selves we were created to be. When we move closer to Jesus, and develop an intimate personal connection to him, this opens up our spiritual senses. We are now more astute and aware of spiritual communication. It takes time to develop those senses, but they are available to each of us as we go along. Once you experience spiritual communication, it tends to make you yearn for more. Once you can see things around you that you couldn't see before, it's like a small spark on a pile of kindling. You want to make that spark grow. You begin to blow on that tiny fire because it brings light and warmth the bigger it gets.

There's a whole spiritual world out there that you may be missing because you haven't gotten in touch with your spiritual side. I've had many experiences in the past ten years that are "weird" because of this journey, and because I came to the knowledge of the truth. This is just a testimony. I ate at the restaurant and spent the week at the all-inclusive resort. Great food and beautiful beach. We must get in tune and in touch with our spiritual side, because it's critical to our growth and to our journey. Listen to Jesus:

> "Truly, truly, I say to you, unless one is born again he cannot see the kingdom of God."
>
> Nicodemus said to him, "How can a man be born when he is old? Can he enter a second time into his mother's womb and be born?"
>
> Jesus answered, "Truly, truly, I say to you, unless one is born of water and the Spirit, he cannot enter the kingdom of God. That which is born of the flesh is flesh, and that which is born of the Spirit is Spirit. Do not marvel that I said to you, 'You must be born again.' The wind blows where it wishes, and you hear its sound, but you do not know where it comes from or where it goes. So it is with everyone who is born of the Spirit." (John 3:3-7 ESV)

There's a flashing neon sign on this one. It's not difficult to see. When Jesus starts letting loose with the "truly, truly," pay attention. He says "truly" four times here. How much more of a signal do we need? Sometimes it comes down to plain old fairness and common sense. Jesus is going out of his way to tell us and show us what's important.

As Christians, we believe in the Trinity. We receive the power of the Holy Spirit when we accept Jesus as our Savior. This power is available to every one of us, but can be obtained only when we accept Jesus as our Lord and Savior. We have the power of the Holy Spirit within us. We should cooperate with him in our spiritual growth. We accomplish this when we listen and pay attention to the guidance we're being given. My prayer and hope is that some of that guidance will come through this book.

We're responsible for our own spiritual growth and development. It's the journey to realizing our authentic selves. It's on us. It's personal. The Word allows us to get a little closer, and it helps bring out the spiritual side of us. We start to think of ourselves as spirits, which is how God wants us to worship and get to know him, as Jesus said:

> The hour is coming, and is now here, when the true worshipers will worship the Father in spirit and truth, for the Father is seeking such people to worship him. God is spirit, and those who worship him must worship in spirit and truth. (John 4:23-24 ESV)

This is one of those must-memorize verses. Remember, Jesus is telling us what God wants us to know. Jesus is telling us we *must* "worship in spirit and truth." He's telling us that *both* are important: spirit and truth. If I believe Jesus, then I begin to think that being in touch with my spiritual side is important. I also begin to think that maybe the truth is important. It's back to how we think. How we think about our spirits and how we think about truth. If we believe what Jesus is teaching, we spend time and energy seeking truth.

These principles aren't my ideas. They belong to Jesus. One important idea I realized from reading the Word was that before they began their work or their ministries for the kingdom of God, both the apostles *and* Jesus received the Holy Spirit. Jesus didn't begin his teaching until he was given the power of the Holy Spirit. He didn't begin to gather the apostles together to help with spreading the gospel until he was given the power of the Holy Spirit:

> And the Holy Spirit descended on Him in a bodily form like a dove. (Luke 3:22 ESV)

> Then Jesus, full of the Holy Spirit, returned from the Jordan and was led by the Spirit into the wilderness. (Luke 4:1 NIV)

I always thought that was interesting, because he's God, but there must be a good reason that he couldn't proceed until he received that Holy Spirit power.

The apostles didn't start their ministry until the Holy Spirit came down upon them like "tongues of fire":

> And suddenly there came from heaven a sound as of the rushing of a mighty wind, and it filled all the house where they were sitting. And there appeared unto them tongues parting asunder, like as of fire; and it sat upon each one of them. And they were all filled with the Holy Spirit, and began to speak with other tongues, as the Spirit gave them utterance. (Acts 2:2-4 ASV)

After that, they had unusual power and strength and were eager to speak about the gospel. Both Jesus and the apostles were "filled with the Spirit" and were given power and strength to complete their ministries. Those two Bible vignettes illustrate how powerful and how important it is to receive the Holy Spirit. There's an *experience* of the Holy Spirit, in addition. We'll get to that in a bit.

We're all spirits. Believers and nonbelievers. God made everyone that way. Our spirits live on after our bodies die. We receive the Holy Spirit when we accept Christ. Jesus says,

> The Advocate, the Holy Spirit, whom the Father will send in my name, will teach you all things and will remind you of everything I have said to you. (John 14:25-26 NIV)

Notice that Jesus says that the Father sends the Spirit in Jesus's name. Going back to the lunatic, liar, or Lord argument from C. S. Lewis—we can't receive the Holy Spirit if we believe Jesus is a lunatic or a liar. We must accept and believe, the Lord part of the argument. There's no other way.

The following three passages tell us that we receive the Holy Spirit when we accept Jesus as our personal Lord and Savior.

> For by one Spirit we are all baptized into one body, whether Jews or Gentiles, whether slaves or free, and we were all made to drink of one Spirit. (1 Corinthians 12:13 NASB)

Here that point is mentioned again:

> But you are not controlled by your sinful nature. You are controlled by the Spirit if you have the Spirit of God living in you. (And remember that those who do not have the Spirit of Christ living in them do not belong to him at all.) (Romans 8:9 NIV)

Then in Ephesians:

> And now you Gentiles have also heard the truth, the Good News that God saves you. And when you believed in Christ, he identified you as his own by giving you the Holy Spirit, whom he promised long ago. The Spirit is God's guarantee that he will give us the inheritance he promised and that he has purchased us to be his own people. He did this so we would praise and glorify him. (Ephesians 1:13-14 NLT)

Look again at that statement: *The Spirit is God's guarantee that he will give us the inheritance he promised.* That's an essential point. The Spirit is a guarantee of God's promise of our inheritance. Now we see that once we believe and accept and receive Jesus, we're given the Holy Spirit.

I didn't have a true spiritual experience until much later in life. There are many things I still don't understand, but the experience I had was like something I read in a magazine article about the actor Denzel Washington. In an interview with *GQ* magazine (September 2012), he spoke of an encounter with the Holy Spirit that he described as "this tremendous physical and spiritual experience," and he decided, "I'm going to go with it," though the incident frightened him; "I was slobbering, crying, sweating. My cheeks blew up. I was purging. It was too intense."

I know exactly what he's talking about. That happened to me, but for the life of me I don't know why it didn't happen when I was much younger. Why not high school or college? The one thing I remember was that I prayed over and over for the Holy Spirit to come into my heart. I hadn't recommitted to Jesus yet. In my own personal non-biblical-scholar opinion, this is an undeniable prayer. If you pray for the Holy Spirit to come into your heart, he'll begin to guide you and release his power in you.

The Holy Spirit is a person. God is always present with his people today by his Holy Spirit. When you pray, "Come, Holy Spirit," you're asking for an increased sense of the presence of God. That's the key. It's practicing the sensing of the presence of Jesus or God. It occurs only when we're engaging our spiritual senses, not our physical senses. There will be critics who'll argue in a slightly nasal tone, "You don't have to pray for the Holy Spirit, he's already there once you accept Jesus as your Savior." Yeah, I get it. I'm just relating my own personal experience and my own opinion. I don't mean to get into arguments about the stages of how we receive the Holy Spirit. I'm just relating what happened to me.

We'll talk about the experience of the Holy Spirit later, but these ideas are not my own. Look at this:

> When they arrived, they prayed for the new believers there that they might receive the Holy Spirit, because the Holy Spirit had not yet come on any of them, they had simply been baptized in the name of the Lord Jesus. (Acts 8:15-16 NIV)

This description in the book of Acts is early in the history of the Christian faith, but it's important. That's what I believe happens to each of us as we learn to experience and understand the presence of Jesus and the Holy Spirit.

Here's a good prayer to the Holy Spirit:

> Come Holy Spirit, fill the hearts of your faithful and kindle in them the fire of your love. Send forth your Spirit and they shall be created. And you shall renew the face of the earth. O, God, who by the light of the Holy Spirit did instruct the hearts of the faithful, grant that by the same Holy Spirit we may be truly wise and ever enjoy his consolations, through Christ our Lord, Amen.

As we begin to think of ourselves as spirits and learn these principles, it helps us to discover the nature of our authentic selves. This helps us in our spiritual growth and in our relationship with Jesus. These principles also allow us to discover and develop our true self, the person we were created to be. Notice that it starts as a small spark, "kindle in them the fire." We have to get that fire going. It's on us.

There's significant power in the study of NDEs as we learn to discover and develop our spiritual senses, because every experience that's documented is an experience in "the spirit."

There's power when we can begin to think of NDEs as total and full descriptive experiences of people fully engaged in their spirit. NDEs are unique experiences because there's a total absence of the flesh or the body. You can try to get in tune with your own spirit by escaping your body, but good luck with that. I use the term *flesh* because that's our tie into biblical doctrine. The bridge to the past. People who experience an NDE are separated from the body because the body is dead or incapable of functioning. It's an actual glimpse of the world that's outside our bodies. These experiences occurred only when the person's spirit was freed from the confines of the human body. They don't always occur at the point of death; some people have them during anesthesia or at other times. This allows us to get a peek into the spiritual world that surrounds us.

I know this may be getting a little twilight zone, but hang with me for a bit. Try to think about it like this. Our spirits are trapped in our bodies. They can be released only when the body dies. So when our spirits are free from the enclosure of our bodies, they can see, hear, or feel *more*. It's kind of like trying to use a cell phone in the multilevel basement parking garage of a big building. It's possible to get reception here and there, but you have to walk around and put effort into it. This is similar to being more in tune with our spiritual sides. It takes effort.

Here are some examples of what people have said they were capable of doing or seeing while they were free from their bodies:

> I was startled to see that my vision had changed: I could see everything in the room—every hair on every head, it seemed—all at the same time.[23]

> From where I was looking, I could look down on this enormous fluorescent light...and it was so dirty on top of the light. [Could you see the top of the light fixture?]

Yes, and it was filthy. And I remember thinking, "Got to tell the nurses about that."[24]

The room was much more interesting than my body. And what a neat perspective. I could see everything. And I do mean everything! I could see the top of the light on the ceiling, and the underside of the stretcher. I could see the tiles on the ceiling and the tiles on the floor, simultaneously: three-hundred-sixty-degree spherical vision. And not just spherical. Detailed! I could see every single hair and the follicle out of which it grew on the head of the nurse standing beside the stretcher.[25]

This next one is absolutely fascinating to me:

I got to sense and feel, basically, what everyone around me felt at the same time. I was watching it and doing it. And I got to experience both aspects of it at the same time.[26]

There are many more examples, but I wanted to reference one source, as those quotes were all taken from Dr. Kenneth Ring's *Lessons from the Light*. What I'll argue is that when you get more in tune with your own spirit, you'll be able to see things more clearly. Maybe not to the degree that people can see when they're totally free from their bodies, but you'll be able to see in the way we were intended to see. Kind of like viewing life in high-definition as compared to watching on a clunky old tube television. Once you see a movie or program in high-definition, it's kind of hard to go back and really enjoy that fuzzy picture. That's like living in the spirit.

Remember, Jesus gives us more confirmation of this right at the moment of his death:

Jesus called out with a loud voice, "Father, into your hands I commit my spirit." When he had said this, he breathed his last. (Luke 23:46 NIV)

Let me develop this idea a little, because it does make me think of something. When there's a debate between believers and nonbelievers about the afterlife, nonbelievers tell us that we'll go to a big black nothing after we die. They say things like, "Do you remember anything before you were born?" Well, the way I think about it, if Jesus was a liar, and the resurrection isn't true, and we all go to a big, black nothing—then no one will know, and really no one "wins." No one gets to say, "See? I was right!" But what if the nonbeliever must stand before Jesus and explain why he or she rejected him?

We all must account for what we did with our lives, even the nonbeliever. So for the nonbeliever, the afterlife is either a no-win or a lose-big reality. That's it. There are no other options. Either big black nothing, or else explain your lifelong rejection of Jesus. For believers, it's either a no-win or a win-huge reality. A big black nothing, or a heaven that's beyond our wildest dreams, where we'll experience the profound joy of spending eternity with God and Jesus in love, peace, and happiness. Ever dream of winning a Lotto prize? Me too. This would be bigger.

One little nagging idea, though. I kind of feel like Colombo in that 1970s detective TV show: "Uh excuse me, just one last question before I go." (There's an obvious age revealer.) Stop and think about this. If we're spirits like the above NDEs tell us, and we go to an afterlife, then we'll see and feel *more* after we die. If we're all spirits and go on to another existence, NDEs tell us that our senses are heightened. Increased exponentially. No big black nothing. We'll be in another place with enhanced abilities and awareness.

That sounds like there's much to look forward to, if you believe in heaven. Kind of an eye-opener, if you believe what Jesus said about hell—which would be a reality of pain and suffering experienced with heightened senses.

10 - Near Death Can Bring New Life

We know that the church will mention these type of experiences, but there's clearly a de-emphasis on them. Irish priest Enda Cunningham, who lectures in eschatology (the study of "last things"), explains:

> Sometimes there is an over-emphasis on the miraculous and this can lead to the manipulation of the vulnerable. The challenge of the Christian message is to find God in our daily life and the ordinary.[27]

There's the responsibility to emphasize doctrine and the teachings of Jesus, which makes sense. In my own experience, there's tremendous value in looking at these NDEs if they're consistent with the teachings of Jesus and the Bible. There's true power in these experiences as they help us to look at our own behavior and to really strive to develop our "spiritual vision." They also help us discover and develop our true or authentic selves.

Here's a passage in the Bible that for all the world sounds like a near-death experience to me:

> I know a man in Christ who fourteen years ago was caught up to the third heaven—whether in the body or out of the body I do not know, God knows. And I know that this man was caught up into paradise—whether in the body or out of the body I do not know, God knows—and he heard things that cannot be told, which man may not utter. On behalf of this man I will boast, but on my own behalf I will not boast, except of my weaknesses—though if I should wish to boast, I would

not be a fool, for I would be speaking the truth; but I refrain from it, so that no one may think more of me than he sees in me or hears from me. So to keep me from becoming conceited because of the surpassing greatness of the revelations, a thorn was given me in the flesh, a messenger of Satan to harass me, to keep me from becoming conceited. (2 Corinthians 12:2-7 ESV)

That sounds like Paul was given special revelations to help with his ministry. Could these revelations be available to us? If we believe and understand the depth and height and vastness of the love of God and Jesus, do you think it's so improbable that they wouldn't want us to benefit from these revelations? Why are some people who've undergone an NDE told to go back and tell people about their experiences or write a book?

Let's be clear, I know some of this stuff is written to make money. And I know I fell for the paint-scratch scam. But I ain't stupid. For me, it's simple. God created us to love us. God sent his only Son Jesus to die for us as a sacrifice for our sins, doing so out of pure love, so that we could be saved. So in my humble, non-biblical-scholar opinion, either God is going to do everything he can and give us every chance to come to the knowledge of what's true, or he's just going to sit back and watch us flounder around. If we know God and Jesus and can see them the way they truly are, we know the answer to that.

Jesus promised to reveal himself to each of us in a unique and personal way, but it will only be revealed to our spirits. We communicate with Jesus, and he reveals himself to our spirits. When he walked the earth he performed miracles, but sometimes he refused to do so, and he got angry when the Pharisees kept asking for more and more signs.

In doing miracles, Jesus revealed himself to people's physical senses. Miracles are revelations that we can see, hear, and appreciate in the flesh. It's the spiritual world coming down and being discernible in the physical world. There are still those kinds of revelations today, but not as common. It's much more common that Jesus reveals himself to our spirits.

> When the Pharisees heard that Jesus had arrived, they came and started to argue with him. Testing him, they demanded that he show them a miraculous sign from heaven to prove his authority. When he heard this, he sighed deeply in his spirit and said, "Why do these people keep demanding a miraculous sign? I tell you the truth, I will not give this generation any such sign." So he got back into the boat and left them, and he crossed to the other side of the lake. (Mark 8:11-13 NLT)

Notice: "He sighed deeply in his spirit." Why do you think that got thrown in there?

I've studied NDEs and I've learned a great deal that has helped me in my own relationships. Studying them has helped in my role as a spouse, parent, boss, coworker, son, brother, and friend. They helped me also in my study of the Word. My growth, understanding, and trust in the love of Jesus began first, then learning about NDEs reinforced the knowledge and understanding of what's true.

I believe Jesus is working in ways all around us to save as many people as he can. He's everywhere. We can ignore it, or we can grow spiritually and grow in our love for Jesus. Then we can join the party. So after every foray into NDE land, we come back to truth and doctrine.

Here's more of the kind of doctrine or truth that serves to anchor this whole book:

> The fruit of the Spirit is love, joy, peace, forbearance, kindness, goodness, faithfulness, gentleness and self-

control. Against such things there is no law. Those who belong to Christ Jesus have crucified the flesh with its passions and desires. Since we live by the Spirit, let us keep in step with the Spirit. Let us not become conceited, provoking and envying each other. (Galatians 5:22-23 NIV)

When we change the way we think about our spirits, we can begin to try to live by *the* Spirit. Want a quick check on the spiritual meter? Look at the "fruit" listed there in that verse, then look at your own life. Are love, joy, and peace obvious and shining through? How about patience, kindness, or goodness? Or forbearance? Forbearance really means patience and tolerance; personally, patience is a struggle for me.

Really the whole point of this passage is that all these attributes come about when we spend time in the Word and really try to develop and grow in our relationship with Jesus. These qualities come about by beginning to start good spiritual habits. When we want to strengthen and take care of our physical bodies, we develop physical habits. We get plenty of sleep and rest. We exercise at least three or four times a week. We avoid harmful things like alcohol and tobacco. Those are physical disciplines. When we begin to understand the value of spiritual growth, we develop spiritual disciplines or habits.

The one habit that changed my life was getting up before everyone else and spending time in Bible study and prayer and especially writing down my thoughts and prayers. Also, being quiet. Learning to listen and hear the guidance of the Holy Spirit or the voice of God or Jesus.

Really, if we look at the life of Jesus, any habit of his that we emulate or try to acquire is beneficial. It will never hurt us. Spending time reading the Bible? Never hurts you. Spending time in prayer and listening to the guidance of the Holy Spirit or to the voice of Jesus? Never hurts you. Memorizing Scripture? Never hurts you.

If we look at the life of Jesus, he really valued this time in prayer to God:

> Very early in the morning, while it was still dark, Jesus got up, left the house and went off to a solitary place, where he prayed. (Mark 1:35 NIV)

> Then Jesus came with them to a place called Gethsemane, and said to the disciples, "Sit here while I go and pray over the over there." (Matthew 26:36 NKJV)

Jesus didn't need to keep a spiritual journal, because he knew the entire Old Testament by heart, and he essentially spoke the New Testament into existence. Plus, he was even described as the Word:

> The Word became flesh and made his dwelling among us. We have seen his glory, the glory of the one and only Son, who came from the Father, full of grace and truth. (John 1:14 NIV)

It's tough trying to start three or four new habits at a time. Just start with one and build on that.

Yes, there are bad habits, but there are good habits too. These spiritual habits won't just change your life; *they'll change your eternity.*

If we begin to develop and get more in tune with our spiritual side, this means by necessity we'll be able to minimize or deemphasize our fleshly side:

> So I say, walk by the Spirit, and you will not gratify the desires of the flesh. For the flesh desires what is contrary to the Spirit, and the Spirit what is contrary to the flesh. They are in conflict with each other, so that you are not to do whatever you want. But if you are led by the Spirit,

you are not under the law. The acts of the flesh are obvious: sexual immorality, impurity and debauchery; idolatry and witchcraft; hatred, discord, jealousy, fits of rage, selfish ambition, dissensions, factions and envy; drunkenness, orgies, and the like. I warn you, as I did before, that those who live like this will not inherit the kingdom of God. (Galatians 5:16-21 NIV)

I want to develop this idea of walking in the flesh, because in our society and culture today, we see significant amounts of time, effort, and energy devoted to the idea of "life watching"—either watching someone else's life or getting others to watch our lives. If you look at social media and reality television and our modern culture, there's an obsession with this. We're becoming a "look at me" kind of society.

There's a kind of competition for followers on Instagram or Twitter. There's nothing wrong with engaging in social media as a pastime. Looking at Instagram or Facebook and seeing posts from family and friends is a good way to keep up with the people closest to you. It's a good way for people to communicate and interact. That's all good. The danger is when these activities become like idols, and we're spending inordinate amounts of time looking at everyone else's life and ignoring our own children or the people we love around us. It's almost like we're no longer participants in our own lives. We aren't as actively engaged in our lives as we ought to be because we're spending inordinate amounts of time looking at other people's lives.

We can't make our own life fascinating when we're obsessed with everybody else's life. How many people are you following, even people you hardly know or have no real friendship with? We can see whole families at restaurants all looking at their cell phones and not engaging or interacting with each other. Do you think that's what Jesus had in mind?

A study done at Baylor University showed the following:

> Women college students spend an average of ten hours a day on their cellphones and men college students spend nearly eight, with excessive use posing potential risks for academic performance, according to a Baylor University study on cellphone activity published in the *Journal of Behavioral Addictions*. "That's astounding," said researcher James Roberts, Ph.D., the Ben H. Williams Professor of Marketing in Baylor's Hankamer School of Business. "As cellphone functions increase, addictions to this seemingly indispensable piece of technology become an increasingly realistic possibility."[28]

These numbers are clear evidence that there's a problem with how much time is being devoted to being on cellphones engaging in social media. That time could be used productively for activities that have value and help us discover and develop our authentic selves.

If we're spending so much time "life watching" or trying to get others to watch our lives, we should be able to look at time spent and try to determine if there's real value in this activity. People spend significant amounts of time looking at the details of the lives of celebrities, or they're posting pictures of the blueberry muffin they had for breakfast. Looking at reality television, we can easily see "idolatry, hatred, discord, jealousy, fits of rage, selfish ambition, dissensions and factions, envy and drunkenness." It's like the apostle Paul could watch *The Real Housewives of Jerusalem* two thousand years ago.

If you notice on those shows there'll always be a train wreck or big fight or some big blowup. Why? Everyone slows down to look at a train wreck. No train wreck, no eyeballs, no ratings. It's hard not to rubberneck when you drive by a car wreck. So there's always some "dissension, jealousy, discord, fits of rage, selfish ambition, or envy." And don't forget a dash of "drunkenness." Always.

Think about what's the most recognizable cultural phenomenon right now. It's hard to argue that it isn't the "selfie."

Look around. I just heard Facebook described as an adult "show and tell." The problem with this, especially for young people, is that they see the lives of peers as better than their own. And they begin to become depressed or feel deprived. Social media distorts their own view of reality, and it can be detrimental to self-esteem. This is a mere observation.

Our own focus on the self and our own focus on watching the lives of others or working to get people to become interested in our lives is devotion to the physical or the fleshly part of our selves. Any time devoted to watching other people's lives is time robbed for the discovery and development of our authentic selves.

This brings me to another important verse:

> Then Jesus said to his disciples, "Whoever wants to be my disciple must deny themselves and take up their cross and follow me." (Matthew 16:24 NIV)

Notice what's first: deny the self. Remember, we want to develop healthy self-awareness. We can't deny the self if we aren't even aware of the self. Especially the physical self. The fleshly self. If we want to be in touch with our spiritual self, we deemphasize the flesh.

Remember the many benefits of being in touch with our spiritual and authentic self: we can communicate with Jesus and the Holy Spirit; we begin to see the world way more clearly; we acquire the real fruit of the Spirit—love, joy, peace, kindness, patience, and self-control; we benefit, and the people around us benefit; and we get closer to authenticity.

To me, it's all about the changes within us. God is everywhere and always has been. The change occurs in us. We begin to be able to pick up on his presence through a relationship with Jesus. We begin to understand that we're really spirits within a human body.

We have our senses of sight, touch, smell, taste and hearing—the physical senses we need to physically survive on this planet. We don't begin to see spiritual things until we live in the power of the Holy Spirit. We spend time in the Word and in prayer and meditation. Those are spiritual habits and disciplines. As we begin to see with the "eyes of Christ," it becomes clear that living in the Spirit is desirable and yields the fruit of the Spirit. We can begin to see love, joy, and peace in our interactions with others. Kindness, goodness, and patience also develop.

It doesn't happen overnight. It's easy to slip back into fits of rage and discord and jealousy, especially if you're married and raising children.

When we begin to live in the Spirit, things change, as we can see and understand more. Think of it like special vision or seeing in high-definition. Like Keanu Reeves when he becomes Neo in *The Matrix*. We all have this ability. People who've had NDEs talk about special degrees of empathy where they can actually feel or experience the emotions of others. Our spiritual abilities are masked by our bodies. When our bodies die, our spirits live on and last forever. Our spirits are where the power resides. We can see more. We can feel more. We acquire wisdom. We understand what's important and what isn't. Sure, the critics and cynics will scoff and laugh. "And those who were dancing were thought to be insane by those who could not hear the music."

As I was growing in my own understanding of living in the Spirit, I've always wondered about fasting. What's the deal with fasting? Why stop eating as part of your faith? Here's something Jesus said about that:

And when you fast, do not look gloomy like the hypocrites, for they disfigure their faces that their fasting may be seen by others. Truly, I say to you, they have received their reward. But when you fast, anoint your head and wash your face, that your fasting may not be seen by others but by your Father who is in secret. And your Father who sees in secret will reward you. (Matthew 6:16-18 ESV)

Notice Jesus says *when* you fast, not *if* you fast. Some pastors talk about how your mind is sharper and more clear when you fast, so that's one of the reasons for doing it. I just started to realize that when you fast, you're denying the physical body of food. What are you left with? The spirit.

God is spirit and Jesus speaks to our spirit. Every form of communication is by spirit. My assertion is that you don't need to have an NDE to live in the Spirit, enjoy the fruit of the Spirit, or communicate with Jesus. This is my testimony. This is my experience.

11 - A Spirit of Service

This is a good time for an inventory. There's so much focus on how we think, because that's the most powerful way to change our behavior and our vision.

> From that time on Jesus began to preach, "Repent, for the kingdom of heaven has come near." (Matthew 4:17 NIV)

Repent means to turn and refers to turning from sin. But it also means, in the Greek (*metanoia*), "a change of mind" or "renewing of the mind."

> Do not conform to the pattern of this world, but be transformed by the renewing of your mind. Then you will be able to test and approve what God's will is—his good, pleasing and perfect will. (Romans 12:2 NIV)

If we change our minds about our relationship with Jesus—there'll be huge benefits in this life and in eternity.

If we change our minds about choice, love, truth, and the Bible—there'll be huge benefits in this life and in eternity.

If we embrace the idea of getting in tune or in touch with our spiritual side or authentic selves—there'll be huge benefits in this life and in eternity.

How you *think* about every topic we've discussed will form and shape your behavior and your spiritual growth, and will have a major impact on your life today and in eternity.

We began with how we think about our relationship with Jesus. Do we have a "rich relationship"? Then we talked about choice and free will. How do we mentally process our freedom to choose to grow in our relationship with Jesus? What about our choice to go to heaven? What about truth? How important is that in our thinking? Do we spend any time thinking about how important truth is and how much time we spend pursuing truth?

What do we think about the Bible? Do we think there's any value in studying the Scriptures?

What about love? Can we see the value of learning how to love as outlined by Jesus, and as further strengthened by the phenomenon of the NDE?

What do we think about our spirits? If we think there's real value in being in tune with our spirits, we'll spend time and effort on spiritual growth.

I like lists so that I can keep all these ideas manageable. Here's a good one of vital topics for our thinking:

1. "Rich relationship" with Jesus.

2. It's a personal choice to grow that relationship.

3. It's a personal choice to go to heaven.

4. Learning to love God and others is life's main goal.

5. Seeking truth is important.

6. The Bible is a gift and a guide for this life.

7. We are spirits living in a physical body.

8. Living in the spirit gives us the fruit of the spirit.

We've already said that the main goal of life is to learn how to love. But love is an *action*. How do we put that love into action? And what does how we *think*—our mental attitude—have to do with that? Jesus points the way:

> Your attitude must be like my own, for I, the Messiah, did not come to be served, but to serve, and to give my life as a ransom for many. (Matthew 20:28 TLB)

The Christian life is about service. We're to love others by serving others and by *thinking* about the needs of others before our own. That's the essence of love. A loving mother or father will put their children's needs before their own. That's true love. We model this by putting the needs of others before our own. It's one of the most difficult things to do in this life. The reason that it is so difficult is that our fleshly body is concerned only with the preservation of the self. Our brains are hard-wired to focus on serving the flesh. So when we pursue true authenticity, we are in a battle with ourselves, and the battle occurs within our minds.

There are many verses in the Bible that talk about our service and how we're to use our time and gifts for the benefit of others. My favorite parable is the parable of the talents:

> For it [the kingdom of heaven] will be like a man going on a journey, who called his servants and entrusted to them his property. To one he gave five talents, to another two, to another one, to each according to his ability. Then he went away.
>
> He who had received the five talents went at once and traded with them, and he made five talents more. So also he who had the two talents made two talents more. But he who had received the one talent went and dug in the ground and hid his master's money.
>
> Now after a long time the master of those servants came and settled accounts with them. And he who had received the five talents came forward, bringing five talents more, saying, "Master, you delivered to me five talents; here, I have made five talents more." His master said to him, "Well done, good and faithful servant. You

have been faithful over a little; I will set you over much. Enter into the joy of your master."

And he also who had the two talents came forward, saying, "Master, you delivered to me two talents; here, I have made two talents more." His master said to him, "Well done, good and faithful servant. You have been faithful over a little; I will set you over much. Enter into the joy of your master."

He also who had received the one talent came forward, saying, "Master, I knew you to be a hard man, reaping where you did not sow, and gathering where you scattered no seed, so I was afraid, and I went and hid your talent in the ground. Here, you have what is yours." But his master answered him, "You wicked and slothful servant! You knew that I reap where I have not sown and gather where I scattered no seed? Then you ought to have invested my money with the bankers, and at my coming I should have received what was my own with interest. So take the talent from him and give it to him who has the ten talents. For to everyone who has will more be given, and he will have an abundance. But from the one who has not, even what he has will be taken away. And cast the worthless servant into the outer darkness. In that place, there will be weeping and gnashing of teeth." (Matthew 25:14-30 ESV)

From this parable, it's clear that each of us has been given a gift or talent. Here's a description of a "talent":

According to the *New Nave's Topical Bible*, one who possessed five talents of gold or silver was a multimillionaire by today's standards. Some calculate the talent in the parables to be equivalent to twenty years of wages for the common worker. Other scholars estimate more conservatively, valuing the New Testament talent somewhere between $1,000 to $30,000 dollars today.[29]

In this parable, we can assume that Jesus was making a point about the value of the gifts we're given. He chose a large sum of money that was given to each servant. In my humble, non-biblical-scholar opinion, he's telling us that we're each given a valuable gift to use, and then receive a return on that investment. He wants us to use our gifts and talents in serving and helping others. We're to bear fruit. Our gifts and talents and even our passions and interests were given for the benefit of others, not ourselves.

From the parable, we can see that some of us have one talent, some three talents, and some five. Those who are given more have more responsibility.

Notice how Jesus says, "Well done, good and faithful servant. You have been faithful over a little; I will set you [put you in charge] over much. Enter in the joy of your master." He's giving us an idea of the reward waiting for us if we use our talents, money, and gifts in ways that are wise. In ways that benefit others. We'll be put in charge of much, and we'll celebrate with Jesus in heaven. This is an illustration of our responsibility for our unique eternity.

Why unique? Because our gifts are unique to each of us, and how we choose to use or ignore these gifts has a direct influence on what kind of responsibility or work Jesus will assign to us. But we can also see how he isn't happy with the servant who buried his talent and just gave it back to his master. When we're not seeking the full extension of our gifts and exploring our potential, we're hiding and burying our gifts.

We begin to discover our gifts and passions while in the Spirit, and we begin to see with the eyes of Christ. We discover and develop our authentic selves. We can see what God's idea or dream is for our lives.

This parable also gives us a unique insight or glimpse into the personality of Jesus and what he considers to be most important. Look at the power and depth in describing the master's anger: "You wicked and slothful servant! You knew that I reap where I have not sown and gather where I scattered no seed? Then you should have invested the money with bankers so that I could have at least gotten interest [my paraphrase]. So take the talent from him and give it to him who has ten talents. And cast the worthless servant into the outer darkness. In that place, there will be weeping and gnashing of teeth." Wow!

Jesus uses three words there that really should drive this deep into our hearts: *wicked, slothful* (which means "lazy"), and *worthless*. Why do you think he uses those words, and gets so emotional and animated?

If we start trying to really understand the depth of his love for us and of his sacrifice on the cross, he's driving home how important it is that we don't waste our talents or our lives. He's emphasizing a very strong idea. It's like he's screaming: "Don't waste your gifts or your lives!"

The real-world example I'm reminded of is the professional athlete who's out of his or her sport in only a few years. The comments are always the same: "He had so much talent, he just didn't want to put in the work." And in interviews after they're not playing anymore, they always admit, "I didn't put in the time and effort. I was very immature and I didn't understand what it took to get to the next level."

Tim Tebow won two national collegiate football championships as a quarterback for the Florida Gators, and he says, "Hard work beats talent when talent doesn't work hard." That should be a lesson for every one of us, because these talented athletes are still alive and they can do something valuable with their lives outside sports. There's a plan beyond a life of sports for them. If we come to that realization after we die, it's too late. We know that Jesus sees us as lovable, valuable, forgivable, and acceptable. Just look at the cross. He's making a point. A very strong point. Then he throws in this: "Cast the worthless servant into the outer darkness where there will be weeping and gnashing of teeth." This talent stuff is serious business.

12 - Making Your Life Fascinating

Joseph Campbell said, "We must let go of the life we have planned, so as to accept the one that is waiting for us."

I've heard people say, "Well, my life's not very interesting." But we have the choice to discover, explore, and seek our unique gifts and talents to use in this life, which makes life interesting, exciting, and worth living to our fullest potential. It's our responsibility, because no one's going to do it for us. We can make our own lives as boring or as interesting as we choose.

We can choose to spend time merely "life watching." We're free to learn as many details of other people's lives as we can, but we aren't free from the consequences of that choice. We should remember the truth. We know the truth from the Bible, one that's reaffirmed in NDEs: we'll be held accountable for how we lived *our* life. We won't be asked about or shown anything from anyone else's life.

In books on the phenomenon of NDEs there's a common occurrence known as the "life review." Guess what—the life shown is the life of the person undergoing the NDE. No one else's. Usually they're shown interactions with other people. Our lives are about relationships. That's what matters.

In my humble, non-biblical-scholar opinion, there's no more interesting life than the life of Jesus. The life of Jesus is the most interesting and fascinating life we need to be concerned with. It's a two-way street that yields real value in this life and the next. We receive love, guidance, grace, and blessings, which will make our life not only more interesting, but fascinating.

This also has an impact on our eternity. Our eternity is our responsibility. Can we get that from Twitter or Instagram? Jesus has our salvation in his hands and our eternity in his hands. Are you interested?

We're to spend our lives becoming more like Jesus, and our lives are as interesting and fascinating as we want to make them. God has a plan for every one of us. We're to grow in our relationship with Jesus and develop and fully use every gift and talent he has given us.

It's absolutely mesmerizing. That's one huge idea that people forget. Boredom isn't part of the plan. Boredom is our own fault. It's the unwillingness to explore our unique and authentic selves. It's our unwillingness to examine our passions. We're never bored when we pursue activities and actions that fully realize our individual uniqueness and authenticity.

We need to remember that what other people are doing is not our business. We may be watching other people become who *they* were meant to be, while we're wasting time ourselves in *not* discovering and realizing our own full potential.

We're in the love business. We're to use our unique gifts and talents in loving service to others.

As I'm writing this, it's around Christmas time. Every year I get reminded of the many different versions of the story *A Christmas Carol* by Charles Dickens. Early in the story, Jacob Marley tells Ebenezer Scrooge, "Mankind was my business. The common welfare was my business; charity, mercy, forbearance, and benevolence were *all* my business." People in need all around us—that is our business. Which celebrity is doing what with who is none of our business. Sitting back and judging celebrities or criticizing them or anyone else is none of our business either.

When we put Jesus at the center of our lives, that's the wisest thing we can do. He gives us more in return, in this life and the next. He yearns for us to spend time with him, and God yearns to bless us in this life and the next. There's nothing more valuable or interesting than that.

Now we come to what NDEs are telling us. We've already mentioned that one of the most common phrases that's conveyed to a person experiencing the NDE is this: "What do you have to show me that you've done with your life?" That direct quote is from *Life after Life* by Dr. Raymond Moody.[30] Another person relates, "The being pointed out to me that I should do things for other people, to try to do my best."[31] In some instances, people describe being given a choice to go back and to live, usually because their request to do so was made unselfishly, or because God or the being apparently had some mission in mind for them to fulfill. Here I would argue that God has a mission in mind for each of us to fulfill. In addition, he has an image of us in his mind when he created us. One part of his plan was for us to use our talents and gifts in a way that benefits others.

Remember the description Jesus gave to Howard Storm in his interview:

> The world is like God's garden. And God made you and everyone else to bloom in that garden. And to be beautiful. And God made every one of you unique and special to be beautiful in your own way.[32]

Unique and special. We should think about ourselves the way Jesus does. Every one of us is unique and special, and we bloom when we fulfill God's plan for our lives.

In *Lessons from the Light*, Dr. Kenneth Ring writes,

> In examining the lives of the NDErs we have met in this chapter, do you not feel that all of them, to various degrees, have been aided to live more authentic lives, much more in keeping with their previously dormant gifts and propensities, and emboldened to throw off the

social shackles, where necessary, that previously constrained them?[33]

Boom! There it is. That paragraph cuts to the bone of what this book is about. Living *authentic lives,* lives that are more closely true to what God had in mind. Much more in keeping with our own previously dormant gifts and passions. That is self-awareness.

Do you have dormant gifts and passions? Dormant gifts and passions are exactly what Jesus is talking about in the parable of the talents. The talent is buried. The definition of *dormant* is "being in a state of rest or inactivity, inoperative." Life becomes exciting only when you explore your passions and your gifts. They're already there, and have always been there.

It may be that we're too busy taking on life wave after wave, and we don't feel much like digging for our gifts. When we can learn to brave the wave, we use the power of the troubles to get us closer to our authentic selves. The waves become opportunities. Just as *we* have a purpose, so also each wave has a purpose.

Are you living a life that's authentic and consistent with what God had in mind? Or do you have social shackles that inhibit the full realization of your authentic self?

Some of these shackles could be the opinions of others or the pursuit of goals with limited or questionable value. Maybe there's an obsession with how others are living their lives. This sums it up nicely, as we go further in Dr. Ring's documentation of an NDE account:

> The Light told Peggy, in effect, that she should "follow her love," and that yielding herself to it was, in fact, to do the most unselfish and constructive thing in the world. The Light seems to be telling us, each of us, that we have a unique gift, an offering to make to the world,

and that our happiness and the worlds are both served when we live in such a way as to realize that gift, which is no less than our purpose in life.[34]

Discovering and realizing our gifts and offering them to others is the key to happiness. This is an interesting point Dr. Ring makes:

I have talked about this authentic or true self as something that is the Light's function to disclose to the individual. How does it do that? The answer is, often by first showing the NDEr his or her false or socially conditioned self.... In other instances, however, the NDEr is given a direct perception into the nature of the false self and is thereby allowed intuitively to understand that the person one has identified with and habitually thought of as one's essential self was nothing more than fiction.[35]

Boom! There's power in that last statement, if it helps us get a glimpse of our own false or fictional self.

The most obvious point is that we may be living a lie. There's real value in looking at the "false or socially conditioned self." Could you be living a life based on an inauthentic or fictional self? Dr. Ring is saying that the NDE experience reveals this false self. Think about this. What if God is allowing these near-death experiences so that people can identify their false or socially conditioned self?

My argument is that you don't *need* an NDE to recognize this false and socially conditioned self.

It bothers me when I see how much our society emphasizes values that are temporary and not eternal. There's so much time, energy, and money wasted on things that have limited value. I'm a witness to this because I've lived it.

There's value in looking at the NDE experience because it allows for a direct perception into the nature of the false self. For the rest of us, we're going to have to do this for ourselves.

In *Imagine Heaven*, John Burke writes this about Howard Storm's NDE:

> The reason Jesus did not love what I did was because it distracted from who I was meant to be. Like when you see someone who not only is failing to live up to their potential, but is actually denying their potential. I was made for one purpose and one purpose only. And that was what I was missing.[36]

We can't achieve our purpose if we can't even see that we're operating with a "false or socially conditioned self." We may be pursuing activities that we think are valuable or acceptable to our society, but not true to our own passions, gifts, or unique talents. It's living a lie by not being true to our real or authentic selves.

We must be cognizant of our own unique and special talents. The backpack on the journey comes into play because it can carry our supplies, but we can also fill it with our burdens. Let's look inside.

Let me stop for a second to make one important point. If you go back and reread the last few statements and begin to look at your own life, this is where you can begin to change the way you think. *Metanoia*. This self-examination is critical, and it requires brutal honesty with yourself. This process begins with your being able to recognize any evidence in your life that you're being driven by a "socially conditioned self." Do you spend large amounts of time watching other people's lives? Do you spend time and energy trying to entice others to watch *your* life, or trying to inspire envy in other people? Are you shackled or constrained by the opinions of others, as you work hard to impress other people?

Or are you actively trying to discover and develop the passions, talents, and gifts you already have? We all have them.

Brutal honesty is required here. Real change develops when we can be self-aware and totally honest about ourselves.

Spending inordinate amounts of time trying to impress others is especially dangerous because it leads to pride. From my own experience, we want to avoid pride like the plague.

Is there any misery or depression or unhappiness in your backpack? You may be investing yourself in pursuits that you actually have no talent or passion for. You may just be trying to make a lot of money. You may be stuck in a job because you have to care for your family or support your parents.

You may have to look at your own talents and try to see if your authentic self is being expressed in your daily life. That's a real key to fulfillment. Is your authentic self being expressed in a beautiful and unique way every day? The reason some task or labor makes you happy and brings fulfillment is that you're doing exactly what you were created to do. Albert Einstein said, "Everybody is a genius. But if you judge a fish by its ability to climb a tree, it will live its whole life believing that it is stupid." There's genius in everyone. Everyone's good at one thing at the very least. You may be the fish trying to climb a tree.

Are your passions and gifts being expressed in a way that benefits others and brings you joy? If not, that could be a source of unhappiness. What about low self-esteem or sense of value?

We've talked about our "rich relationship" with Jesus. When that relationship grows and develops, our own sense of worth and self-esteem grows. When we work to develop a real understanding of how much love Jesus has for us, our sense of worth and value skyrockets. When that's true, how could we *not* have value? Look at the sacrifice and suffering Jesus endured for every one of us.

How about bitterness, anger, resentment? Those are heavy weights in our backpack, because they don't allow for the love of Jesus to enter our hearts. Not enough room. We should forgive the people who hurt us and move on from that bitterness or anger, because if we don't make room for the love of Jesus, we can't express that love to others.

If we're Christians in the love business, we need to have plenty of inventory in our hearts. To be honest, we need as much love as possible. Get rid of that resentment and bitterness. Remember that you're the only who's suffering or losing by holding on to bitterness or resentment.

What about fear and anxiety? The antidote to fear is love. Remember that a mother will run into a burning house and sacrifice her life for her children. She has no fear, because it's overwhelmed and totally suppressed by sacrificial love.

Here, once again, the love of Jesus will enter our hearts and allow for boldness. Especially if we live in our spirits and by the power of the Holy Spirit. It takes time, but we're beginning to travel in the way God intended. Boldly.

> For the Spirit God gave us does not make us timid, but gives us power, love and self-discipline. (2 Timothy 1:7 NIV)

This is the second time I've mentioned this verse, because fear is one of the largest impediments to success. There's only one thing worse than failing, and that's not trying. People don't try most often because of fear.

We should look at the feeling of fear and try to see if it controls or dominates our lives. Is fear calling the shots? Are you a slave to those feelings? Are you paralyzed by your own fear? Fear will totally restrict your ability to reach your authentic self.

It may take some time to discover your authentic self, because you may have to try some things that make you uncomfortable and uneasy. That's a very good indicator that the activity you're pursuing is within the will of God. Remember, faith pleases God, and we can't stretch or grow our faith without some type of task that forces us to trust or rely on him. *Audentes fortuna iuvat*—fortune favors the bold.

The following NDE account really sums everything up nicely. It's from *Imagine Heaven: Near-Death Experiences, God's Promises, and the Exhilarating Future That Awaits You* by John Burke, where the author writes,

> Lindi heard a Voice [she assumed from Jesus] giving another person a life review, saying, "Let's look at all the things you've done to serve Me, to love other people well; let's look at the relationships in your life and how you've loved them well and therefore served Me through them." Lindi recalls, "What was interesting is it was all about relationships. There was nothing about accomplishments, nothing about our 'successes'—all about how you've loved other people." Then came the part she feared, but the Voice said, "Let's look at the missed opportunities to love Me better. Let's look at how you could have loved other people better, and the missed relationships and how you could have loved them better and therefore served Me better." Then the Voice said, "Welcome home, thank you for loving me so well throughout your life."[37]

There's no better summation of what's important in this life.

From my own experience, I know that studying these accounts and growing in my relationship with Jesus have had an impact on every single relationship in my life. Every one. There's more love, joy, peace, kindness, goodness, and patience. My role as parent, spouse, sibling, and son have been impacted in a very positive way. I ate at the restaurant and the food was great; no claims of perfection—I just said the food was great. The resort is awesome and the beach is beautiful.

Each of us is just a WIP (as I am too): a *work in progress*. That's WIP, not wimp. We're WIPs looking for WOTs: *wastes of time*. If we begin to eliminate more and more WOTs, we get closer to our authentic selves. We may stumble, fall, and get angry and frustrated, and make huge mistakes and experience epic failure. But we get back up, dust ourselves off, and keep going.

PART II - WHAT WE BELIEVE

13 - THE BEDROCK OF BELIEF

As we're going through this journey, it's helpful to remember that any endeavor must be built on a foundation. A solid bedrock. The thought, idea, or conviction should be undeniably, absolutely, and indisputably true in your mind, in your heart, and most importantly your soul. Spiritual truths and beliefs are the solid rock or foundation of any valuable or worthwhile undertaking.

Ask yourself these questions: Am I right now, at this moment, close to the image God had in mind for me when he created me? Am I using the talents and gifts God granted me in meaningful ways that add value to my life and endeavors? Whose image am I realizing? Do my habits, passions, and pursuits reflect the image God has in mind for me? Is this *my* idea, or God's image for me?

Asking yourself these kinds of questions is part of the self-examination that leads to self-awareness. Sometimes the path isn't so clear, but that's the whole idea behind faith.

To help sustain and carry us on our journey, two bedrocks of faith are (1) the life, teachings and resurrection of Jesus, and (2) the promises of God in his Word.

Jesus told us that he did miracles and fulfilled prophecy so that we might believe:

> After all, the Father set me apart and sent me into the world. Don't believe me unless I carry out my Father's work. But if I do his work, believe in the evidence of the miraculous works I have done, even if you don't believe me. Then you will know and understand that the Father is in me, and I am in the Father. (John 10:36-38 NLT)

We know that Jesus existed. Even atheists concede this point. Most biblical scholars feel that the current evidence available to us favors the resurrection of Jesus as occurring. It's the best explanation of what the evidence is showing us. This is discussed by Dr. Gary Habermas in *The Case for the Resurrection of Jesus*. Regarding miracles, Habermas argues the following:

> Two recent researchers, both leading scholars in the historical Jesus discussion, have written almost 500 pages each on Jesus's miracles. John Meier found that in almost half of the miracle accounts recorded in the New Testament, we have enough data to conclude that something like that particular historical scene occurred. (For details, see Vol. 2 of Meier's set *A Marginal Jew.*) The second, Graham Twelftree, concluded that about three-quarters of the Gospel miracle accounts were confirmable; again, at least that historical details in the accounts could be verified. (For details, see Twelftree's volume, *Jesus the Miracle Worker.*) They did not say that all these accounts were verifiable miracles, but that these particular miracle scenes have verifiable historical checks and balances, according to the normal standards applied in recent historical Jesus research. Admittedly, that's still rather outstanding, as well as surprising. Traditionally, many have said that if the resurrection occurred, then lesser miracles are more easily confirmed. But in light of this research, now we have specific historical considerations in favor of the miracle accounts themselves.[38]

There are many references regarding the proof of the resurrection and the historical veracity of the life of Jesus. This book is not about history or trying to prove the existence of Jesus. I've done enough research and work to satisfy myself as an individual. That investigation is enough for me, but if you need further study, I invite you to challenge the reality of the life, teachings, miracles, and resurrection of Jesus. Do the research and the work if you need further confirmation.

I'm going to admit that I'm the king of the skeptics. But when it comes to the historicity of Jesus and the veracity of NDEs, the evidence is overwhelming. However, don't let me stop you from doing your own research. You can start with the references in this book.

Faith and belief are critical for the next stage of the journey. They're absolutely required. Jesus showed us as much:

> And they took offense at Him. But Jesus said to them, "A prophet is not without honor except in his hometown and in his own household." And He did not do many miracles there because of their unbelief. (Matthew 13:57-58 NASB)

If we want Jesus to work miracles in our own lives, our faith must be developed, nurtured, and grown.

There's a very important scene in the New Testament involving the raising of Lazarus from the dead. The whole account is in John 11:1-44. I'm going to quote a few verses from that longer account because they really spell out what Jesus thinks is important.

> So then he told them plainly, "Lazarus is dead, and for your sake I am glad I was not there, so that you may believe." (1:14-15 NIV)

This sounds to me like Lazarus *had* to die so that Jesus could make a point and strengthen the faith of the apostles when he brought Lazarus back to life.

The account continues:

> Jesus said to her [to Martha, the sister of Lazarus], "I am the resurrection and the life. The one who believes in me will live, even though they die, and whoever lives by believing in me will never die. Do you believe this?" (11:25-26 NIV)

This is important also because Jesus says whoever lives by believing in him will never die. He's trying to tell us that this is the only way to live. We live by believing in Jesus. We have eternal life, but we also have faith, power, and strength while in this life.

He also said later on this occasion, in kind of an irritated tone, "Did I not tell you that if you believe, you will see the glory of God?" (11:40 NIV). We should remember that Jesus is fully human and fully God, so we get a glimpse here of what he thinks and how he feels, because he has a human side. So you can see that he gets a little annoyed. Kind of like a parent. It's like he's saying "What's with you guys?"

This is my own personal, layman, non-biblical-scholar opinion, but it seems to me that *believe* is mentioned so many times by Jesus, I don't think we can really ignore it. He's sending us a message. Not only do we believe in him, we *live* by believing in him. We believe so that he can work miracles in our lives and so that we can see the glory of God. When we live by believing, he reveals more of himself to us and then we begin to see others and ourselves the way we truly are. We develop the "eyes of Christ." We begin to see more of the spiritual side of who we are.

Believing and accepting that Jesus was telling us the truth is just the beginning of the journey. The real work begins when we *act* on those beliefs.

A good first step is realizing that we have a distorted and fuzzy view of how we're to live. We may be spending too much time settling. We get comfortable. We get into a routine that we think is "good enough." It kind of reminds me of when pro football players describe another player as "just playing for a paycheck." Our vision may be blurry because we haven't developed the "eyes of Christ." God doesn't want us to live our lives "playing for a paycheck," or thinking, "Well, I believe, so I'm going to heaven, and that's all that counts."

We need to clarify the word *believe* when it comes to Christ, because there's a very important contrast between the Greek definition and the English definition. You may already be aware of this distinction. I mention it because it's huge, and I just learned it recently.

Believe (in English) basically means "to accept something as true."

Believe (that is, the Greek word *pisteuo* that's translated as "believe") means "trust in, rely upon, commit to."

This distinction involves action. When we believe in the way Jesus had in mind, we trust in, rely upon, and commit to him. We *act*. We act on what we know to be true.

We've already gone over the idea that wisdom is the combination of knowledge and obedience. We act by using Jesus as our guide. We can look at our thoughts, beliefs, and values right at this very moment and get a snapshot of where we are in our relationship with Jesus. We should be able to look at our lives and get a clear idea of the value we place on our relationship with Jesus. We're all at different places on this road, but the goal is for all of us to get closer to Christ. The closer to him we get, everything else falls into place. We get closer to that sculpture or picture or painting God had in mind for us—our authentic selves.

> For God so loved the world, that he gave his only begotten Son that whoever believes in him should not perish but have everlasting life. (John 3:16 NLT)

Accepting something as true is passive. We just accept. Like accepting our fate. And there's a difference between (a) just sitting and accepting and (b) actually growing in our relationship.

People should ask themselves, "Okay, if I change my relationship to *trust in, rely upon,* and *commit to*—what's the payoff? What's in it for me?"

My response: *everything.* Everything's in it for you. Nothing will change until you really believe that a growing, thriving relationship with Jesus has real value. If you don't believe you need Jesus, you won't be inclined to do anything differently.

As I've described, I was frustrated, angry, and anxious because of a series of repeated failures and events that really shook me. Sometimes it takes an event or series of events in your life for God to get your attention.

When we understand that God is sovereign and he controls those events, those waves, we can use them to get closer to authenticity. It hinges on our ability to see them as a means of shaping us and allowing us to grow closer to our authentic selves. We must remember that these difficulties come from pure and inexhaustible love. They're for our own good.

We're all on different paths along this road, this spiritual journey. Some of us are just standing still. I was just existing. Total zombie walk. Just going about life focusing on surviving and acquiring. Getting more things. I was ripe for this warning from Jesus, and the illustration he then gave:

> Then he said, "Beware! Guard against every kind of greed. Life is not measured by how much you own." Then he told them a story: "A rich man had a fertile farm that produced fine crops. He said to himself, 'What should I do? I don't have room for all my crops.' Then he said, 'I know! I'll tear down my barns and build bigger

ones. Then I'll have room enough to store all my wheat and other goods. And I'll sit back and say to myself, "My friend, you have enough stored away for years to come. Now take it easy! Eat, drink, and be merry!"' But God said to him, 'You fool! You will die this very night. Then who will get everything you worked for?' Yes, a person is a fool to store up earthly wealth but not have a rich relationship with God." (Luke 12:15-21 NLT)

This passage is there to point out how the rich man was totally consumed with building barns and storing all his goods. Look around next time you're driving. Look at how many storage businesses there are for people to store their possessions. You know where you *won't* find any storage unit businesses? Poor countries. We don't even realize how wealthy we are in this country. We have businesses to store our excess "things." Desiring and acquiring.

I myself wasted decades of time, energy, and money when I had no thriving or growing relationship with Jesus.

I also came to realize that we all have a relatively short amount of time left. Everything was not lost, though. Once you begin to see the WOTs (wastes of time) in your life, there's still enough time to make real changes. It's never too late.

When you begin to believe that the things you can't count have the most value, your life changes.

I remember being in a business meeting with some of my partners, and one of them was going on and on about profits and threats to our business. I was looking straight at him and just thinking to myself, "Wow, he doesn't even have a clue that not one thing he's talking about has any real value." My eyes were open, and I could clearly see that most of the things we were discussing and spending so much time on really didn't mean anything.

Some business owners and accountant types will probably say, "Hey, how are you going to take care of yourself and your family?" I get it. I understand. We have to survive. But there's a difference between surviving and acquiring versus surviving and *thriving*. That's what Jesus is saying in that parable. Focus on your relationship to God. That's where the real value is.

When we die, the only thing we'll possess is our relationship with Jesus. Things don't really start to change until we get serious about Jesus. The Christian life is serious business. Until we believe that Jesus is valuable, we won't get serious.

14 - The Choice to Believe Is Ours

The waves are coming. We know that. Whatever age you are, you've felt them.

I'll say it again. It doesn't matter who you are, how much money you make, how smart you are, or what you believe; you *will* have waves, storms, trials, and troubles. There's no avoiding them. There'll be bumps, storms, obstacles, and waves to face. That's reality. You may as well learn that. Teach it to your kids.

It's simple truth, as Jesus says:

> I have told you all this so that you may have peace in me. Here on earth you will have many trials and sorrows. But take heart, because I have overcome the world. (John 16:33 NLT)

I chose this version because it mentions "many trials and sorrows." Some other versions read "trouble" or "tribulation" instead of "many trials and sorrows." If you've lived any significant amount of time, you know well that "many trials and sorrows" sums it up better. There may be a few people out there who can say, "Oh yeah, I've had a little trouble here and there." Good for them. For the rest of us, it's a boatload of trials and sorrows. If you know you've been through all these storms, and you're very aware that more are coming, why not build your relationship with Jesus?

When you have him with you, you can endure any trial. More importantly, how you see those trials will give you the strength and wisdom to see them as opportunities. Opportunities to build your faith and to bring you closer to who you were created to be. When you can brave the wave and ride it, that's when life becomes more interesting and fulfilling.

I've come across people in my life who have little or zero faith. I've seen the look in their eyes at the death of a loved one. One thing's missing. Hope. Not the hope of wishful thinking, but the hope of the Bible.

Biblical hope is conveyed by the Greek word *elpis*, meaning "confidence" or "trust." Our hope is to be more like eager expectation. I've seen this kind of hope in people of faith when they're nearing death. Sometimes they're eagerly awaiting it, almost like they're in line for a ride at Disneyland. Excitement and eager expectation. Smiling and waiting. They have total confidence in the beauty and wonder of the place that Jesus has prepared. They believe Jesus when he says,

> Let not your hearts be troubled. Believe in God; believe also in me. In my Father's house are many rooms. If it were not so, would I have told you that I go to prepare a place for you? And if I go and prepare a place for you, I will come again and will take you to myself, that where I am you may be also. And you know the way to where I am going."

After saying that, Jesus was asked (by the disciple Thomas), "Lord, we do not know where you are going. How can we know the way?" Here's the answer from Jesus:

> I am the way, and the truth, and the life. No one comes to the Father except through me. If you had known me, you would have known my Father also. From now on you do know him and have seen him. (John 14:1-7 ESV)

We either believe Jesus about heaven or we don't. We either believe this promise or we don't.

The people of faith who are excited about dying and being with Jesus believe this statement down to their very bones. You know who else has no fear of death? People who've had near-death experiences. The majority of them lose their fear of death. They believe they now know exactly what it's like, and that's one of the traits of people who've undergone those experiences. No fear.

We need to decide whether we believe and trust Jesus. There will be trouble, but he's with us. We'll die, but he has prepared a place for us. We have the Bible's brand of hope: eager expectation, not wishful thinking.

If we build our lives on the words of Jesus, there's no downside. We trust and have joyful and confident expectation of eternal salvation (Acts 23:6; 26:7; Romans 5:4; 12:12; 15:13; 1 Corinthians 13:13; 1 Peter 1:3; 3:15—you may want to go over all those verses).

Think about it for a second. Why is this hope mentioned so many times? Could it possibly be so that we may come to believe and trust in the words of Jesus? Luke, Paul, and Peter tell us in all these passages about our joyful, confident, expectation of eternal salvation. That's how we're supposed to think. Why? I believe it's because this allows us to change the way we think about what's temporary and what's eternal. It allows us to separate the seen from the unseen. The spiritual versus the fleshly.

We're to be serving and loving others. We're to be consumed with the business of loving others. That's the family business. Nonbelievers always bring up hell in their arguments. "So I'm going to hell because I don't believe in Jesus, right?" Our best response? "No one gave me the keys to the gates of heaven. No one gave me the power to send anyone to hell. That's between you and Jesus."

As Christians, we're in the love business. We're open for business, and business should be booming.

It's very easy in this life to get caught up in worldly or materialistic goals. It's the rat race and the consumerism and the competitive lifestyle engendered in this modern world.

Many people have an idea that if they won the Lotto or had plenty of money, all their problems would be solved. Jesus talked more about money than he did heaven or hell. Why do you think that is? Money and material wealth are the things most likely to become idols, and they interfere the most with our relationship to him. When you have all the money in the world, it seems that you don't have a need for God.

We need to rely on, trust in, and commit to Jesus. That's the meaning behind *believe*. It means a real relationship. It's like a marriage. You trust in, rely on, and commit to your husband or wife.

Think about this. Two of the wealthiest men on earth are agnostic. An agnostic is defined as "a person who believes that nothing is known or can be known of the existence or nature of God or of anything beyond material phenomena; a person who claims neither faith nor disbelief in God." This comes back to the lunatic, liar, or Lord argument. When someone claims neither faith nor disbelief, they've chosen not to decide. *But it's still a choice.* They've chosen to believe that Jesus was a lunatic or a liar. If they believed he's Lord, they would be screaming it with their words and actions.

We know Jesus was real and existed, and we have his Word. If we choose to ignore him, then we make ourselves God. Everybody has a god. Everyone. If you don't believe in the real God, you made yourself your god. And if there's one thing we've learned from history, it's that we humans make horrible gods.

Compared to God we are puny, weak, and we make stupid decisions. (That sure sounds like me.)

Remember humans are humans. Again, I'm not saying we're stupid. I'm arguing that we say and do stupid things. We all do. So learn from history.

God wants a relationship with every one of us. He wants us to depend on him. That's one of the wisest things you can do. Look how many times we screw up when we depend on our own power or wisdom. Look how many times the world screws up when it depends on its own wisdom. It's not hard to see that we're destroying our own planet.

God wants us to grow in our relationship with Jesus. If he were to give us a bunch of material wealth, we most likely would be unable to handle it, because we're not living for spiritual fruit. Remember that self-control is in there (in the list of the fruit of the Spirit) beside love, joy, peace, patience, kindness, goodness, faithfulness, and gentleness.

For example: "Seventy-eight percent of NFL players go bankrupt within two years of retiring. Within five years of retirement, sixty percent of former NBA players are broke. Numerous major league baseball players have been similarly ruined."[39] You should ask yourself a question: Is there a correlation with being an elite athlete and the inability to handle money? Or is there a problem with discipline and self-control in handling large amounts of money? What seems to be more likely?

Many times God wants to bless us, but he's just waiting for us to grow up. Hey, don't believe me—believe Jesus:

> And I tell you, ask, and it will be given to you; seek, and you will find; knock, and it will be opened to you. For everyone who asks receives, and the one who seeks finds, and to the one who knocks it will be opened. What father

among you, if his son asks for a fish, will instead of a fish give him a serpent; or if he asks for an egg, will give him a scorpion? If you then, who are evil, know how to give good gifts to your children, how much more will the heavenly Father give the Holy Spirit to those who ask him! (Luke 11:9-13 ESV)

There are several points to mention about this passage. One is that this is one of those undeniable prayers. Jesus is telling us that the heavenly Father will never deny the Holy Spirit to us. "How much more" will God give us the Holy Spirit! If you pray for the power of the Holy Spirit to come into your heart and into your spirit after accepting Jesus, it will never be denied. The Holy Spirit is our promise from God, and he's available to all believers. There's real power in the Holy Spirit, and nothing in the New Testament got done (including the ministries of Jesus and the apostles) until the power of the Holy Spirit descended on them.

As a father or mother, we know the joy and satisfaction we get when we give our children gifts or something special. When they've been kind or good or they've accomplished something after hard work or sacrifice, we really want to reward them. Why would God be any different? Plus, we should remember that he loves us more than we love our own children, and he has an unlimited ability to bless us. He has a huge storehouse of blessings he wants to give us. He wants to bless us more than we want to be blessed.

Here's a good verse to memorize:

I am the LORD, the God of all mankind. Is anything too hard for me? (Jeremiah 32:27 NIV)

God can do anything. He's waiting for us to believe. He wants us to grow up and be more mature. He wants us to think about others and to take our spiritual growth seriously.

Notice that Jesus said, "What father will deny gifts to his children"? God our Father is waiting for us to come to him and ask. He's waiting for us to become blessable.

When we believe we have the choice, things change. We choose how close to Jesus we want to be. When we can recognize the value of a relationship with Jesus, we choose to spend time with him.

We've already talked about heaven being our choice. Likewise, hell is the separation from God by our choosing to reject him. But we can also choose to accept and embrace him. We can begin to see Jesus as our best friend. We can begin to live our lives the way he had in mind: discovering and embracing our authentic selves.

Jesus wants us to get to know him. He desires our love.

I remember one time I came home from medical school on Christmas break, and my father pulled me aside and said, "Son, I'm getting worried about your mother. She's going to church every day. I think she's addicted to religion." I remember thinking that there could possibly be some type of addiction to faith that we hadn't gotten to in my psych courses.

That was years ago. I just recently figured out what was going on with my mom back then. She *chose* to go to church because of her love for Jesus. She wanted to spend time with him. She valued her relationship with him, and it was a priority in her life.

One of my aunts thought she was spending so much time at church, and she made a comment that my mom was having an affair with another man. My mom replied, "I am. I'm having an affair with Jesus."

I get it. I enjoy spending time with him during the week also. It brings me joy.

Sometimes there's a fear that we'll change so much when we commit to Jesus that we won't recognize our own selves. It's quite the opposite. God made you. He knows your personality, quirks, traits, and gifts. You can't reach your full potential or realization of your authentic self *without* a relationship with Jesus. He is truth.

If my life hadn't changed ten years ago, I wouldn't be able to see the things I can see now. I wouldn't understand all the things I now understand. I wouldn't have received all the love, joy, and peace that I've received, plus many more blessings. (Notice I didn't emphasize self-control; I'm a work in progress.)

God is waiting, yearning, and craving for us to seek him. He promised many times that if we seek him, we'll find him:

> Then you will call upon Me and come and pray to Me, and I will listen to you. You will seek Me and find Me when you search for Me with all your heart. (Jeremiah 29:12-13 NASB)

Can you hear the yearning and longing in his voice? He *wants* us to love him. Notice that he says we're to search for him with *all our heart*. This search can't be half-hearted. We need to have a conviction and a passion. He wants all our hearts, not just a part. That's why living within the confines of a false self that's fiction deprives us of the full experience of a relationship with Jesus. If we're pursuing worldly goals, our hearts and our desires aren't fully invested in our pursuit of a thriving relationship with Jesus.

Jesus died so we could have all this. Some people aren't even aware of their own potential. They don't see Jesus as someone they need. But we can't fully realize our full potential and live our lives the way God had in mind without Jesus and the power of the Holy Spirit.

What we believe about money and possessions has a real impact on our spiritual growth. The reality is that we don't own anything. We're just borrowers. God gives us gifts in this life, and then he watches how we use those gifts. It kind of reminds me of those big plastic ant farms where you can see the ants working and building tunnels. God then drops a gift and watches and sees what we do with it.

> Here's the lesson: use your worldly resources to benefit others and make friends. Then, when your earthly possessions are gone, they will welcome you to an eternal home. (Luke 16:9 NLT)

Here Jesus is telling us to use our financial resources to benefit others and bring more people to him. That's part of our whole reason for living. Telling others about the good news. Telling others about Jesus. We're to use our money to help others who are less fortunate. The musician Prince said it well: "The best use for money is to give it to the ones who need it most." We must remember that fifty percent of the world's population lives on less than two dollars a day. We're truly blessed in this country.

Sometimes you don't want to see, even if you believe. Sometimes you tell yourself that *you* know what's best for *you*. "I mean who knows me better than me?" Jesus does. And when you ask Jesus for direction, remember that if you believe, you'll be shown the best path. It might not be the easiest path, and you may even fail, but if you believe in the promises of God, it's always the best for you *at that time*. Just like a comedian or an actor delivering a funny line; it's all in the timing.

So in faith, we trust him and believe his promise. No matter what the outcome, even if it brings bumps and bruises or it fails, it's for our own good:

> For we know that God causes everything to work together for the good of those who love God and are called according to his purpose for them. (Romans 8:28 NLT)

Sometimes God sends us on a tough path because he wants to grow us up. Whenever you're getting frustrated and you're asking God for something, sometimes he's waiting for you to *act*. It's like a parent who has a special gift for one of their children, and they're so excited to give it to them. Then their teenager walks through the door with a report card showing straight F's across the board. How excited would you be to give that son or daughter the special gift?

Whenever there's unanswered prayer, the first place to look is ourselves and our own behavior. God has revealed Jesus to us, so we have a good idea who our role model is. But many times, we're our own worst enemy. Are we allowing something in our own lives that we absolutely know is not within God's will? If you want beautiful wood floors in your living room, you need to take out the stinky, dirty, stained carpet.

Sometimes when our prayers aren't being answered, it's just not the right time. His blessing for you will come at the exact right time. Sometimes he's going to bless you in ways you can't see. There are blessings of peace or good health. Blessings of love and joy. Blessings of family and good friends. Blessings of true intimacy with Jesus—the most valuable diamond in the world. There are blessings of wisdom and insight. You may be shown something that you've never been able to see before. Wisdom, insight, and understanding are gifts also. These are all true spiritual riches.

> If you are faithful in little things, you will be faithful in large ones. But if you are dishonest in little things, you won't be honest with greater responsibilities. And if you are untrustworthy about worldly wealth, who will trust you with the true riches of heaven? And if you are not faithful with other people's things, why should you be trusted with things of your own? (Luke 16:10-12 NLT)

Spiritual riches are way more valuable, because you take them with you into eternity. We all get into this world of see, feel, touch, and count, but Jesus wants us to live above those things. What we can see, feel, touch, and count usually do *not* count. You can't count love, joy, peace, or patience.

When we trust in, rely on, and commit to Jesus, that's when things change. We learn to let go, believe, trust, and rely on him. When we let him into our finances and into our job and into our marriage, all those are stronger. Put Jesus into your marriage and see what happens. If two people in a marriage think like Jesus, the marriage is easier and instantly better. How? Jesus loves with unconditional, pure, sacrificial love. The Greek word for this love is *agape*. That's the kind of love Jesus loved us with. He put us before himself when he died on the cross for us. If a husband puts his wife and family first and loves sacrificially, the marriage is stronger. If a wife puts her husband first and loves sacrificially and unconditionally, the marriage is stronger. Pure, unconditional, sacrificial love by both husband and wife in a marriage is difficult, but when two people are committed to that goal, the marriage is stronger. No question. Much of the difficulty in marriages can be broken down to selfishness, immaturity, and pride. But if two people can deny themselves and put the needs of the other first, the marriage thrives. There's struggle when only one partner is committed to that goal.

Also, we can learn from seeing with the "eyes of Christ." Things get easier when we allow our spouses and children to be themselves. It's also helpful when we allow our spouses and children to be imperfect. God created us to be ourselves and to develop a clear idea and understanding of who we are. His will isn't some overbearing rule or law to control us. God's will is an expression of his love for us. Things get easier if we allow our spouse to be imperfect. Jesus allows *us* to be imperfect; that's the whole reason he came, because we can't be sinless. If we can allow our children and our spouses to be imperfect as we are imperfect, things get easier.

> Make allowance for each other's faults, and forgive anyone who offends you. Remember, the Lord forgave you, so you must forgive others. (Colossians 3:13 NLT)

Notice the word *must* in that verse. This is nonnegotiable.

If you look closely at your own marriage or relationships around you that are in difficulty, it's easy to see pride, selfishness, or immaturity causing the problem.

Remember, the family is the laboratory of love. *Agape* is something we strive for—but it's very hard. Just look at the current divorce rate.

Stop and take some time to look at the arguments in your marriage or other relationships. Look carefully and ask yourself: Was I being prideful? Was I being selfish? Was I being immature?

Notice that it starts with you. Did you start with what the other person was doing? Was he or she being prideful, selfish, or immature? Sometimes we can't even see our own pride or selfishness. Sometimes your spouse can't see their own pride, selfishness, or immaturity. When you can see your own pride, immaturity or selfishness, and you accept responsibility for your part in an argument, the relationship grows. When two people in a marriage have self-awareness and can see their own fault in an argument, things get easier.

Most of the time there's blame being thrown around like confetti at a New Year's Eve party. That's our culture right now. It's always someone else's fault. But pointing fingers is childish and immature. Looking at our own role in a conflict is what adults do. If we all accepted responsibility for our mistakes and became more self-aware, everyone would be better off.

You know how to develop self-awareness? Go to the Word. Spend time with Jesus. My marriage got stronger because I became very aware of my own selfishness. I started to be on the lookout for pride. My family got stronger because I began to think the way Jesus had in mind.

Want a stronger marriage? Put Jesus in the center of it.

It's not going to happen overnight. It takes time before we start to feel comfortable allowing Jesus into every area of our life. When we trust more and believe more, then we can ask for guidance in more and more areas.

People go through this life buffet style. They pass on the salad, choose an entree and a dessert, and then go to their table. They say, "You can be in my nighttime prayer life, Jesus, but stay out of my finances." Or, "I'll take the salvation you offer, Jesus, but don't get involved in my big decisions." They don't turn to him for guidance in some of the biggest decisions in their lives.

It will take time to move from the "accepting as true" type of believe to the "trust in, rely on, and commit to" type of believe. There's no instant remake of our spiritual lives. The most important thing to realize is that the *believe* mentioned in John 3:16 is about action.

We've already mentioned the fact that only thirty percent of people in this country read the Bible regularly. So no big decisions from the other seventy percent? People aren't consulting God in their daily lives. But when they get a diagnosis of cancer, you never hear, "Jesus, stay out of my health issues, okay? I got this. I really don't need you now."

Notice that people don't talk about faith or prayer too much, and Jesus doesn't come up in a conversation, until someone's in the hospital or has died. We don't talk about Jesus much unless we're in church or Bible study. It's always, "My thoughts and prayers are with you." When people get closer to death and they can see the finish line, that's when vision becomes the clearest. We'll go over that later. Vision becomes crystal clear.

It's when you think you have plenty of time that you tend to put off your relationship with Jesus. You may think, "Oh, I believe in Jesus, but I don't want to get caught up in all the rules and going to church on Sundays."

This book was written for the "nones" also. I was one of those too. People in this group have an acquaintance with Jesus, but are put off by organized religion or by the rules and regulations or the hypocrisy of those who have authority in the church. They got put off by some bad experience, or they feel they don't get anything out of church services. They say, "There's no need." When we have that approach, the problem is that we're blocking out voices of truth. You eliminate all voices, and you tend to miss out on living a life that's way more full, rich, and satisfying.

Jesus wants to be our best friend not only when we're on our deathbed, but when we're healthy and happy. He says,

> The thief's purpose is to steal and kill and destroy. My purpose is to give them a rich and satisfying life. (John 10:10 NLT)

He doesn't want the genie role. He doesn't want to be the judge ready to pounce whenever we slip up. He wants to be our best friend. He wants us to love, rely on, and commit to him, like you would with your spouse. He wants us to know and love him the way you would your own child, wife, husband, significant other, mother, or father.

Do you love Jesus like that?

> I keep asking that the God of our Lord Jesus Christ, the glorious Father, may give you the Spirit of wisdom and revelation, so that you may know him better. I pray that

the eyes of your heart may be enlightened in order that you may know the hope to which he has called you, the riches of his glorious inheritance in his holy people, and his incomparably great power for us who believe. (Ephesians 1:17-18 NIV)

There's that word *believe* again. Remember: rely on, trust in, commit to.

15 - CHOSEN TO PRODUCE

To really *know* someone, you must spend time with them. There are no other options. Think about how long it took to really get to know your husband or your wife. Think about the things you do because you know your child or spouse so very well. You're at the grocery store, and you think, "Oh, let me get this, because I know they'll really love it." Or you did something you know will make your spouse or your child angry or upset. They get home, and you know you should tell them, so you hang your head in a pitiful way. "I have something to tell you."

Jesus want us to *know* him like you do your spouse or your child. It's *personal*.

People don't understand how much Jesus yearns, desires, and wants so badly for us to be in a close loving relationship with him. He says,

> There is no greater love than to lay down one's life for one's friends. You are my friends if you do what I command. I no longer call you slaves, because a master doesn't confide in his slaves. Now you are my friends, since I have told you everything the Father told me. You didn't choose me. I chose you. I appointed you to go and produce lasting fruit, so that the Father will give you whatever you ask for, using my name. This is my command: Love each other. (John 15:13-17 NIV)

This is one of those stop-reread-and-absorb verses. When he's talking about laying down one's life for one's friends, he's not only talking about his sacrifice on the cross, but about *us* laying down and donating our lives back to him.

If we stop and self-examine, we can figure out what we're living for very quickly. For most moms, the kids come first. They live for their families. Dads can be focused on career and looking for promotions or making more money. Some people want social status, or they want to be admired or envied. Everyone's living for something. What are you living for?

Notice that Jesus emphasizes that we didn't choose him, he chose us. He may be choosing you now. Calling you to get to know and love him. He's challenging us to go and *produce lasting fruit*. Can you see any fruit in your life?

When we accept the sacrifice Jesus made for us on the cross, and begin to develop our relationship, we should remember the price he paid and that we were purchased. We belong to him. But what people forget is that he willingly, lovingly belongs to us. He wants to belong to us. It goes both ways. We were bought with a price, so we belong to him also. And he's our most valuable possession—the most valuable diamond in the world—just as we're his most valuable possession.

We should spend time with him in prayer. He wants to be our friend and confide in us. Think about it. Do you share your most important secrets with the girl who makes your latte at Starbucks? How about the lady who does your nails? You share your closest secrets with your closest and most trustworthy friends.

The part about choosing is important. If you feel compelled, or you feel a deep moving or stirring in your heart to start on this road, pay attention. He gives us many chances to come to him.

There's no downside to developing a stronger relationship with Jesus. None. You may have waves and trials and testing and tough paths, but they're all worth it. When we can begin to understand that those waves and trials serve a purpose, we look at them as opportunities to get closer to Jesus. We learn to brave the wave and turn and get ready to ride it, because we know and understand that at the end of the ride are spiritual insights and understanding that make it all worth it. Not to mention the rewards that wait for us in eternity. The benefits in this life of knowing Jesus are so many it's incredible. The rewards later can't be described in words, as the NDEs tell us.

We should accept responsibility for our own eternity. Your eternity is your responsibility, and no one else's. It's personal. It's unique to you.

We read the Gospels to absorb the words of Jesus. We get to understand how he thinks and what's important to him. We begin to see him the way he truly is. We spend time with him to learn to be able to recognize his voice. We communicate with him.

He wants us to get to know him. He yearns for our love also. Everyone needs Jesus. There's the real value. You can bet your life on him. The good news is that once you do, you've already won.

Things will not change until we believe in Jesus the way he intended. He wants us to get to know and love him.

Which means we must act. Love is an action. As Amy Carmichael said, "You can give without loving, but you cannot love without giving." Jesus wants our time. He wants to know our love is genuine by our effort. As he said,

> Now that you know these things, you will be blessed if you do them. (John 13:17 NLT)

We don't sit and accept. I don't accept where I am now, and I hope you don't want to accept where you are now. The New Testament mentions our responsibility to grow eight times. How many do we need to take it seriously?

We're to love God and love others. Love is an action. One of the most effective first steps is starting at least one good habit. Bad habits are hard to break, but so are good habits. Starting each day in a quiet time in prayer and in Bible reading and meditating on the Word will start the day out the right way. The most important thing you do every day is love God and spend time with him. That's exactly what Jesus did:

> Very early in the morning, while it was still dark, Jesus got up, left the house and went off to a solitary place, where he prayed. (Mark 1:35 NIV)

What you do every single day matters. It matters in this life, and it has a major impact on the next. Starting off in the morning with Jesus is the best way to start our day. You don't have to spend hours and hours to get something out of a quiet time. Fifteen to twenty minutes a day will make a difference. As you grow in your relationship, you may want more time. That's a very good sign. When you love someone, you yearn to be with them. But it takes time, energy, and effort. Every relationship does.

What we believe about Jesus is very important of course, not only because of the value of our relationship with him, but also because it influences what we believe about ourselves. It happens automatically. As I mentioned, maturity and improving our relationships with our family and spouses begins to develop when we begin to see our own behavior more clearly. But we also begin to see ourselves the way Jesus sees us. For our lives to change for the better, we begin to see ourselves as valuable, acceptable, lovable, and forgivable. We know we have value just by looking at the cross. When you look at yourself, you can truly believe, know, and understand: "Yeah, he really did die for me." That's when things change. It's personal. That's the main goal of this book: personal, powerful, practical.

Here's some personal. As I said, when you accept him, he belongs to you. The tough part for many people is realizing that you belong to him:

> God paid a high price for you, so don't be enslaved by the world. Each of you, dear brothers and sisters, should remain as you were when God first called you. (1 Corinthians 7:23-24 NLT)

When we can look at ourselves the way Jesus does, we can see that we have value. People become depressed when they see themselves as worthless. They begin to believe there's no hope in their lives. When they have no hope, they can get suicidal. They don't see their lives as valuable or having any worth. That's a huge lie. Everyone has worth and value. We're loved beyond our capacity to describe in words.

NDEs confirm that. When someone who had an NDE is describing the love they felt, but they don't say, "It's hard to put into words," then you know they didn't really have an NDE. The only person I spoke to who had an NDE said, "The love I received seemed to be dripping out of every pore of my skin, I can't describe it adequately."

Remember that Satan is the father of lies, so whenever you or anyone you know begins to believe they have no worth or value, they're believing a total lie. *Every* person's life has value and worth. *Every* person.

We must try to understand the depth of love that God has for us. Saint Augustine said, "He loves each and every one of us as if there is only one of us." And Jesus said,

> As the Father has loved me, so have I loved you. Now remain in my love. If you keep my commands, you will remain in my love, just as I have kept my Father's commands and remain in his love. I have told you this so that my joy may be in you and that your joy may be complete. (John 15:9-15 NIV)

You see love and joy mentioned there. Those two in combo bring peace. The first three of the spiritual fruits come from our proximity to Jesus. Clearly, we're valuable and lovable. He calls us friends, and he has let us in on the family business. We're in the love business. We can start by loving ourselves and then opening our hearts so they can be filled with the love of Jesus. That's our job. Spreading his love to everyone. We begin to believe we're acceptable and forgivable. This can be very hard. We often believe that we've done so much sinning, there's no way God can forgive us. I still struggle with that one. Really believing that I'm forgiven.

Jesus once said,

> Therefore, I tell you, her many sins have been forgiven—as her great love has shown. But whoever has been forgiven little loves little. (Luke 8:47 NIV)

In this scene, a woman who led a sinful life had been weeping at the feet of Jesus, wetting them with her tears and wiping them with her hair. An act of great love. The point of this is that if we've been forgiven much, we should love much. We're humbled and grateful, and we develop the heart and mind of a servant.

That's why reading the Bible is so important. We can learn so much by reading about all the people in the Bible. This story of the sinful woman gives us confidence and illustrates the mercy of Jesus.

We can see many flawed and imperfect characters in the Bible. Moses, Abraham, David, Peter, Timothy, Thomas, Adam, and Eve. That's just a few.

It's my humble nontheologian opinion that God doesn't want us walking around with a backpack full of rocks (that's the guilt that hinders us), because he makes this promise:

> I will put my laws in their minds, and I will write them on their heart. I will be their God and they will be my

people. And they will not need to teach their neighbors nor will they need to teach their relatives, saying, "You should know the Lord." For everyone, from the least to the greatest will know me already. And I will forgive their wickedness and I will never again remember their sins. (Hebrews 8:10-12 NLT)

Several things to notice in this passage. God is saying he's putting the Word in our minds and in our hearts. So God clearly wants the Word in our minds and in our hearts. He says that everyone will know him already. And the kicker on this is that he'll forgive our wickedness and never again remember our sins.

Relationship experts say that it's counter-productive to continually bring up the past. There are some relationships where the past is never forgotten nor forgiven. Always bringing up past transgressions or mistakes or something someone did is just not helpful in developing a strong marriage. For that matter, it's not very useful in parenting either. Sometimes I forget, and I'll bring up past hurts or mistakes to my wife and my kids. It's immature and not productive.

God is telling us that he forgives our sin and he forgets about it. When we easily forgive and forget, we're more like Jesus.

As someone has said, "The first to apologize is the bravest, the first to forgive is the strongest, and the first to forget is the happiest."

16 - APOLOGIZE, FORGIVE, LOVE

When we begin to see ourselves as acceptable and forgivable, it's easier for us to forgive, and it's easier for us to ask for forgiveness. It becomes easier to apologize when we do or say something that hurts our spouse or children or a close friend. We cut people some slack because we want others to cut us some slack. But if you feel the need to apologize because you hurt someone you love, don't give in to the urge of coming up with some excuse, reason, or explanation: "The reason I hurt you is that you did this, or you said that." It takes the emphasis off the hurt person and puts it on yourself. "If you could just listen and hear my explanation, then everything will be alright." That's *blame* spelled as *be lame*. We blame it on circumstances or other people's behavior.

If we hurt someone by our actions or by our inaction, we should take responsibility. When we take responsibility and apologize for our mistake, everyone wins.

We're not perfect. Our spouse isn't perfect. Our kids aren't perfect. But the family is the laboratory of love. They're gifts from God that teach us the most important lesson in life.

We're here to learn how to love. When we hurt someone by being selfish, immature, or prideful, we should just apologize. In my personal non-parenting-expert opinion, it's good for parents to apologize to their kids. When we don't, it makes it seem like we don't care that we caused them pain. Bad idea. Also remember that it's an opportunity for them to learn to forgive others. Isn't that one of the big lessons Jesus wants us to learn? This applies to our husbands, wives, or significant others. If we hurt them in some way by an action or inaction, assume responsibility and show love. Everyone wins. They feel better. You feel better.

> Therefore, if you are offering your gift at the altar and there remember that your brother or sister has something against you, leave your gift there in front of the altar. First go and be reconciled to them; then come and offer your gift. (Matthew 5:23 NLT)

We all know of rifts between family members that go on for years—siblings estranged from each other, or parents and children estranged from each other. *Estranged.* "Estranged often implies replacement of love or belonging by apathy or hostility." Why? Pride gets in the way. No one wants to apologize or accept responsibility for their part. Immaturity. Pride. Does that sound like what God had in mind?

We're here to learn how to love. Jesus said not to even bother bringing a sacrifice to him if you're having a disagreement with a brother, sister, wife, or child. In other words, that's not allowed. Nonnegotiable. Apologize or forgive *now*. When is the best time to apologize? *Now.* When's the best time to forgive? *Now.*

Are you having a disagreement with a friend, spouse, or child? Put the book down and apologize *now*. You may be already coming up with an excuse. "You don't understand what they did to me." Jesus says, "Sorry, not interested." That's his idea, not mine.

Go back and reread the above verse from Scripture. We don't get to keep our pride while having a loving relationship with Jesus.

One good way to apologize is this: "I'm deeply sorry for hurting you, I have no excuse. I was unkind and inconsiderate. I'll do my best to not repeat that behavior." You know why that's so effective? No excuses, and a willingness to accept full responsibility. That leads to maturity. It gets us closer to our authentic selves. It helps both parties in the relationship. When you can apologize like that, it makes the person you hurt feel better that you acknowledged that they were hurt, and that's the most important thing. It also helps the person apologizing because it develops maturity and helps us focus on our behavior and how we can change that behavior.

In no way am I saying that it's easy. It takes time and work to think and act that way. What's easy is to come up with an excuse for everything we do that's negative to another person. It's much harder to look at yourself honestly and see the things you can do to make yourself more like Jesus. In my humble, non-marriage-counselor opinion, there must be an "I'm sorry" somewhere in the relationship. Really, in any relationship, but especially in marriage. Hopefully many.

If you're like me, you tend to screw up many times. Same thing with parenting. I screw up and blow it as a parent all the time. When we don't say "I'm sorry" to our spouse, significant other, or child, that's like saying we never made a mistake by saying or doing something that hurt your husband, wife, significant other, or child. Frankly, that's impossible. Humans are human.

We should be able to see ourselves as acceptable and forgivable, and to examine ourselves to see if we're having a problem with asking for forgiveness when we make a mistake.

We've talked about pride. Pride is a luxury that we can't afford. No one can. You can see it in people in politics and throughout history. Pride will destroy any relationship.

I've had people I know tell me their husband or wife has never told them they were sorry in a marriage that spans twenty years. Not once. Are we to assume that they never made a mistake? That they never hurt their spouse or significant other by what they said or did? Or maybe by not doing something they knew was important to the other person?

We have all had the thought, "I'm not saying I'm sorry, because I was right in this situation!" But what's the big deal with being right? Where did this come from? No one is always right. If you're right about something, does some oompa loompa on a tricycle ride up and give you a lollipop? Does some bespectacled banker walk up to you, shake your hand, and pose for a picture with one of those huge five-foot checks, just because you're *right*? (I'm still waiting.)

Forget about right. Work on being kind. Kindness, gentleness, patience. Being right has nothing to do with fully realizing our authentic selves. When we focus on being right, we're focused on ourselves. Remember, when you think you're right in some disagreement, that means someone else is wrong. You're the "winner," but for you to win, who loses? You feel great, but how does your wife or son or daughter feel? Like a loser?

Being right is not only pride, it's stupid pride, blind pride, useless pride. There's no advantage to not apologizing if you know you harmed someone. Especially a child who hasn't developed coping mechanisms to deal with a parent who's being selfish or immature. Do some parents act in selfish and immature ways sometimes? Uh, that would be me.

Who wins when I refuse to say that I'm sorry? In my marriage, if I refuse to say I'm sorry, *I* lose and *my wife* loses. If I, as a parent, say or do something that hurts my child or neglect to do something that's important to them, I need to take responsibility for that. If I refuse to apologize, *I* lose and *my child* loses. I'm also denying my own child an opportunity to learn how to forgive.

We'll come later to what Jesus says about our own ability to forgive. When someone refuses to say they're sorry, they're choosing pride over the hurt feelings of their spouse or child. When you refuse to say you're sorry, you lose also. You move further away from your authentic self, because you've avoided a chance to be more mature and humble. You've chosen not to ask for forgiveness and admit fault. There's another example of everyone losing.

The family is the classroom of love. There's the morning bell.

One of the smartest things we can all remember is that God *hates* pride. It's the one thing he can't stand. Why is this the biggest thing Jesus wants us to let go of? Because it totally hinders our relationship with him. We begin to think we know better than God, which is total madness and stupidity.

Pride will get you into big, big trouble, and you'll be smacked down hard. There are definite discernible repercussions to excessive pride. I've been through the "parade of punch-backs" that you get when you're full of pride. It was no picnic.

> In his pride the wicked man does not seek him; in all his thoughts, there is no room for God. (Psalm 10:4, NIV)

Don't forget this ever popular verse:

> Pride leads to destruction, and arrogance to downfall. (Proverbs 16:18)

It's a daily battle for me. When we have pride, we don't depend on Jesus. We don't depend on the power of the Holy Spirit. It interferes with our ability to be close to Jesus. It's a huge boulder on the path to our authentic selves. We try to make it on our own power and our own wisdom. It also begins to separate us from his Word and his truth.

When we're humble and contrite in spirit, God *seeks* us:

> But this is the one to whom I will look: he who is humble and contrite in spirit and trembles at my word. (Isaiah 66:2b, ESV)

Being humble, contrite, and willing to ask for forgiveness are all good traits. When we have those, we tremble at his Word. We take his Word seriously. That's what he means by "trembles at my word."

We know the statistics that seventy percent of the population ignores the Word. This brings me to the idea of entitlement. Entitlement is bad for the wealthy and the poor. That's another idea that tends to interfere with our relationship with Jesus and everyone else. If we think we're entitled to know and understand everything God does, we're expecting something that's never promised to us. He'll reveal more to us when we develop our relationship with him, but he doesn't owe us an explanation for anything that happens in our lives. He never promised that he would explain everything. There are no promises that we'll understand *everything.*

The easiest, simplest way to remember all this is that we don't deserve anything. Nothing. Zero. Everything we have—including salvation, life, energy, talents, money, joy, love, peace, and the privilege and honor to serve Jesus—are all gifts. So are wisdom and understanding, which we should seek, and when we do, they'll be revealed to us.

All those gifts are totally at God's discretion. We should be grateful and have an attitude of appreciation. A grateful attitude for everything we have brings joy. But an attitude of entitlement brings immaturity and unmet expectations. Unmet expectations lead to frustration, anger, misery, and a bad attitude.

The two most dangerous words in my life are *I* and *deserve.* I like the line from the Clint Eastwood movie, *The Unforgiven.* Clint has a gun pointing at Gene Hackman, who says "I don't deserve to die like this. I was building a house!" Clint squints and says, "Deserve's got nothin' to do with it." Love that line. Everyone should memorize that line, because it's true. Deserve's got nothing to do with it.

Think about breaking a diet, or buying something you don't need when you can't afford it. It's very easy to say, "I deserve it." I always say, "You know what I deserve? A big swift kick in the butt." Everything else I receive is a gift of God's love, grace, and mercy.

That attitude brings joy. God is in total control. He is sovereign. This not only helps us remember who we're to serve and who we're to grow in our relationship with—it also gives us peace. He wants us to love him and get to know him more than we want to do the same. If we love, trust, obey, and rely on Jesus, and we develop and get closer to our authentic selves, we all win.

Now here comes the oompa loompa on the tricycle.

We'll never see other people as acceptable or forgivable until we can see ourselves that way. It's seeing the way that Jesus does.

We should allow ourselves to be imperfect. We also allow our spouse, significant other, or children to be imperfect. When we can do that, we become more like Jesus. We can apologize and forgive and forget more easily. What does all that lead to? Joy and peace. (Sound familiar?) Also, when we don't have hurts resolved properly and we haven't forgiven and forgotten, the only thing that's left is anger, resentment, and bitterness. Those things just grow in our hearts, and they limit us.

That's why apologizing and forgiving are two big components of growth in the laboratory of love. Before we can fill our hearts with the love of Jesus, we must remove the bitterness and anger. No other options. Someone may have hurt you in the past, but now they've already died, or you don't see them anymore. Forgive and forget. It really has an impact on how much love is in your own heart. It really does hinder your ability to reach your authentic self.

Can you begin to see how these things are related? Apologizing, forgiving, and forgetting have a direct impact on our joy and our peace. Removing bitterness and resentment create space in our hearts for the overwhelming love of Jesus.

If you think about it, it's easy to see people who are angry, bitter, or resentful all around us. Grocery store. Car wash. Our workplace. They're everywhere. They're the ones who need more love and patience. Extra love is required to be around these people. Extra patience is required. That's our business. The problem is not the love of Jesus, the problem is the space we create for his overwhelming and overflowing love. You can't feel the love of Jesus or experience it when your own heart is full of anger, bitterness, and resentment.

Raymond Moody makes this interesting observation in his book *Life after Life*:

> What is perhaps the most incredible element in the NDE accounts I have studied, and certainly the element which has the most profound effect on the individual, is the encounter with a very bright light.... Despite the light's unusual manifestation, however, not one person has expressed any doubt whatsoever that it was a being, a being of light. Not only that, it is a personal being. It has a very definite personality. The love and the warmth which emanate from this being to the dying person are utterly beyond words, and he or she feels completely surrounded by it and taken up in it, completely at ease and accepted in the presence of this being.[40]

This love of God is overwhelming and inexhaustible. Filling our hearts with the overwhelming and inexhaustible love of Jesus is our goal. We can't get there with a closed and tiny heart. We need to get rid of that anger, resentment, and bitterness. Holding on to those really hinders our growth.

Sometimes what we believe about ourselves is molded by what others have said to us. Parents, siblings, teachers, friends. I remember people laughing at me when I mentioned I wanted to be a doctor. This isn't a pitch for pity. I've never been into self-pity, because it's of zero use and unhelpful. I share because I care, and I hope to prevent someone else experiencing that. We should be positive and give affirmation to people around us. The negative things we say can be like tapes that run in a loop in their brains. It's a disadvantage beginning medical school with a tape loop running constantly that says, "You aren't smart enough to be a doctor." I was constantly thinking to myself, "Am I good enough? Am I smart enough?"

I wish I'd known Jesus then the way I know him now. I would have understood that people say stupid things. Jesus would have told me, "Dude, really? Of course, you're good enough and smart enough. This is the plan I created for you. I would have never set you on this path without giving you everything you need. Just look in your backpack."

Start listening to Jesus. He's never said anything stupid, he doesn't lie, and he doesn't make mistakes. If you have tapes running in your head telling you that you're not valuable or not good enough, or that you're worthless, those tapes are lies. Those things were said by humans. We humans say stupid things. I know I do. Jesus says you're lovable, valuable, forgivable, and acceptable. Believe him. We know he doesn't lie, because he can't.

So in the laboratory or classroom of love, our family and closest friends are there to help us learn how to love. When we believe that there's value in developing our relationship with Jesus, and we can see ourselves as valuable and forgivable, we start to see others in the same way. We learn how to love, forgive, and apologize. We can learn how to release anger and bitterness.

This has an impact on every relationship in our lives for the better. We try to minimize pride and be more grateful for the gifts we have and the mercy we've received. We learn that loving others and learning to love are the most important pursuits of this life. This brings joy and peace.

There will be waves and storms, but the power of love is true no matter who you are, what you believe, or how much wealth you have.

There will be storms for everyone. Those storms and waves serve a purpose. They bring us closer to our authentic self. Why not endure these waves and storms with an attitude of joy and peace and with a desire to learn how to love? The waves and storms help us grow our faith and develop endurance and character. When we learn to maintain our joy and gratitude in the midst of trials, and we learn to brave the wave and ride it, we benefit in this life and much more so in the life to come.

There's one big problem as we're learning how to love the people around us. As we're beginning to see people with the "eyes of Christ," those who we're to see as lovable, acceptable, valuable, and forgivable can make it very difficult to do so. It's not easy to love people who are trying their absolute best to be unlovable. Rude, difficult, selfish, mean, and disagreeable. Plus, the most frustrating thing is a total lack of self-awareness when they're engaging in this behavior. These are the jaw-droppers. Their behavior is so outlandish, it leaves you speechless. You just open your mouth in utter shock.

You can easily find examples in politicians, celebrities, or people around you. We ourselves may have acted in a jaw-dropping way. One example that comes to mind is Kanye West interrupting Taylor Swift when she was receiving an award and about to give her speech. Jaw-dropper. Have you ever seen anything like that in any live televised award ceremony? The only thing Kanye could have been thinking was, "No, you voters who decided to give this award to Taylor are all wrong, and my opinion is more important than yours." Wow. Can you see a total lack of self-awareness?

Here's a jaw-dropper story. When I was in training, I saw a forty-year old gentleman as a patient in the emergency room who was to be admitted to the hospital. He was having a heart attack, and we were admitting him to the ICU for the cardiology service. He was having some discomfort, but he was able to give me his medical history.

As I was looking down scribbling notes, one of the nurses yelled out, "Hey, he's coding!" I looked up quickly. The patient's eyes were rolled back, his skin was grayish, and he wasn't breathing. He was on the monitor, and I could see he was in ventricular fibrillation.

We needed to cardiovert him immediately. Just like you see in the movies. The nurse began to charge up the paddles, and I was scrambling to get his gown up and position myself. There were two or three nurses in the room, so we were running around like a bunch of clowns in a circus.

I positioned the charged paddles on his chest and pushed the button. Boom! He opened his eyes and let out a kind of deep guttural groan. He was back in a normal heart rhythm, and we began infusing IV medications to stabilize him. He was admitted and transferred to the cath lab for further evaluation.

The next day I thought to myself, "I wonder how Mr. Wilson is doing? I think I'll drop by the ICU to check on him." I was just curious. I walked into the ICU and asked one of the nurses where Mr. Wilson's room was. She pointed to a corner area with curtains drawn, but I could see the bed below the curtains. I kind of peered in between them and could see him. He was reading a newspaper with some reading glasses on. I thought, "He's okay!" I slowly proceeded forward to the bed. "Mr. Wilson! How are you? How are you feeling?"

He slowly looked up and said, "Hey, I know *you*. You're the guy that shocked me with that thing. Yeah, I recognized you. You know, I just wanted to let you know that really hurt my chest. I'm really sore right here." He slowly rubbed his chest with three fingers.

I wasn't necessarily expecting praise or thanks from this man, but that was the last response I was expecting. I backed away from his bedside, turned around, and went on to continue my rounds and see other patients. Jaw-dropper.

Here's another one. I remember once being involved in the resuscitation of a twelve-year old boy. It's kind of a blur regarding the circumstances of why we were working on him; I can't remember the details. I do remember that it was a long and emotionally exhausting resuscitation, and we tried everything. We worked and worked, but after maybe an hour and a half, we lost him.

Losing a child affects everyone in the room. It's impossible to not be emotionally scarred when you realize that nothing's going to work, and that child is not going to make it. It's very tough.

The one thing I remember was being drained and feeling very sad and a little beat up. I was working in the emergency room as part of my training, and it was very difficult to pull myself together to go see another patient after an episode like that.

I went to a back area of stretchers where there were patients who had minor ailments. I thought to myself, "I'll see a few patients with a cough or sore throat, so I can get myself together." I walked to a back stretcher to see another twelve- or thirteen-year old boy waiting with his mother to be seen. Walking in to introduce myself, the boy's mother began to yell at me angrily and pointed her finger in my face, "Doctor, we've been waiting here for at least forty-five minutes. My son is sick and no one has come to see us or tell us anything!"

I could feel myself getting angry and frustrated. Fighting to remain calm, I said, "Ma'am, I apologize, but most of the staff was tied up trying everything we could do to save a very sick twelve-year old boy. We tried for at least an hour and a half, but he died."

She looked at me and said, "Well, I don't need to hear anything about all that stuff." Jaw-dropper.

Luckily, those examples are rare, but I'm sure you have come across a jaw-dropper or two in your own life. If you look at those examples and think about them, you see a total lack of self-awareness. Each of us can probably think of examples where we acted like a jaw-dropper. Hopefully there weren't many. Most people are appreciative, patient, and understanding. They act appropriately and are cordial and thankful. Thank you, Jesus! But those stories remind us that *some* people can make it difficult to love them or to be patient with them. Plus, this total lack of self-awareness tends to cloud their judgment.

We should develop self-awareness and emphasize self-awareness in the classroom of love. How can we get to our authentic selves without it? We need to be able to clearly identify our false self so we can see our authentic self. If people can see their own behavior in a clear light, they would understand that they were acting like jaw-droppers. Don't let a lack of self-awareness cloud your judgment.

Sometimes God teaches us how to love by putting the difficult-to-love in our path. Sometimes it's the people closest to us. They're the ones who feel the most comfortable being rude or unappreciative, or who take us for granted.

I just heard a comment by Tom Brady's wife: "Tom wants to go to work and be happy and feel like he is appreciated." Wow. Tom Brady has been the quarterback for the New England Patriots for eighteen years and has won six Super Bowls. If you don't know much about professional football, six Super Bowl victories is a big deal. He has had all this success, and he still feels unappreciated at work. That's amazing.

It's difficult to deal with feeling unappreciated and being taken for granted. Being loving, kind, and patient while not seeing any of that in return—that's tough. We should remember that God deals with that every day. We learn to deal with it when we can understand that there are people fighting their own battles. They have their own difficulties and struggles just like we do.

One of the most important lessons to master is that we learn peace in stressful situations. We learn joy in difficult circumstances. We learn how to love and be patient when God sends the jaw-droppers into our lives. Some of these people are seemingly unlovable, but when we see with the "eyes of Christ," we can see them as lovable.

The haunting image I come back to is the Roman soldier driving a nail into the hand of Jesus, and he looks over at him with eyes of love. That's all that he's capable of. He looks at us the same way, and he looks at the jaw-droppers the same way.

It sounds simple. Love God and love others. It's really a simple concept—but it's very, very difficult.

17 - THE PATH TO THE WELL

There's a trap on this spiritual journey that we need to watch out for. We're evaluating what we believe about others and seeing others as acceptable and forgivable is our goal. As we grow closer to Jesus and grow in the power of the Holy Spirit, we begin to see more. Sometimes we begin to see things about others that they themselves may not be able to see. That leads to judging, condemning, and criticism.

But Jesus says,

> Judge not, that you be not judged. For with what judgment you judge, you will be judged. And with the measure you use, it will be measured again for you. (Matthew 7:1-2 MEV)

Christians have a bad rap. We tend to point out flaws in others, which makes them feel uncomfortable. As we mentioned, humans are human, and we all say stupid things. This realization is to help us grow in our authenticity and understand that what other people say about us may be a total lie. It also helps us to release anger or bitterness. It's not so that we can judge or criticize other people.

Remember, we aren't in the judging business or the damning-to-hell business. That's none of our business. We're in the love business. It's kind of an easy trap to fall into. But remember, when you throw mud at others, you can't avoid getting dirty yourself.

We start to feel good about ourselves and the things we're doing and the spiritual things Jesus is showing us, and we start to get a little prideful. This opens a door for our becoming critical and judgmental. That attitude hinders our own growth and hinders our ability to share the love of Jesus.

Instead of being eager to point out flaws in others, we should be eager to meet the needs of others. That's exactly where Jesus started:

> Jesus went through all the towns and villages, teaching in their synagogues, proclaiming the good news of the kingdom and healing every disease and sickness. (Matthew 9:35 NLT)

When we focus on the needs of others rather than their flaws, we become more like Jesus. When we're judgmental or critical of others, we're assuming the role of God. It also interferes with relationships around us. It's way more easy and comfortable for us to look around at others and point out their flaws. The devil would prefer a world full of critics, because when you criticize, you're taking the focus off your own spiritual growth. It's much easier to point and criticize than to look at ourselves. It takes maturity to look at our own behavior and habits to see our own flaws, and to try to improve on those first.

One warning sign that we're becoming judgmental is when the *think* word pops up in our mind or our speech: *he thinks... she thinks... you think.... they think....* "He thinks he's so smart!" "She thinks she's so much better than me!" "You think I'm stupid!" Be careful with starting any sentence with he (or she, they, or you) *think....* God is the only one who truly knows what other people think.

If we go to our backpack and see what we're packing, we should start seeing some improvement in our self-esteem. We have value and we're lovable, and the love Jesus has for us is incomprehensible. When we truly believe that, it's easier to let things bounce off you. Especially when you hear negative comments or critiques about who you are.

Here's my favorite answer: "Yes, I'm different from everyone and a little weird, but God made me this way, and God doesn't make mistakes." Embrace your weirdness. It feels good.

Hopefully when we understand the role that anger, bitterness, and resentment have, we can let go of that heavy package or at least take those three weights out of our backpack. It makes the journey that much easier.

As you go along on your journey, you begin to more easily see the hurts and struggles in others, without even trying. As we begin to develop our spiritual vision, it's easy to see anger or bitterness in others. We can also begin to see despair or emotional pain. When we truly understand that our eternity is our responsibility, and that we choose to accept salvation, that brings peace.

Jesus had a choice also. He was praying in the garden of Gethsemane and struggling with what he knew was coming (in the form of suffering and crucifixion):

> He went on a little farther and bowed with his face to the ground, praying "My Father! If it is possible, let this cup of suffering be taken away from me. Yet I want your will to be done, not mine." (Matthew 26:39 NLT)

He chose to love us by dying for us. We have the choice to accept or reject his offer of salvation. It's within our power and within our own personal free will. When we begin to understand that what we do with our relationship with Jesus is totally up to us, this brings joy and fulfillment. We have the power to choose. We should remember that we have control over our own attitudes, and if we're holding on to anger or bitterness, that's because it's our personal choice to do so. True freedom happens when we can let that baggage go.

All those choices are ours regarding our journey on the path to our authentic selves. We can choose what we bring for strength, and we can let go of that extra baggage to lighten our load.

One of the most commonly reported reasons that people hate their jobs was stated this way: "Because they have no power. Many people lack control over even the most basic aspects of their jobs. If you feel powerless at work, you're not going to clamor to go to the office each day."[41] Once you realize that you have the power to choose to take your spiritual growth seriously and you accept that responsibility, it gives you a sense of joy and freedom.

It's your choice, and you have the free will to either embrace this journey or ignore it. But if you look at what gives you the freedom, it's knowing the truth:

> Jesus said to the people who believed in him, "You are truly my disciples if you remain faithful to my teachings. And you will know the truth, and the truth will set you free." (John 8:31-32 NLT)

You must *pursue* truth before you can *know* truth. Jesus wants us to come to him willingly. From my own experience, the more truth you know, the more you want to know. When you understand more, it makes you want to understand even more. When you get a glimpse of a light behind a black curtain, you want to get closer and fling the curtain out of the way.

It's an exciting life. The more Jesus reveals of himself, the more you want to learn, know, and see. He's waiting for us to pull the curtain back.

Here's a clear invitation and promise from Jesus to everyone:

> Here I am! I stand at the door and knock. If *anyone* hears my voice and opens the door, I will come in and eat with that person, and they with me. (Revelation 3:20 NIV)

It's interesting that in my Bible study group there's always one topic of discussion among the participants. We consistently lament the fact that family members or loved ones are resistant to coming to Jesus or coming back to church services. We get frustrated because we would do anything we could to bring a brother, sister, mother, brother-in-law, or father-in-law to the knowledge of the truth. It always brings the image to my mind of being in the desert and stumbling along with all my family members. It's hot, and our lips are chapped and dry. The wind is blowing hard, and sand is getting in our eyes. We look over, and there's Jesus standing in an oasis right next to a well. He's drawing water from the well. It's hard to make him out because of the sand in our eyes.

A few of our group will then fight the wind-driven sand and wipe it from our eyes, as we make our way to where Jesus is standing next to the well. It's much calmer there, and we can see Jesus. We're dying of thirst, and he gladly gives us a drink. He's smiling at us and looking at us with eyes of love. We start drinking the water, and then he starts to give us food. We're laughing and joking, and then Jesus looks over at some of my family still out there in the desert with sand in their eyes, walking aimlessly. And he says, "What about them?"

We're trying to get them to come to the oasis. We wave our arms wildly and shout, "Come over here. We have food and water!" But our loved ones say, "No, we're okay over here." They continue to stumble around in the desert with the wind-driven sand in their eyes.

I'm telling you, I've been in both places, and being next to Jesus is so much better. There's not only water in the oasis, but also a garden and fruit trees and many wonderful things, things you can't see from outside. There's a whole world that opens to you when you stand next to Jesus and accept the water from the well.

We need to wipe the sand out of our eyes.

We've gone over what Jesus said about believing. We've reviewed what we believe about Jesus and what we believe about ourselves. We've focused on what we believe about others and how judging and criticism interfere with our own growth. Now we look at what we believe about the world.

Why do we have to spend time on this? Because we're living in the world and surrounded by the world, but it's important to realize that we're supposed to live insulated from it.

We need to be able to see the world the way Jesus does. We learn, believe, and see that the world with all its beauty is broken, imperfect, and fallen. One of the things nonbelievers say is, "How can a loving God allow so much pain and suffering in this world?" Two things we need to understand. First, we live in an imperfect place. Everything is imperfect. People, places, governments, churches, and on and on and on. A great recipe for frustration is seeking perfection in an imperfect world. We try to do the best we can, but trying to be a perfectionist in an imperfect world is a lonely and frustrating job.

Don't get me wrong. We need those types of people. My home contractor should be as much of a perfectionist as possible. I don't want my walls falling on me. But people look for perfection in places where it doesn't exist. It's easy to criticize churches because they're run by people and they have flaws. They all do. We allow the world, governments, and institutions to be imperfect. Look at the United States government. We can't control our spending. Twenty trillion dollars in debt, and it's only growing. Try running your home finances like that. Talk about imperfect.

What you believe about Satan is closely tied to what you believe about the world, because Satan can roam the earth. The smartest thing Satan has done is to convince people that he doesn't exist, that hell doesn't exist, and that he's not active on this planet. He's not called the "father of lies" for nothing. God is sovereign and has total control, but God allows Satan to work in a limited way.

We see this when Jesus told Simon Peter, "Simon, Simon, behold, Satan has demanded permission to sift you like wheat; but I have prayed for you, that your faith may not fail; and you, when once you have turned again, strengthen your brothers." Peter's reply sounded fearless: "Lord, with you I am ready to go both to prison and to death!" But Jesus told him, "I say to you, Peter, the rooster will not crow today until you have denied three times that you know Me" (Luke 22:31-34 NASB).

There are many learning points we can take from this passage, but I want to emphasize just two. First, Jesus says Satan has demanded permission to sift Peter. Stop and think about that. Did you ever demand to have permission to do something? "I demand that you allow me to go to the movies with my friends, right now!" Doesn't that seem a little unusual? If we believe Jesus, then we know Satan exists. We also know that Satan must ask for permission to do anything on this planet. God is sovereign and has total control. The devil can't do anything without God's permission, especially when it comes to his children. When you take your spiritual growth seriously, and start to try to bring others into the faith, that's when Satan says, "It's on. Let's get ready to rumble!" Spiritual warfare is as real as it gets. As much as Jesus loves us, Satan hates us. He desires to see every one of us fail. He's a liar and a hater.

Jesus loves us, and his words are truth. That's why we study them. Jesus is our biggest cheerleader and supporter. So there's no reason to be terrified of the devil, but it's foolish to just ignore or not believe in Satan, or to doubt that there are demons in this world. The reality of evil in the world is obvious.

If you're fighting a battle, you need to know your enemy. Our enemy is not going to lie down.

If we accept that Jesus is really the Son of God, then he must be telling the truth about the devil and about hell. I've heard people in the church say that the best approach with this type of spiritual warfare is to take it seriously, but not to focus on it too much. But spiritual warfare is as real as it gets, and the more in tune with your spirit you become, the easier it is to recognize that warfare.

The other thing we need to understand is that not everything is going to be explained to us while we're here. As we've discussed, there's a sense of intellectual entitlement where people believe they're owed an explanation for every major disaster or why there's suffering. You hear it in nonbelievers when they question God's power and wisdom and call him impotent. Atheist writer Sam Harris says, "Either God can do nothing to stop catastrophes like this, or he doesn't care to, or he doesn't exist. God is either impotent, evil, or imaginary. Take your pick, and choose wisely."[42]

I remember atheist Richard Dawkins was asked in an interview, "What would you say to God if you died and you were in heaven and you find out that he really did exist?" his response was "I'd say, Why did you go out of your way to keep yourself completely hidden?" This kind of idea or line of reasoning irritates me. Some of this just comes down to plain old vision and common sense. Hidden? Impotent? Imaginary? I can see God everywhere and at all times.

This is one of my most favorite quotes in the Bible:

> The wrath of God is being revealed from heaven against all the godlessness and wickedness of people, who suppress the truth by their wickedness, since what may be known about God is plain to them, because God *has made it plain* to them. For since the creation of the world

God's invisible qualities—his eternal power and divine nature—have been clearly seen, being understood from what has been made, so that people are without excuse. For although they knew God, they neither glorified him as God nor gave thanks to him, but their thinking became futile and their foolish hearts were darkened. Although they claimed to be wise, they became fools and exchanged the glory of the immortal God for images made to look like a mortal human being and birds and animals and reptiles. (Romans 1:18-22 NIV)

There are several points to be made here, the most important being that phrase, "God has made it plain to them." God has revealed his invisible qualities and has shown them clearly to people; those qualities can be understood from what he has made on the earth. So my simple response is, "Don't believe? Take a trip to the local zoo. Go to the beach. Look at the mountains and the forests. Look closely at a rose."

Hidden? God went way out of his way when he sent Jesus, his only Son. It's not like Jesus was trying to be discreet with that bringing someone back from the dead trick (John 11:38-44). How about that walking on water thing (Matthew 14:22-33)? Oh, and let's not forget about his own resurrection (Luke 24). That was so well hidden and kept secret from the world.

But wait, that's not all. Then God allows thousands of people to get close to him and experience his love in lucid and enlightening NDEs. He tells some of these people to go back and tell others about the importance of love and relationships. He asks about loving him.

Go back and read the above passage from Romans. Now examine all the ways he has revealed himself to the world. God isn't hiding. He's screaming. He has revealed enough of himself to justify our love and worship. He sent Jesus as a human reflection of exactly who he is, so that we can develop and grow in our relationship to him. He even left us the gift of the Bible, his precious Word. He doesn't promise to explain everything, but it's patently clear to me that he has shown plenty.

My favorite part of that Romans passage: "People are without excuse."

But the sense of intellectual entitlement is illustrated in atheist Stephen Frye's response to the same question about what he would ask God if he found out he really existed:

> "Suppose it's all true, and you walk up to the pearly gates, and are confronted by God," asked Bryne. "What will Stephen Fry say to him, her, or it?"
>
> The 57-year-old replied: "I'd say, bone cancer in children? What's that about? How dare you? How dare you create a world to which there is such misery that is not our fault. It's not right, it's utterly, utterly evil. Why should I respect a capricious, mean-minded, stupid God who creates a world that is so full of injustice and pain. That's what I would say."
>
> Byrne's second question, "And you think you are going to get in (heaven), like that?" only served to fuel his fervor.
>
> "But I wouldn't want to," Fry insisted. "I wouldn't want to get in on his terms. They are wrong."[43]

Can you see the absolute arrogance in feeling entitled to an explanation for everything that goes on in the world? It also illustrates our choice to go to heaven. Here Stephen Fry is rejecting heaven. He's not only rejecting heaven, but he says God is wrong. If you reject God, and you say he's wrong and you're right, then you're trying to make yourself God. As Dr. Phil would say, "How's that working out for ya?"

If you think about the biggest, dumbest, worst decisions you've ever made in your life, most likely you didn't confer with God before making them.

There are plenty of reasons why humans make lousy gods. We make stupid decisions, we say stupid things, we sometimes have bad judgment and compared to God, we are puny and weak. What a great combination for a god!

God reveals things to us when we seek him. We read his Word and *humbly* ask for his guidance, because we know that he knows what's best for us. He knows the outcome of every decision.

Plus—hello?—he's omniscient. This is one of my favorite verses:

> Trust in the LORD with all your heart; do not depend on your own understanding. Seek his will in all you do, and he will show you which path to take. Don't be impressed with your own wisdom. Instead fear the Lord and turn away from evil. (Proverbs 3:5-7 NLT)

That's the problem with the attitude that God is "wrong": it's an attitude that comes from being impressed with your own wisdom rather than fearing the Lord and turning away from evil.

Just look at your own life. What's more likely: me wrong, or God wrong?

Here comes that backpack again. I would look inside and make sure you have some self-awareness in there. You'll need it for the journey. It's as essential as water. If you walk around thinking God is wrong and you're right, that's when the trouble begins. We've been wrong and way off base many, many times. If you can't see that in your own life, it's time to look back and think.

Here's a little exercise for you. Write down examples of when you exercised bad judgment or made mistakes that could have been avoided in your spiritual journal. Here's the header: "Major Mistakes I Made When I Failed to Consult God." You may need a few extra sheets of paper. If you're being honest with yourself, you'll find plenty of examples.

Let me share a difficult personal story to give you an example from my own life about feeling we're owed an explanation for everything. I honestly believe that part of the reason this happened was so I could share it with you.

About ten years ago, I was innocently waiting at a stoplight when I got this overwhelming feeling or impression to go visit my dad. My mom and dad lived about a four-hour drive away by car. We had a newborn baby at the time, so I wasn't thrilled about making a long car drive with a screaming two-month old. But this feeling was very strong. Not being very spiritual at the time, I didn't stop to pray or ask questions. There was just a strong feeling that I needed to see my dad. (This is a good lesson to pay attention to impressions.)

So my wife and children and I drove to visit my father and mother for the weekend. My dad had been struggling with breathing problems for many years due to smoking. He was on home oxygen and wasn't very mobile. In the evening, I got to spend time with my dad alone as he ate dinner on a small tray and we watched an old western together. At the time, I didn't understand the gift God was giving me by being there. I remember my dad telling me, "You know, son, I'm glad you were able to come spend some time with me." I responded, "Yeah, me too, Dad."

Those were some of the last words we spoke to each other. Now that I look back, that was a gift from God I probably didn't deserve. That was pure grace for me.

In Christian belief, grace is "the free and unmerited favor of God, as manifested in the salvation of sinners and the bestowal of blessings." What I couldn't see then was the grace given to me and my mom from my being there.

Anyway, being tired and knowing my wife was on kid duty by herself, I said good night to my dad and went to help with getting our kids situated. As I was getting ready for bed and moving things around the bedroom, I could hear my dad going into the restroom near the bedroom we were going to sleep in. He seemed to be struggling with his breathing, but it didn't seem to be anything out of the ordinary. I went to lie down and dozed off.

About twenty minutes later, my brother rushed into the room and roused me. "Mom needs you! It's Dad. He's having problems breathing!"

Running into their bedroom, I could see my dad sitting up on the window ledge struggling to catch his breath. His face was gray and ashen, and he was losing consciousness. We laid him on the carpeted floor and my mom calmly said, "Call 911."

The paramedics were there within four to five minutes, and they started to put IVs in my father. I let the paramedics know that I was a doctor, so they kind of allowed me to run the "code." After multiple rounds of CPR and medications, I looked over at my mom, and just shook my head; together, we knew dad was gone. The look on mom's face is burned into my mind. She kind of looked at me, nodded, and said, "Okay." We stopped the resuscitation at that moment.

The question burned in me: Why was I given the impression so strongly to go visit my dad? For this? To be the doctor who pronounced my own father dead? At the time, it seemed very unfair, very harsh and unkind. Why did God allow this much pain in my life?

For two years, I struggled with this. Why did this happen?

My questioning was all about me. Why did *I* have to go through this? Remember, I was operating under total or partial blindness. No walk in the Spirit. No reading of the Word. No strong relationship with Jesus.

I'm thoroughly convinced that if something similar were to happen now, I would be able to discern the circumstances more quickly. At the time, I was left to wallow around for two years. Angry with God is a good way to describe my state of mind. I even mentioned it to my mom. She said, "No son, you can't be angry with God, that happened for a reason." She was right. Purely from grace, and totally undeserved.

My impression about that event was explained over time like this: "You were there for one reason only: to be a comfort for your mother and to support her. You were there to give her a sense of power and control over the situation. She's *My* daughter, and I was using you to help her in that most difficult time. Remember that you're lost."

My knowledge or familiarity with NDEs at the time was very limited. But now I can see that it's consistent with what NDErs describe when they have their experience. People or beings are there to help the person go through their experience and to help them so that they're not afraid. We see that it's so very common for a guide to be there with them.

It's commonly seen in children undergoing near-death experiences. Raymond Moody describes this phenomenon in *Life after Life*:

> Quite a few have told me that at some point while they were dying—sometimes early in the experience, sometimes only after other events had taken place—they became aware of the presence of other spiritual beings

in their vicinity, beings who apparently were there to ease them through their transition into death.[44]

In this instance, I believe I was there to ease my mother's transition into a new life without my father. I can imagine that God will provide even more support for her when she dies.

This was kind of a two-for-one situation. Comfort for my mom. God using pain to get my attention. As C. S. Lewis said, "We can ignore even pleasure. But pain insists upon being attended to. God whispers to us in our pleasures, speaks in our conscience, but shouts in our pains: it is his megaphone to rouse a deaf world."

I asked my mom, "Did my being there as a doctor help you in this situation?" She said, "Oh yes, it was easier to accept, and there were more of my children there at the time, so all of that helped."

Now I just smile. God's plan is perfect. Isn't that so much like a loving God to do for one of his most faithful daughters? Plus, for me—the spiritually lost and blind person, walking in the desert with sand in my eyes—he hit me upside the head with a big board. He got me going in the right direction. Toward Jesus. Toward the well. Thanks.

18 – WHEN EVERYONE LOSES

We've talked about what we believe about the world, and when we feel entitled to an explanation about everything that happens to us. I must admit that the supernatural and the spiritual warfare that goes on is fascinating to me. I couldn't resist including the following passage about spiritual warfare, because it's somewhat unique. It's in the book of Daniel, which is where the initial description of Jesus as the "son of man" is found.

What we believe about the world and Satan and demons will influence our spiritual growth. It helps us to remain strong and keep our faith and perseverance. We fight the world, our own flesh, and the devil as we grow closer to the realization of our authentic selves.

In this passage, an angelic being speaks to the prophet Daniel:

> He said, "Daniel, you who are highly esteemed, consider carefully the words I am about to speak to you, and stand up, for I have now been sent to you." And when he said this to me, I stood up trembling. Then he continued, "Do not be afraid, Daniel. Since the first day that you set your mind to gain understanding and to humble yourself before your God, your words were heard, and I have come in response to them. But the prince of the Persian kingdom resisted me twenty-one days. Then Michael, one of the chief princes, came to help me, because I was detained there with the king of Persia. Now I have come to explain to you what will happen to your people in the future, for the vision concerns a time yet to come."

While he was saying this to me, I bowed with my face toward the ground and was speechless. Then one who looked like a man touched my lips, and I opened my mouth and began to speak. I said to the one standing before me, "I am overcome with anguish because of the vision, my lord, and I feel very weak. How can I, your servant, talk with you, my lord? My strength is gone and I can hardly breathe."

Again the one who looked like a man touched me and gave me strength. "Do not be afraid, you who are highly esteemed," he said. "Peace! Be strong now; be strong." When he spoke to me, I was strengthened and said, "Speak, my lord, since you have given me strength." So he said, "Do you know why I have come to you? Soon I will return to fight against the prince of Persia, and when I go, the prince of Greece will come; but first I will tell you what is written in the Book of Truth. No one supports me against them except Michael, your prince." (Daniel 10:11-21 NIV)

One very important point here to emphasize is that all this battling and fighting is happening because "the prince of Persia" and "the prince of Greece" are doing everything they can to prevent the messenger from telling Daniel "what is written in the Book of Truth." Demons and Satan are interested only in lies. The devil is known as the "father of lies." So why go into this long passage and get all worked up about this? Because there are spiritual battles happening all around us. We just can't see them. Just like Daniel didn't know that there was an angel or messenger trying to get to him. It's not a fairy tale.

Plus, there are many things we can learn from this:

1. God hears our prayers from the first day we pray them.

2. Humility in prayer gets God's attention.

3. Most of the time, there's a delay between our asking and God's response.

4. There are spiritual battles going on all around us that we can't see.

5. The devil and demons will fight against the truth.

6. These aren't fairy tales. We should take the supernatural seriously.

By looking to the world, we'll never reach our potential or develop into the people we're to become. We strive to live above what the world values because it's closely aligned with the flesh. What we can feel, what we can see, and what we can count. The true value lies in what is not seen: love, joy, peace, kindness, patience, goodness, self-control.

The world will try to discourage us and try to get us to focus on worldly goals and worldly values. You can see it in advertising. You deserve this. Luxury. Ease. Comfort. It's hard to escape. We're constantly bombarded with images and ads talking about looking and feeling good. Also about acquiring material wealth.

Remember what Jesus said:

> If you belonged to the world, then the world would love you as its own. But I chose you from this world, and you do not belong to it; that is why the world hates you. (John 15:19 GNT)

> Do not love the world or the things in the world. If anyone loves the world, the love of the Father is not in him. For all that is in the world—the desires of the flesh and the desires of the eyes and pride of life—is not from the Father but is from the world. And the world is passing away along with its desires, but whoever does the will of God abides forever. (1 John 2:15-17 ESV)

It's all right there, broken down. The pride of life (looking good). The desires of the flesh (feeling good). The desires of the eyes (getting the goods). Those are the big three. What we believe about the world and what we believe about those big three will influence our behavior and our actions.

You should always have some biblical scholar or pastor or spiritual leader who you can connect with when it comes to Scripture and Bible study. One of my favorites is John Piper. This is one way he breaks down this passage in 1 John:

> The first incentive John gives is that "if anyone loves the world, love for the Father is not in him." In other words, the reason you shouldn't love the world is that you can't love the world and God at the same time. Love for the world pushes out love for God, and love for God pushes out love for the world.[45]

This is powerful to me because I've seen it in my own life. As we grow in our love for Jesus, things of this world are kind of pushed out. They just don't seem as shiny and desirable. This comes from seeing the world as it truly is. When we recognize that real value lies in things we can't see—such as love, joy, peace, and kindness—things change. They bring so much more fulfillment and satisfaction than something that's worldly. Don't get me wrong, I still like shopping for a new car. It's still fun to drive one too. It's just not an obsession or an idol.

We've gone over what Jesus says about believing and what we believe about Jesus. We've talked about what we believe about ourselves and others. We've also addressed what we believe about the world, Satan, and spiritual warfare. The last thing we need to focus on—and it's a biggie—is what we believe about sin. We focused earlier on how sin can influence our behavior, but we should look also at what we believe about sin, because what we believe may be a lie, or we may look at it in a way that's not accurate.

My view of sin has changed from when I was a teenager. Again, I wish someone would have explained it to me more clearly. As I was growing up, sin was about rules and following rules. If you broke this rule or that rule, you got punished. God was depicted as an angry judge just waiting to zap you. Every time you sinned, it was a stain or black mark on your soul. It is probably more helpful to think about sin in terms of relationships. It is probably more practical too because if you think about love and relationships, sin has an impact on relationships also. Mostly in a damaging way. Love strengthens relationships. Sins like pride or anger kill or hurt relationships. Pride kills love too.

I think what we believe about sin should be influenced principally by what Jesus taught, and by what he said and did. Look at how he spoke to the Pharisees about their rules and regulations:

> Woe to you, teachers of the law and Pharisees, you hypocrites! You give a tenth of your spices—mint, dill and cumin. But you have neglected the more important matters of the law—justice, mercy and faithfulness. You should have practiced the latter, without neglecting the former. You blind guides! You strain out a gnat but swallow a camel. Woe to you, teachers of the law and Pharisees, you hypocrites! You clean the outside of the cup and dish, but inside they are full of greed and self-indulgence. Blind Pharisee! First clean the inside of the cup and dish, and then the outside also will be clean. Woe to you, teachers of the law and Pharisees, you hypocrites! You are like whitewashed tombs, which look beautiful on the outside but on the inside, are full of the bones of the dead and everything unclean. In the same way, on the outside you appear to people as righteous but on the

inside, you are full of hypocrisy and wickedness. (Matthew 23:23-28 NIV)

Here we see two references about being clean and beautiful on the inside. He compares the Pharisees to a cup and a tomb. He tells them that inside they're full of hypocrisy, wickedness, greed, and self-indulgence.

Jesus tells us that the origin of sin is within ourselves:

> Are you also still without understanding? Do you not see that whatever goes into the mouth passes into the stomach and is expelled? But what comes out of the mouth proceeds from the heart, and this defiles a person. For out of the heart come evil thoughts, murder, adultery, sexual immorality, theft, false witness, slander. These are what defile a person. But to eat with unwashed hands does not defile anyone. (Matthew 15:16-19 ESV)

Sin comes from within. That's a good starting point to understand what we ourselves believe about sin. As Walt Kelly famously said in his *Pogo* comic strip, "We have met the enemy and he is us." Sin begins within our own hearts, and there's no one to blame except us. The devil can suggest with a thought, but we have free will. There's no finger-pointing other than at ourselves.

The most effective and powerful thing we can do is take responsibility for our sin. There's no benefit to blaming others or our circumstances. Don't give in to the notion so prevalent in our society: "It's not my fault."

The life of a Christian is a perpetual struggle with our natural self—our chemistry, brain structure, and reward system. We have our authentic and spiritual selves, and we have the natural or fleshly selves. As we grow closer to our spiritual sides and value the authenticity of our spiritual selves, we become closer to Jesus.

As mentioned above, one of the most important things I came to realize is that sins like adultery, anger, envy, pride, lying, laziness, stealing, or lust have a negative effect on our relationships. Sin disrupts the very thing we should be focused on. Remember, the family is the laboratory of love, and relationships are the most valuable things we have.

The sins listed above hurt other people. Someone else is involved. Usually someone else is hurt. Stop and think about it for a moment. Do you think God isn't aware of the pain and damage all these types of sins have on our relationships? Think about a society where lying to your customer was a normal part of doing business. We already have enough of that going around in our society. (Remember the car scratch scam?) Thankfully, some businesses value providing a service or product in an honest way. But think about a society where stealing or giving the wrong change back in a transaction was a normal part of doing business. If lying and stealing were a normal part of business transactions, there would be chaos, and no one would trust anyone.

I remember listening one time to a home improvement radio show, and the host was telling a story about how a foundation repair contractor once told him, "I'm a good businessman. For every three foundations I repair, only one really needs it." That isn't to say foundation repair is a business rampant with dishonesty. I'm sure there are many honest and reputable foundation repair businesses. This kind of dishonesty is out there in all types of businesses. (See Tyco, Enron, WorldCom).

Even when we have outlines for behavior in the teachings of Jesus and in the Ten Commandments, there is dishonesty. Can you imagine the chaos if cheating, lying, or stealing were considered normal?

What about adultery? I've seen marriages and families totally blow up when a spouse commits adultery. Everyone loses in that scenario. There are no winners. The husband or wife who cheated loses. The man or woman who cheated with him loses. The wife who was cheated on loses. The kids lose, as they go through tremendous amounts of pain. This happens at a time when they haven't developed coping mechanisms to deal with divorce. They're forced to adapt to less time spent with a mother or father.

All that suffering and pain—for pride, lust, deception.

God can see all this before we can. He's not making up all the rules to keep us under control. *He knows what is best for us.* Period. If we live in the Spirit, we can see the damage that pride, envy, greed, and adultery do to our very lives and to our relationships.

One other thing we should be looking at here is that Jesus doesn't want a legalistic type of a relationship with us. If we believe that keeping laws and rules is what makes us acceptable to God in his eyes, we've missed the point. What we believe about sin is backward and wrong. It also tends to lessen the value of grace—God's grace to us.

A nice description of grace is God's unmerited favor—his goodness toward those who have no claim on, nor reason to expect, divine favor. The principal manifestation of God's grace has been in the form of a gift. Salvation is not our achievement, but it's a gift from God. Salvation is indeed the most extraordinary expression of God's grace. If you're like me, the phrase "not of works, lest any man should boast" (Ephesians 2:9) has been pounded into your head. It's a gift. Yes, we get that. You've also been pounded with sin sermons and "God hates sin."

We all sin. I'm a sinner. Yes, we all get that. Someone close to me once said, "Yes, what you said is true, but you have to remember that you're a sinner." Really? Are you kidding? How is that helpful to remind everyone that they're sinners?

It's probably more important to remember that God doesn't expect perfection from anyone. Jesus doesn't expect us to be perfect. It's impossible for a human to be sinless. God fully understands that we don't have the power to be sinless. We know this because he sent his one and only precious Son. An act of great love. But it's entirely possible for every single human on this planet to sin *less*. That's our response to God's love and our love for Jesus.

We can now see the relationship between the power of love, our love for Jesus, and the ability to resist sin. That's within everyone's power, unless we lie to ourselves and try to convince ourselves we don't have control. Jesus allows us to be imperfect, but he asks that we allow imperfection in others. We don't condone sin, but we don't judge others either, if we do as Jesus says:

> Judge not, that you be not judged. For with the judgment you pronounce you will be judged, and with the measure you use it will be measured to you. Why do you see the speck that is in your brother's eye, but do not notice the log that is in your own eye? (Matthew 7:1-3 ESV)

There's that speck and log thing again.

The Bible acknowledges that we aren't perfect:

> For everyone has sinned; we all fall short of God's glorious standard. Yet God, with undeserved kindness, declares that we are righteous. He did this through Christ Jesus when he freed us from the penalty for our sins. For God presented Jesus as the sacrifice for sin. People are made right with God when they believe that Jesus sacrificed his life, shedding his blood. This sacrifice shows that God was being fair when he held back and did not punish those who sinned in times past, for he was looking ahead and including them in what he would

do in this present time. God did this to demonstrate his righteousness, for he himself is fair and just, and he declares sinners to be right in his sight when they believe in Jesus. (Romans 3:23-26 NIV)

This is an "everyone's welcome to the party" verse. There's no need to feel like your sin is so much worse than everyone else's. The difference is that we believe in, we trust in, we rely on, and we commit to Jesus. We focus on knowing Jesus and learning to love him. That's what he's interested in, not our mistakes.

This is what I think God thinks about me: "Yeah, this guy, he screws up a lot. He repeatedly stumbles when he lets pride, anger, and selfishness get the best of him, but he loves me. He spends time with me and he knows me. Boy, does he have a long way to go." This has been a ten-year marathon, and I'm only on the first leg.

Our relationship with Jesus is personal. No one knows or is privy to my relationship with Jesus or yours. I'll never comment on someone else's relationship with Jesus because I don't know. Just as we don't know fully what anyone else thinks, so also we don't know what anyone else's relationship with Jesus is. Only God can know the human heart. We can make observations based on how people spend their time, energy, and money, but we still don't know their hearts. We can observe to see if there's spiritual fruit in their lives, but we really can't make judgments, because we don't know anyone's heart.

Remember that love is the essence, fabric, and focus of this life. We've gone over how love and sin are related. When we develop our relationship with Jesus, we learn to value that relationship. We don't want to hurt or damage that relationship. We don't want to let anything interfere with it.

Plus, we learn that part of following Jesus is that we deny ourselves. That's the first step. We deny ourselves the pride, anger, lust, or fleshly indulgences. Jesus says,

> Whoever wants to be my disciple must deny themselves and take up their cross daily and follow me. (Luke 9:23 NIV)

That means we deny our own plan and our fleshly desires and instead pursue a more valuable, spiritual, loving relationship with Jesus. No one said it's easy. It's extremely difficult, because our brains are wired for self-preservation and species preservation.

Remember that we're spirits surrounded by a physical body or self. There are neurotransmitters in the brain that give us a sense of reward and pleasure when we eat or have sex or even when we buy something new. Some of those feelings of pleasure or reward are necessary for the survival of the self and the species. As we grow, we learn to control those urges, because we want to develop our spiritual side.

We're no longer a primitive hunting and gathering type of people. As a species, we need to grow up. We begin to look at sin like kryptonite for Jesus and God, who are pure and righteous and holy. So when we sin and rebel, they can't get close to us. Our cell phone reception gets spotty, and our spirits are not in direct communication with God or the Holy Spirit.

Love is the answer for our sin problem. It doesn't make us perfect, but along with the Holy Spirit, it gives us the power to help with the temptation to sin:

> Most important of all, continue to show deep love for each other, for love covers a multitude of sins. (1 Peter 4:8 NLT)

We're going to sin after being saved. We'll stumble. It will happen to everyone. But God wants us to grow in becoming like

Jesus. That's part of the journey to our authentic self. It's the process of sanctification. It will take our entire life.

You need to cut yourself some slack. Spiritual growth and becoming like Jesus will take time and discipline. We've all developed habits over many years. We have patterns of thought and behavior totally ingrained in our very nature, patterns going back ten, twenty, or thirty years. It takes time to change those patterns.

We should allow ourselves to be imperfect. No one's perfect, and we're all going to stumble sometimes. Also, cut your family, your spouse, or significant other some slack too. Their habits and patterns of thought and behavior have been established over years based on family life, culture, friends, and relationships. Again, this will take work and effort. It won't happen overnight.

The one verse that sticks in my head when I screw up is this one: "Like a dog that returns to its vomit is a fool who repeats his folly" (Proverbs 26:11 NASB). Every time I screw up or let pride take over or act in a selfish immature way, that verse just slides right on through my head. Happens all the time.

> I keep asking that the God of our Lord Jesus Christ, the glorious Father, may give you the Spirit of wisdom and revelation, so that you may know him better. I pray that the eyes of your heart may be enlightened in order that you may know the hope to which he has called you, the riches of his glorious inheritance in his holy people, and his incomparably great power for us who believe. (Ephesians 1:17-18 NIV)

Our understanding and belief about sin at its very core is to appreciate how it's disruptive to every relationship that's important in our lives. We've extensively gone over the importance of love and our relationships with others as seen in NDE accounts. It's the focus of those experiences. We've talked about the family as a laboratory or classroom of love. Sin interferes with every relationship, but especially those close to us.

Let me tell you a story I'm not proud of, but it had a direct impact on my ability to control anger and helped me understand the real damage that pride can do. Pride and anger can really affect your relationship with Jesus, your spouse, your family, and your friends. No one is an island. Anger and pride do real and extensive damage to our relationships.

One bright sunny afternoon, I was having a conversation with my teenage daughter. She wanted to go out with her friends, or something along those lines, and the conversation turned somewhat contentious. (I'd been drinking alcohol, which was a bad sign already.) She's very intelligent, but she made a mistake in forming her argument, as fifteen-year-olds tend to do. So, Mr. Smarty (what a dummy I was), started to belittle her in a condescending, prideful way. When I think about it now—years later—it makes me sad and makes my eyes well up.

Our argument became heated, and I just kept belittling her in a mean, horrible, shameful way. She became quiet, and I just kept going on about my business doing something in the room, when I looked out of the corner of my eye. There she was, my baby girl, her head down, not fighting back, just quietly sobbing. Totally beaten down by a prideful, stupid, selfish, arrogant, idiot.

The pain from that scene lasted three or four days, even after apologizing for days and being forgiven. That kind of pain tends to open your eyes.

I still have bouts of anger, but now it's easier to see and feel the kind of pain I inflict on the people most important to me. Plus, one more little cherry on the cupcake of pride is that not only will I probably relive that scene again, but it will be relived from my daughter's perspective. I get the privilege of feeling the pain inflicted upon her by me. When I see that scene again, I'll get to feel that pain.

That's the power of studying NDEs. More on that later.

You can see what kind of havoc and suffering you can inflict on those you love. Anger and pride kill the family relationship and inflict the most pain on those we love, those we care about most.

Anger is a sin because no one wins. I lost big time, and my daughter lost, and our relationship lost. No one wins. Only Satan smiles.

Pride is at the center of most arguments between husband and wife. It's a total disrupter of marriages and relationships.

So we know the origin of our sinful behavior, but we know that God has made a provision by sending Jesus. Our belief makes us righteous in the eyes of God. We begin to produce fruit in our lives as evidence of this belief. But remember, *belief* means to trust in, rely on, and commit to. It's a little more involved.

When we commit to Jesus, that carries responsibility. When we trust in and rely on Jesus, he expects us to work on our hearts. He talks about cleaning "the inside of the cup." He talks about "bones and everything unclean" in those whitewashed tombs. There's some work and effort involved.

The righteousness God gives us is given freely, but it isn't cheap or easy. Some may argue that free by itself is cheap. If someone gave you the gift of a $500,000 home, that doesn't make it cheap. Half a million dollars is an expensive home. Salvation is a gift, but the value is priceless. It's not cheap; it's the most valuable thing you own, and it manifests in our daily lives as our relationship with Jesus. That's part of the fully loaded Benz. It cost Jesus his life, and he paid for our sin with his precious blood.

Sin interferes with our intimacy with Jesus, and it places a pall or distance between us and those around us. Pride, lying, adultery, excessive alcohol, stealing, laziness, greed and lust all hurt our relationships to those closest to us. And most importantly, they interfere with our closeness and intimacy with Jesus.

These sins are all about the flesh and the world, and they're all temporary. When we choose to live above the world and in tune with our spirits and the Holy Spirit, we acquire love, joy, peace, kindness, goodness, patience, and self-control. These fruits are eternal. This is the spiritual fruit that makes our relationships full and satisfying and more enjoyable.

That's what I mentioned in the beginning of this book. Every relationship in this world is impacted in a positive way when we believe that the essence, fabric, focus, and goal of our lives is love. Love and relationships. Jesus understands that we aren't perfect and we sin, but we can strive or work toward perfection by loving those close to us. That's the closest we can get to perfection: when we love, sacrifice, and serve, forgoing the self.

> Put on then, as God's chosen ones, holy and beloved, compassionate hearts, kindness, humility, meekness, and patience, bearing with one another and, if one has a complaint against another, forgiving each other; as the Lord has forgiven you, so you also must forgive. And above all these put on love, which binds everything together in perfect harmony. (Colossians 3:12-14 NLT)

We can't be sinless. No one can. But everyone can sin less. That's within our power. We can all love in a way that's selfless and giving. We can participate in this "perfect harmony." Each of us has the power right now, at this very point in time, to sin less and love more.

Guess who wins in the classroom of love? *You* do. And your own family. And everyone. It becomes evident and visible in our interactions, action being the key component of interaction.

This is the fruit that allows us to experience the presence of Jesus. We enjoy an intimacy and closeness that allows us to experience the love, joy, and peace that God had in mind for us. It also means we're closer to reaching our authentic selves. It brings the love, joy, and peace we all desire. It's the peace that passes all understanding.

19 - The Hindrance of Guilt

H*omologeo* the Bible's Greek word for confession. There are different approaches to confession in the varied Christian faiths, but they all agree that it's important. God knows every little sin, every lie, every lustful thought, all of it.

In the New Testament lexicon, *homologeo* means "to say the same thing as another, to agree, to concede." We acknowledge that we were wrong and we'll try to do better. Jesus wants us to be on the same page with him. We know what we did was wrong and we confess our sin.

Once you confess, God doesn't want you walking around with a heavy burden and backpack full of guilt. As essential as self-awareness is for this journey, guilt is a hindrance that interferes with our ability to grow. If we're constantly telling ourselves, "I'm not worthy," more than likely we'll be ineffective in fulfilling what he wants us to do with our life. We should be focusing on the road ahead and not spending too much time looking in the rearview mirror. We glance quickly in the rearview mirror to learn from our mistakes, but the road ahead is the focus.

Look at these quotes from the book Evidence of the Afterlife: The Science of Near-Death Experiences by Jeffrey Long, MD:

> As he took a walk through this heavenly place, Mark began to hear a voice that seemed to be "from nowhere, yet everywhere": "Mark! You must go back!" "Go back? No! No! I can't go back!" Again, the voice said, "You must return, I have given you a task, you have not finished."[46]

Another NDEr says, "The Being of Light told me it was my choice to stay or go but that there was more for me to do in that life and it wasn't quite time for me to leave."[47]

Another NDEr: "I was made to understand that it was not my time, but I always had the choice, and if I chose death, I would not be experiencing a lot of the gifts that the rest of my life still held in store."[48]

Is it possible that those statements apply to you or me? Are we missing out on the gifts that the rest of this life has in store?

From my own experience, walking in the Spirit has given me more gifts than I could have imagined. If I hadn't gone on this journey, I would have missed out on so many spiritual blessings and a totally new and thriving relationship with Jesus.

There are gifts in this life that we all could be missing out on when we focus on the things the world values, or if we don't believe and trust in the mercy of Jesus. This is important, because Jesus doesn't want us walking around with a bunch of guilt. It's like walking around with a backpack full of rocks. It hinders our ability to love and serve him and others.

It also has an impact on what we believe about ourselves. He wants us to be confident and sure of ourselves. It robs us of our joy when we're walking around wondering if Jesus is thinking about something we did twenty years ago. It also interferes with our ability to see and recognize the vastness and power of his love.

You may have had a bad experience when you were young, and possibly someone associated with a church made you feel guilty, ashamed, or unworthy. I myself went through this type of guilt as a measure to control.

When you realize that your real mentor, friend, and guide is Jesus, the closer you get to him. It's also easier to see people or institutions for who they are. You have an advantage, because you can measure what they're telling you and see how it stands up to the perfect truth of the Word. Jesus. He is the truth. The more you get to know him and how he thinks, and the more you know about what he thinks is important, the easier it is to recognize BS. You can see, feel, and smell rubbish (that's not how I wanted to put it; "rubbish" sounds too proper).

Honestly, I want to curse right here to make a point. People, including ministers and clergy and others associated with the church, are not perfect. I'm not saying you should ignore the church, clergy, or priests; it's just that many people get alienated from the church because of a bad experience with one person.

There's a growing trend of people listing "none" when they're asked to identify their religion. The "nones" are growing in number, and that's not a trend consistent with what Jesus desires for his family.

As we grow spiritually, we truly believe that he forgives us and loves us and wants us to do better. We then grow in our love for him. It's our own unbelief and guilt that hinders the relationship. We don't trust in his mercy and his love. This is critical, because when we learn to trust in his mercy and grace, then we learn to be more forgiving and merciful to others. It's easier to be kind and merciful to others when we can appreciate the love and mercy shown to us by Jesus.

Remember what he told the Pharisees: "You give a tenth of your spices—mint, dill, and cumin. But you have neglected the more important matters of the law—justice, mercy, and faithfulness." If we stop and think about what Jesus is telling us, we begin to see that what's important are the big principles. But focusing just on rules and regulations and the details of the law can make us blind and neglectful toward the most important ideas he wants us to learn.

The important ideas are mercy, faith, and peace. You can see in this encounter Jesus had:

> And he said to her, "Your sins are forgiven." Then those who were at table with him began to say among themselves, "Who is this, who even forgives sins?" And he said to the woman, "Your faith has saved you; go in peace." (Luke 7:48-50 ESV)

Our faith is extremely valuable. We should be making every attempt to grow in faith, because saving faith brings value to our lives. Also, Jesus is telling us to go in peace. When we confess, when we agree (*homologeo*) with him about our sin, then he forgives us, remembers our sins no more, and allows us to go in peace. Peace is a component of the fruit of the Spirit, along with love and joy and more. When we believe we're forgiven, that brings peace.

This idea of "nones" is something I want to address, because that's exactly how I would describe myself. When it came to the question of which religion I belong to, I could have easily put "none" on a questionnaire, just like plenty of other people:

> A growing share of Americans are religiously unaffiliated, including some who self-identify as atheists or agnostics as well as many who describe their religion as "nothing in particular." Altogether, the religiously unaffiliated (also called the "nones") now account for 23 percent of the adult population, up from 16 percent in 2007.[49]

So the number of people describing themselves as "nones" seems to be growing. There's an idea that's kind of attached here, and it's this: "I can be spiritual and still be nonreligious or an atheist."

People who put down "none" when it comes to religion can be broken down as follows:

—Don't believe: 49 percent

—Dislike organized religion: 20 percent

—Religiously unsure/undecided: 18 percent

—Inactive believer: 10 percent[50]

I myself could be described as an inactive believer, or unsure, or maybe with a little dislike of organized religion. There was more of an "accept as true" kind of belief—not a rely on, commit to Jesus kind of belief. You could best describe me as a casual, occasional dabbler in religion.

When it comes to belief in Jesus, one of the most interesting books that I've read is *The Case for Christ* by investigative reporter Lee Strobel.[51] There's so much compelling evidence to consider that it's worth the time to explore.

From my own experience, I can just tell you that I didn't automatically go back to church services and embrace religion and all the trappings of practicing my faith. I began to study the Bible and listen to different pastors, and I slowly developed my relationship with Jesus. Reading and rereading the New Testament and asking questions and studying different views on faith is what I focused on. From my own experience, I put my focus on Jesus. That's the best place to start. It's important to listen to different pastors and teachers who can answer some questions in a way that speaks directly to you. But it's also important to ask questions. Asking questions makes it personal, because the answers are tailored to you.

Here are some examples of questions you could ask: Who is this Jesus? Why should I listen to him? What does he think is important? Where's the payoff for me? How will he help me in my current difficulty? How can he help me in my marriage? How can he help me with my finances? How can he help me raise my children? How can he get my boss off my back? How can he help me with my alcohol or drug habit? How is he going to help with my anxiety or panic attacks? How is he going to help me deal with my abusive spouse?

That's just scratching the surface.

This is a personal journey. You're looking to reach a fully developed picture of who God created you to be. Your authentic self.

The other day I was having dinner with some of my friends discussing these ideas, and it made me think about how many people in that restaurant were within spitting distance of their authentic self—the person who God created them to be. Is it thirty percent? Sixty percent? These are the questions I ask myself.

Right now, there may be a small tiny stream between who you are now and who God created you to be. You can just step across the stream. For me it was the Grand Canyon. The distance between who we are now and our authentic self may be a crack or a chasm. This book is to help you get closer to the image God had in mind when he thought you up.

As you develop a relationship with Jesus and he reveals more and more to you, you begin to realize the vision he had in mind. Religion is defined as "an organized system of beliefs, ceremonies, and rules used to worship a god or a group of gods." That's a Merriam-Webster definition of religion. It's not what Jesus had in mind, as we can see from these words he spoke to the Pharisees:

> For God commanded, "Honor your father and your mother," and, "Whoever reviles father or mother must surely die." But you say, "If anyone tells his father or his mother, 'What you would have gained from me is given to God,' he need not honor his father." So for the sake of your tradition you have made void the word of God. You hypocrites! Well did Isaiah prophesy of you, when he said: This people honors me with their lips, but their heart is far from me; in vain do they worship me, teaching as doctrines the commandments of men. (Matthew 15:4-9 ESV)

God is interested in our hearts. He's also saying we waste our time teaching or learning ideas that man came up with.

Doctrine is a belief or set of beliefs taught by a church. Those beliefs or set of beliefs must be consistent with the teachings of Jesus. Remember that every word that came out of his mouth is truth. Start with the red. He wants us to know him. He wants us to know how he thinks. He has a *relationship* in mind. Organized system, rules, ceremonies—that isn't what being a Christian is all about.

Going back to the book *My Descent into Death*: Howard Storm tells of asking the beings, "Which is the best religion?" and he reports the answer he received:

> I was expecting them to answer with something like Methodist, or Presbyterian or Catholic, or some other denomination. They answered, "The religion that brings you closest to God. Religions are a vehicle to take you to a destination. The purpose of religion is to help you have a personal relationship with God. Religion is only a means to find God. Religion is not the destination. True religion is the love of God in every word, thought and

deed of the person. God loves all people and is pleased by religions that seek him in spirit and in truth."[52]

There's that spirit-and-truth idea again. Must be important, don't you think?

As we begin to grow in our faith and our understanding of who Jesus really is, it's important to remember that God wants us to be a part of a church. He wants us around and working with other believers. Look at this verse:

Therefore, as we have opportunity, let us do good to all people, especially to those who belong to the family of believers. (Galatians 6:10 NIV)

That one was very difficult for me, because I prefer to be a hermit at home doing my studying and learning in a corner by myself. I had to get out of my comfort zone and join a Bible study group.

As we read the New Testament, we see that the early Christians were always praying together and having common meals. They supported each other and shared everything they had with each other.

Jesus wants us around other believers. The purpose of this life is loving and serving others, and it starts by being around other believers. Some of us aren't as social as others and have a hard time with all that, but that isn't an option.

Also, we can learn from others who are further along in their journey or have had experiences or wisdom to pass along. And as you grow in your spiritual life, you can pass along to others the things Jesus has revealed to you personally.

Some of us have had a bad experience with the church or we have a negative view of organized religion. Here are some reasons given for not being associated with a church:

"I see organized religious groups as more divisive than uniting."

"I think that more harm has been done in the name of religion than good."

"I no longer believe in organized religion. I don't attend services anymore."

"I just believe that religion is a very personal conversation between me and my creator."

"Because religion is not religion anymore. It's a business…it's all about money."

"The clergy sex abuse scandal."[53]

When I was younger, I remember someone complaining that "the church always has its hand out asking for money." Now that I'm older and have a business of my own, I understand that the church is required to pay the light bill and the rent or mortgage, just like anyone else. Money is needed for everything that any church is trying to do. Especially when it's trying to bring others to the knowledge of the truth.

There is false doctrine, and there's the "prosperity gospel" that's popular right now, but that's where a relationship with Jesus and study of the Word have real value. I've come to realize that a relationship with Jesus is personal, but becoming part of God's family is also what Jesus had in mind:

> My prayer is not for them alone. I pray also for those who will believe in me through their message, that all of them may be one, Father, just as you are in me and I am in you. May they also be in us so that the world may believe that you have sent me. I have given them the glory that you gave me, that they may be one as we are one—I in them and you in me—so that they may be brought

to complete unity. Then the world will know that you sent me and have loved them even as you have loved me. (John 17:20-23 NIV)

When Christians come together as a family and love and support each other in meaningful, selfless ways, it's a witness to the world. We exhibit love, service, and support for each other. But we should be careful looking to judge, criticize, or seek perfection in any pastor, priest, or church. There's no perfect pastor, priest, church, or biblical teacher. They're all flawed, just as we are, and we shouldn't be surprised by any flaws or imperfections.

Review the answer Howard Storm received above when he asked about the "best" religion. This is a good answer to the question, Which church should I become a member of? Many times it comes down to what you grew up with and the environment you're comfortable with.

Everyone should become a member of a local church. To me, local just means convenience. You don't have to drive too far. It should be where you're comfortable and the doctrine or teaching lines up with what you already know to be the teachings of Jesus. Become a member of a church that brings you closer to God and seeks to love God in every word, thought, and deed.

We've talked about waves and storms, so we need the words of Jesus to build the foundation of our lives in order to withstand the storms:

> Therefore, everyone who hears these words of mine and puts them into practice is like a wise man who built his house on the rock. The rain came down, the streams rose, and the winds blew and beat against that house; yet it did not fall, because it had its foundation on the rock. But everyone who hears these words of mine and does not put them into practice is like a foolish man who built

his house on sand. The rain came down, the streams rose, and the winds blew and beat against that house, and it fell with a great crash. (Matthew 7:24-27 NIV)

We need to know the teachings of Jesus so well that when we hear something that's shaky, we recognize it. I'll admit I've channel-surfed through religious channels and come across a guy preaching, and I say to myself, "Whoa, wait a minute; that doesn't sound like Jesus." We have a standard to use to make sure that what a church is teaching is lining up with the words of Christ.

As you grow in your spiritual journey, you'll start to see things in your own church that seem off. Observe only. Resist the urge to judge. Remember that the church is known as the "bride of Christ." If you love Jesus and trust in, rely on, and commit to him, you aren't going to walk up to him and say, "Hey I trust you and I commit to you and I'm learning to love you, but I think your wife is ugly."

I myself went into this hypercritical mode of pointing out every flaw of the church and getting this kind of arrogant prideful attitude about it. Then I came to realize that if I see something that's so wrong, then isn't it my responsibility to make it better? Critics point out flaws but never lift a finger.

Let me share one of my favorite descriptions of critics by Teddy Roosevelt. You may be familiar with it already.

It is not the critic who counts; not the man who points out how the strong man stumbles, or where the doer of deeds could have done them better. The credit belongs to the man who is actually in the arena, whose face is marred by dust and sweat and blood; who strives valiantly; who errs, who comes short again and again, *because there is no effort without error and shortcoming*; but who does actually strive to do the deeds; who knows great enthusiasms, the great devotions; who spends himself in a worthy cause; who at the best knows in the end the triumph of high achievement, and who at the worst, if he fails, at least fails while daring greatly, so that his place shall never be with those cold and timid souls who neither know victory nor defeat.

I couldn't resist highlighting "no effort without error or shortcoming," because that's what will happen on this bumpy road. Expect it. Bank on it.

One thing I want to home in on is the last sentence from Howard's NDE: "God loves all people and is pleased by religions that seek him in spirit and in truth." There's that spirit-and-truth thing again. It's important to realize that Howard Storm had no religious involvement at all. He was an atheist. So this gives more credence to the idea that he was given a special experience. We can all learn from it.

Also, if you go and look at interviews with Howard on YouTube, he tells of needing to be in therapy for post-traumatic stress disorder for twenty years because of his glimpse into what hell was really like. Some skeptics say that NDEs are just dreams. Have you ever heard of anyone having post-traumatic stress disorder and needing therapy for years just because of a dream? Me neither.

20 - The Gift of Experience

That brings me to what we believe about our spirits. If we believe we're spirits—as I've pointed out, and shown many examples from both NDEs and the Bible—then by extension we believe in God. God is spirit, and he communicates with us in spirit.

Jesus describes this:

Blessed are you, Simon son of Jonah, for this was not revealed to you by flesh and blood, but by my Father in heaven. (Matthew 16:17 NIV)

God reveals truths to us in spirit to our spirits. We can't receive any communication or revelation in our flesh or our bodies unless we have a vision or special revelation, and those are extremely rare. Our bodies are set up to communicate and survive on earth. Our spirits are meant for heaven and are configured or wired to function in heaven and to communicate with God.

That brings me to a question. When people say they're spiritual but not religious, what does that mean? Atheist writer Sam Harris says that he's spiritual because he believes he can be "one with the universe." Here's an excerpt from a debate between Sam Harris and Rick Warren:

Warren: Sam, do you believe human beings have a spirit?

Harris: There are many reasons not to believe in a naïve conception of a soul that kind of floats off the brain at death and goes somewhere else. But I don't know.

Warren: Can you have spirituality without a spirit?

Harris: You can feel yourself to be one with the universe.[54]

This brings me to the idea of experience. In this world, experience matters. If you have to have brain surgery, who wouldn't want it done by the surgeon who has done that exacting and detailed surgery one hundred times before, instead of the shaky handed and inexperienced resident? Or ask a veteran commander of troops if he'd prefer leading into battle a thousand men who've never had a weapon fired at them, or just a hundred battle-hardened troops. Soldiers tell you that you never know how anyone will react in battle until the bullets start flying.

Experience is powerful. When you experience the intimacy and proximity of Jesus, it changes you.

When I hear debates on God's existence, some Christian apologists will argue that a personal experience with Jesus is one of the most powerful proofs we have of his very existence. Of course, there's plenty of scoffing about this. My argument is that the experience of the Holy Spirit in our lives is another powerful, faith-affirming experience that's available to us as believers.

One of my go-to Christian teachers I listen to is Ravi Zacharias, a Christian apologist. He says that the Christian worldview is the only one where Jesus gave us proof of his divinity by two actions. First, he affirms and fulfills all the prophecies that were made about him. (Take a year or two and go study that one little topic.) Plus, Jesus goes a step further. He reveals himself to us individually and give us an experience of his presence. The Holy Spirit comes to us in powerful and life-changing ways, as I described in Denzel Washington's experience.

John Piper describes it very well in this excerpt:

> I would start by saying that in the book of Acts, everywhere the receiving of the Holy Spirit is described,

it is experiential. What I mean is that it's not just a logical inference that has happened to you only because something else has happened. Instead it has effects that are clearly discernible. In the book of Acts a person knows when he receives the Holy Spirit. It is an experience with effects you can point to.

Let me illustrate this from Acts 19:2. The situation is that Paul has come to Ephesus and found there some disciples who, as it turns out, only know the baptism of John the Baptist and have not been baptized into the name of Jesus. Paul detects something wrong and breaks the whole thing open by asking a key question in verse 2: "Did you receive the Holy Spirit when you believed?"

Now that is a remarkable question for contemporary American evangelicals who have been taught by and large that the way you know you have received the Holy Spirit is that you are a believer. We have been told that you can know that you have the Holy Spirit because all who believe have the Holy Spirit. It's a logical inference. So if we want to know if someone has received the Holy Spirit, we would ask, "Have you believed on Jesus?" If the answer is yes, then we know the person received the Holy Spirit. Receiving the Holy Spirit is a logical inference, not an experience to point to.

But Paul's question isn't like that, is it? Paul says, "Did you receive the Holy Spirit when you believed?" We scratch our heads and say, "I don't get it, Paul. If you assume we believed, why don't you assume we received the Holy Spirit? We've been taught that all who believe receive the Holy Spirit. We've been taught to just believe that the Spirit is there whether there are any effects or not. But you talk as if there is a way to know we've received the Holy Spirit different from believing. You talk as if we could point to an experience of the Spirit apart from believing in order to answer your question."

And that is in fact the way Paul talks. When he asks, "Did you receive the Spirit when you believed," he expects that a person who has "received the Holy Spirit" knows it, not just because it's an inference from his faith in Christ, but because *it is an experience with effects that we can point to.* That is what runs all the way through this book of Acts. All the explicit descriptions of receiving the Holy Spirit are experiential (not inferential).[55]

The phrase I highlighted—*it is an experience with effects that we can point to*—is the gist of all this. It's cause and effect. We can point to and point out the effects that are a result of the *experience*. That is exactly what I can attest to.

Nonbelievers argue that man evolved from a combination of chemicals into complex proteins, then complex organisms, all happening randomly under the auspices and direction of the principle of natural selection. Okay, we understand that. But how did we get a spirit? What chemical or protein combo randomly created a spirit?

If we're in tune with our spirits, or in touch with our spiritual sides, how can that be accomplished without the Holy Spirit and God? Doesn't being spiritual mean being in tune with our spiritual side?

Here's a definition of being spiritual by a nonbeliever:

Well, my definition of spiritual is: We are all connected in some way by an invisible, energetic force. This force can be tapped into when we raise conscious awareness of ourselves and others. Some of you will be thinking the force I am talking about is God; the force I am talking about is not governed by laws and dogma, it is created and enhanced by the energy of everybody around us and raising our consciousness can make this force and energy flow quicker. In order to raise our consciousness our thinking should not be stifled and diminished by dogmatic ways, mainly religion. Religions tell us what to believe, they don't allow room for questioning or thinking freely therefore our consciousness cannot be raised to as high a level as it could.[56]

These ideas sound okay—that we are energy and conscious awareness, and that we can raise our awareness. But what the bleep is he talking about? In my own humble, non-philosopher, non-spiritual-guru opinion, either we believe we're spirits surrounded by a physical body or we don't.

Our spirits are supernatural. They exist above and apart from the physical realm. NDEs are not natural experiences. They're all supernatural events that fully occur only in the spirit of the person near death. They're unhindered by the dulling of our spiritual senses due to our human bodies.

Revelations or experiences of the Holy Spirit are supernatural also. You don't have to die to experience them. They're available to all believers as we grow more in tune with our own spirits.

In the practice of medicine, there's a book called the *Physicians' Desk Reference,* or PDR. It's a large reference book that lists almost every drug with prescribing information. Every so often, the PDR will publish a "black box warning" about a drug, essentially telling doctors how dangerous it is. Drug manufacturers are terrified of this type of warning because usually doctors are too afraid to prescribe drugs with such a warning. Here's my black box warning in this book: don't seek an "experience" with the Holy Spirit or with Jesus. Seek a relationship with Jesus first, and spend time in the Word. Seek the truth of the Word and the guidance of the Holy Spirit. Remember what we talked about regarding NDEs, and the observation of Enda Cunningham: "Sometimes there is an over-emphasis on the miraculous and this can lead to the manipulation of the vulnerable. The challenge of the Christian message is to find God in our daily life and the ordinary." So I want to make that crystal clear.

Remember what Jesus says:

> Those who accept my commandments and obey them are the ones who love me. And because they love me, my Father will love them. And I will love them and reveal myself to each of them. (John 14:21 NLT)

You don't start with the revelation, unless you're the apostle Paul. That's like wanting a Ph.D from Harvard, and skipping junior high and high school and just showing up at Harvard for your diploma. You start with accepting Jesus's commandments to love God and to love others. When we take those commands seriously and grow in our love for Jesus, that's when he reveals himself to each of us, at his own discretion. If we seek the experience first, we'll be disappointed.

Look at this passage, where God is confronting his prophet Elijah:

> And he said, "Go out and stand on the mount before the LORD." And behold, the LORD passed by, and a great and strong wind tore the mountains and broke in pieces the rocks before the LORD, but the LORD was not in the wind. And after the wind an earthquake, but the LORD was not in the earthquake. And after the earthquake a fire, but the LORD was not in the fire. And after the fire the sound of a low whisper. And when Elijah heard it, he wrapped his face in his cloak and went out and stood at the entrance of the cave. And behold, there came a voice to him and said, "What are you doing here, Elijah?" (1 Kings 19:11-13)

Whispers and promptings of the Holy Spirit are more likely. If you seek the miraculous, you'll be disappointed. Plus, it's kind of annoying to Jesus:

> The Pharisees came and began to question Jesus. To test him, they asked him for a sign from heaven. He sighed deeply and said, "Why does this generation ask for a sign? Truly I tell you, no sign will be given to it." (Mark 8:11-12 NLT)

Notice that Jesus "sighed deeply." Faith and trust on our part are what's pleasing to Jesus, not seeking a "sign." That's not to say we shouldn't pray for the presence of Jesus or for guidance or wisdom. But if we're attached to the world and focused on worldly values and pursuits, it's difficult to have spiritual experiences. This is just my testimony from my own experience. This is the great meal at the awesome restaurant.

You may already know or understand exactly what I'm talking about. As we grow closer to Christ, he reveals himself to us individually. Those revelations are gifts for those who actively seek his presence and a growing, loving relationship with him.

Sometimes there's tuition to pay before we get a spiritual revelation or insight. The tuition can include waves, storms, and troubles, plus one other big ingredient. *Pain.*

Pain has an impact. It molds and shapes us into who we are. For sculpting us into our real, true, and authentic self, our painful experiences are just as important as happy or joyful experiences. Sometimes, they are even more important. We're given a more profound experience of the Holy Spirit when we endure these painful trials and keep trusting and depending on Jesus.

These spiritual highs occur at times when we don't expect them. They often occur during times of trial and suffering, when the waves keep coming at us. They can be painful and difficult, but they bring excitement and new revelations that we couldn't get otherwise. That's why we should accept and be willing to ride the wave.

Honestly, I don't remember any revelations from the Spirit when I was lying on a beach drinking a margarita. Don't expect many revelations then. Usually it's in a desperate or painful circumstance when we choose to trust in God and believe that he'll come through for us. *Rely on, trust in, commit to.*

But the experience is discernible and real. We can point to the effects of the experience. The experience strengthens our faith and fortifies our convictions. We grow in our hunger for intimacy with Jesus and for the guidance of the Holy Spirit on our path to fully realizing our authentic selves.

That's where it gets exciting.

PART III - E-VALU-ATE

21 - Our Values, Our Vision

Values drive behavior. Values drive habits. We can look at our habits right now and get a good idea of who we are and what we value.

We've looked at our thoughts and our beliefs, and now we'll get down and dirty to find if we can really see what we value. This is another of the most important drivers of human behavior.

For one thing, you picked up this book, so you have some interest in trying to improve in one area or another. Mind, heart, or spirit. Hopefully all three. You must value growing in one or all these areas or you wouldn't have spent two of the clearest indicators of anyone's values: time and money.

If you look closely at how you spend your time, you get a clear indicator of what you value. Especially free time. Everyone says the same thing: "I don't have time." You say it and I say it. It's probably the most common excuse people give for not exercising. But for every excuse, it's important to always ask yourself, "Is that really true?"

In his book *Rich Dad, Poor Dad*, Robert Kiyosaki[57] writes that the Japanese teach about three powers: the sword, the jewel, and the mirror. The sword represents the power of weapons and military might. The jewel represents the power of money and finances. The mirror represents the power of self-knowledge, which was the most important because it influences how you use the other powers.

We should be able to look in the mirror and become self-aware. I bet you can think of some politicians or celebrities who don't have this ability. Sadly, there are grown adults in their seventies and eighties who've never looked in the mirror and learned how to be self-aware of their own behavior.

The habit of lying to yourself is a huge obstacle:

> The heart is deceitful above all things and beyond cure.
> Who can understand it? (Jeremiah 17:9)

We need to make a distinction here, because it's really important. Waves and storms are allowed by God for our own good. They're helpful in providing spiritual insight, and they're useful in getting us closer to our authentic selves. But self-deception—with a willingness to accept behavior or accept something about ourselves that we know is a lie—is *our* plan, not God's plan. It's based on pride and a total unwillingness to self-examine. It's a sure sign of immaturity. It will lead to pain, sorrow, and destruction. There's no upside to this type of behavior. None. Even more importantly, it leads to a waste of precious time.

We should just be honest with ourselves. *We all have flaws.* We're all in the same boat. So if no one is better than anyone, and no one is flawless and without sin, then why not look at ourselves? We aren't perfect, but we can grow. We can become closer to the image God had in mind. Our true and authentic self.

We can evaluate what we "value." The one area where we can get a good idea about this is time. That's the excuse we use most. So how do we spend our free time?

Our most frequent lies are those we tell ourselves. *Now* is when you can learn to be brutally honest with yourself. If you lie to yourself in the e-valu-ation part of this, you're believing a lie—and then you'll live a lie. Brutal honesty is the key.

Take out a piece of paper, and write down what you did yesterday with your spare time. Or at least walk through it in your mind. Look at last week carefully, or last month. Take out commute time, time at work, and errands for family. Busy stuff that you do every day just to keep yourself or your family afloat. Focus just on the time where you were basically free to decide for yourself what to do with your time.

This is an exercise in self-evaluation. That's it. No judging. There's no right or wrong answers. It's just so you can be able to say to yourself, "Oh, this is what I'm spending most of my free time on." It's useful in helping you see if you're deceiving yourself.

We all say the same thing. "I just don't have time for that." But we spend four hours a night watching reality TV or sports. I myself am the sports-watching guy. Or maybe we spend large amounts of time on social media like Twitter or Facebook. We all do it. The point is realizing how much time we may be wasting.

According to a study in *Social Media Today*, the average person will spend 116 minutes (that's nearly two hours) on social media every day, which over a lifetime totals up to five years and four months.[58] In this modern era, social media is taking over the time spent watching television. How much value is there in spending time engaging in social media? What about spending hours watching television? This is just a question that I think we need to ask ourselves and answer for ourselves, individually. The reason we look at this is to see if we're making excuses about not having time to start a good habit like a quiet time with Jesus. What are we getting out of hours of engaging in social media and watching television?

When we think about the value of time, it's important to remember that time is the one thing we can't get any more of. People who are given a diagnosis of cancer and have a limited amount of time understand that they need to spend time wisely. When we're young and healthy, we don't even think about time. As we get older and closer to death, it kind of moves to the forefront of our thoughts.

I'll never forget sitting on the floor of a hospital room talking to a twenty-year old AIDS patient. I was a young medical student doing clinical training. He told me that when you know you're going to die, and you don't have much time left, "you think about death one hundred or two hundred times a day." Then he started crying, and said, "I've never been this scared in my entire life." He died about three days later. Wish I would have known then what I know now.

Maybe we should be thinking about death a little more, so we can value the time we have today. When people are close to dying, and they can see the finish line, they start to see the things that are most important. Family, relationships, other people. They also start to think about the things they wish they'd done.

In his book *Resisting Happiness*, Matthew Kelly[59] made a list of regrets he compiled from interviews with hospice nurses. Here's a list of some of the most common regrets expressed by people who were dying:

I wish I'd had the courage to just be myself.

I wish I'd spent more time with the people I love.

I wish I'd made spirituality more of a priority.

I wish I hadn't spent so much time working.

I wish I'd discovered my purpose earlier.

I wish I'd learned to express my feelings more.

I wish I hadn't spent so much time worrying about things that never happened.

I wish I'd taken more risks.

I wish I'd cared less about what other people thought.

I wish I'd realized earlier that happiness is a choice.

I wish I'd loved more.

I wish I'd been a better spouse.

I wish I'd taken better care of myself.

I wish I'd paid less attention to what other people expect.

I wish I'd quit my job and found something else I really enjoyed doing.

I wish I would have stayed in touch with old friends.

I wish I'd touched more lives.

I wish I hadn't spent so much time chasing the wrong things.

I wish I'd had more children.

I wish I'd traveled more.

I wish I'd thought about life's big questions earlier.

I wish I'd lived more in the moment.

I wish I'd pursued more of my dreams.

I wish I'd spoken my mind more.

You want real value? There it is. It's like the answers to a test before you take the test.

There's real clarity and wisdom when you get close to the end. When you know your time is very limited, you tend to realize what has real value and what doesn't.

There are some real insights into our lives when we read this list. If we look at it carefully, we can see common themes that can help us right now in our own journey. Why wait until we're dying to look at these regrets? We can start to look at what people really value and then examine our own lives.

Five or six of these regrets deal with the relationships we have while we're alive. As we've discussed in our examples of near-death experiences, relationships with other people are the main scenes that are shown to us. We rarely hear about someone reviewing an episode in their lives when they're alone. Rather, the focus of these experiences is love. We can see from this list of regrets that people are wishing they'd focused more on their relationships with a spouse, significant other, child, or old friends.

Relationships are what's important in this life. Family and friends. Spouses and children. The family is the laboratory and classroom where we learn how to love. Learning to love starts in the family, then branches to friends from school and then friends at work or at church. Those are the things that have real value.

I try to constantly remind myself that spending time with family and friends and developing relationships are what's most important. Loving others and spending time with other people.

There's another theme here that needs to be mentioned because it also focuses on our short-term versus long-term regrets. It involves the idea of regretting our actions versus our inaction. In his book *Chase the Lion*, Mark Batterson discusses what people regret most, and when:

> At the end of our lives, our greatest regrets won't be mistakes we made. It'll be the opportunities we left on the table. Dr. Neal Roese calls them inaction regrets. And timing is a key factor. A study by social psychologists Tom Gilovich and Vicki Medvec found that in the short term we tend to regret actions more than inactions 53 percent to 47 percent. So it's a tossup. But over the long haul, inaction regrets outnumber action regrets 84 percent to 16 percent.[60]

Now look back at this list of regrets and see which regrets are more about inaction. It's the majority.

Why go over all this? Because if we begin to see and understand the truth about what's important, we should act on that information. It's always better to try to do something and fail than to not even try. Knowing and not doing is a problem. Why? Because we'll be held accountable for what's being revealed to us. Especially as an adult.

One good definition of wisdom is *thinking the way God thinks.* Another one: *the combination of knowledge and obedience.* Wisdom requires action.

> What good is it, my brothers and sisters, if someone claims to have faith but has no deeds? Can such faith save them? Suppose a brother or a sister is without clothes and daily food. If one of you says to them, "Go in peace; keep warm and well fed," but does nothing about their physical needs, what good is it? In the same way, faith by itself, if it is not accompanied by action, is dead. But someone will say, "You have faith; I have deeds." Show me your faith without deeds, and I will show you my faith by my deeds. You believe that there is one God. Good! Even the demons believe that—and shudder. You foolish person, do you want evidence that faith without deeds is useless? Was not our father Abraham considered righteous for what he did when he offered his son Isaac on the altar? You see that his faith and his actions were working together, and his faith was made complete by what he did. And the scripture was fulfilled that says, "Abraham believed God, and it was credited to him as righteousness," and he was called God's friend. You see that a person is considered righteous by what they do and not by faith alone. (James 2:14-26 NLT)

Love is an action. Giving is an action. Failing to love or give is a choice; it's knowing the truth and rejecting it instead of knowing the truth and accepting it.

There are regrets listed above having to do with family and relationships. There are regrets having to do with our own personal growth and development. Both require action. We have to *act* if we want to discover and fully realize our authentic selves, becoming the person God created us to be.

There's another theme on this list that I've mentioned before, but it's important to emphasize again. It's a major obstacle to reaching our authentic selves, who we really are. "I wish I'd cared less about what other people thought, and I wish I'd paid less attention to what other people expect." These two ideas kind of get my dander up because I can imagine all the unrealized goals, unfulfilled lives, and wasted opportunities because of those two stumbling blocks. Being influenced or worrying about what other people think can be a huge obstacle for people. We've talked about humans and the stupid things we say. I'm not saying there are no wise people who have good advice for us and have our best interests in mind, but sometimes people are telling us things that just aren't true. If anyone tells you anything negative that contradicts what you *know* Jesus believes about you, there's no value there.

There's no value in a lie. Truth has value. And the truth is that Jesus sees every one of us as lovable, forgivable, valuable, and acceptable.

> Peter and the apostles answered, "We must obey God rather than men." (Acts 5:29 ESV)

When you grow in your relationship with Jesus and your love for him is growing, you'll have more discernment. It starts to become obvious to you who has your best interests in mind. We can look around at this world and see the rampant slavery to the opinions of people. It's obvious and overwhelming. Time, money, energy, and effort all spent on impressing or making an impression on other human beings. One question: From the teachings of Jesus, from the experience of NDEs, from the Word of God, is there any value in any of that?

Jesus said,

> I do not accept glory from human beings, but I know you. I know that you do not have the love of God in your hearts. (John 6:41-42 NIV)

This is an example for us. By the example of Jesus, we should look at our own lives and examine whether we're seeking "glory from human beings." Also, we should be wary of human worship. We need to understand that we're to reserve our worship for Jesus. Just by the gifts of grace and salvation, he's the only one who deserves worship.

In the verse above, Jesus is telling us that he seeks God's affirmation. Remember, we never go wrong and never make a mistake when we emulate Jesus. Think about how many award shows are televised. We love to give each other awards and glory. We humans are experts at giving each other tons of glory and awards. Oscars, Emmys, Tonys. But how valuable is human approval and affirmation? Can we take any of that with us when we die? Are God and Jesus going to ask us about how much approval and glory we received from humans? Do people who've undergone NDEs ever mention that any being of light asked about awards or trophies given by humans? Remember the common themes with NDEs. God and Jesus are asking, "Do you love me? What have you done with your life to show me? Did you learn to love others?" No mention of awards, trophies, or human approval.

What about when people expect you to do something or pursue something that *they* want for your life? I think about parents who want their children to pursue some sport or choose a profession that they view as desirable. The problem is that sometimes it doesn't fit who their child was created to be. The most miserable people I know are the ones who chose to go into a profession or pursue a job for the sole purpose of making a lot of money.

> Work willingly at whatever you do, as though you were working for the Lord rather than for people. (Colossians 3:23 NLT)

We serve people and try to meet their needs. That's very different from working to impress people or attain glory from humans. It's also different from giving glory to humans that should be reserved for God. God is your creator and designer. Jesus is the way to the Father. They have our salvation and the nature of our eternity in their hands. Why not try to please them? Why not try to impress them?

Jesus was once amazed when a Roman soldier demonstrated faith:

> When Jesus heard this, he was amazed at him, and turning to the crowd following him, he said "I tell you I have not seen such great faith in all of Israel." (Luke 7:9 NIV)

In the Gospels, is there any other mention of Jesus being amazed by anything? Or is this the only one? (These are the kind of questions I tend to ask myself.) There is one other time that Jesus was amazed, this time in a negative way:

> He could not do any miracles there, except lay his hands on a few sick people and heal them. He was amazed at their lack of faith. (Mark 6:5-6 NIV)

So there are two examples. Great faith and total lack of faith.

You want to impress Jesus? Then exhibit great faith. Faith pleases God. Their opinion and what they think has the most value. They know the outcome of every decision you make. They know what's best for you. They have the architectural plans of who you were created to be. They know what you were created to do. There's real value in growing in our relationship to God and Jesus, because they'll show us which path to take. Their opinion is the most valuable opinion, and it's all available to us in the Word.

You want real power? There it is.

Another recurring idea on the list of regrets involves having the courage to be yourself. Listen, God made you unique for a reason. And he doesn't make mistakes. Could it be so that you can make a unique contribution to the world? The more you embrace and value who you are, the more you make God smile.

If people say to me, "You're weird," I say, "Thank you."

God made each of us with unique talents, passions, and interests. So don't ignore your passions; they're God-given. You're his design. Find, explore, and develop your passions.

I like the idea that passion intertwined with discipline yields excellence. Look at supreme athletes who are the best at what they do. Michael Jordan and Tiger Woods come to mind. Business people come to mind such as Bill Gates or Steve Jobs. In *On Writing*, author Stephen King tells a story about how he lied to a reporter who asked if he writes every day. He said he told the reporter that he doesn't write on Easter, Christmas, or New Year's. He admits that he lied to the reporter because he does in fact write every day of the year, including those holidays.[61] Passion and discipline. He writes because he loves to write. He writes because he must. It's like breathing for him. But the discipline comes in when he sticks to his own rule that he doesn't stop until he has ten completed pages per day.

Find your passion. Find the thing you *must* do. Remember, we're to use our gifts, passions, and talents in serving. Serving God by using our talents and gifts to the benefit of others. When we focus on using all our gifts and passions and talents for our own benefit, they're wasted. These things are meant to be shared.

I know what my talents are. I know where my passions lie. I also realize what talents and gifts I'm lacking. For all of us, it's important to realize what we're *not* supposed to do. Some of us can't sing. That would be me. Some of us aren't as outgoing or as social as others. Some of us aren't as athletic as others. Being honest about our talents and gifts will prevent us from wasting our time. *Find and fulfill your destiny.* That's a line from the movie *Clash of the Titans*, the 1981 version with Laurence Olivier. My version would be: *Discover and fully realize your authentic self.*

Live your most fascinating life. Be who God created you to be. If we spend time pursuing goals and using our talents for the benefit of others, we won't have regrets, because we can say, "At least I tried."

That list above is a list of regrets. It's always better to learn from other people's mistakes, because you get the wisdom without the pain. The pain of regret is something we want to avoid. We would rather try and fail than regret not trying at all.

The one thing I've learned that really keeps me going is that when I'm pursuing spiritual goals for the kingdom or to bring me closer to Jesus, somehow the Holy Spirit is going to show me something. There's always a payoff. Always. Either a spiritual insight or deeper intimacy with Jesus. Plus, I get a little closer to my authentic self.

Here's a promise:

> And we know that in all things God works for the good of those who love him, who have been called according to his purpose. (Romans 8:28 NIV)

You can't lose, even if you fail in pursuing spiritual goals. As we learn to value our relationship with Jesus and spend time in the

Word and receive more insight, we begin to see life more clearly. It's like seeing in high-definition. Life in high-definition is much better and it tends to make you yearn for more.

Remember, we're each given unique abilities, passions, and talents. If you're saying to yourself, "I don't have any special abilities or talents or passions," you're not being honest. Or you don't want to even try. It's really a way out, an excuse. Just like the "I don't have time" excuse.

Everyone has an ability, talent, or a passion. Don't let fear interfere with the full expression of that talent or passion.

> Therefore, my dear brothers and sisters, stand firm. Let nothing move you. Always give yourselves fully to the work of the Lord, because you know that your labor in the Lord is not in vain. (1 Corinthians 15:58 NIV)

There it is again. You never lose doing the work of the Lord. It takes time to find out what Jesus has in mind for you. Spending time in the Word and in prayer will develop your spiritual vision. It doesn't happen overnight.

Ask for guidance and for the power of the Holy Spirit— remember, it's an undeniable prayer. Jesus is yearning to guide you and be close to you. He has a desire to bless us and guide us.

Sometimes we just keep going on in our daily lives spending time and focusing on things that don't have real value. Like trying to impress others. Look closely at that list of regrets. It's a big warning sign, flashing red. Refer to it often. We just don't want to stand before Jesus with regrets like those, because at that time, there's nothing we can do about it. We're helpless to change the situation. The best time to make changes is now. *Act.* Spend time in the Word and with Jesus. He yearns to know us and wants to guide us and open our eyes.

> The Lord's eyes scan the whole world to strengthen those who are committed to him with all their hearts. (2 Chronicles 16:9 CEB)

This is my favorite version of this verse, because of that word "scan." It has a modern feel to it, and it tells us God is looking over the entire earth for people who are committed to him. He's constantly looking for those who are looking for him. That brings us comfort and helps us feel confident and unafraid.

He wants to be in our lives. He wants us to depend on him. So check that backpack for fear and anxiety, and get rid of some of that.

22 - Life's Biggest Obstacle

W e're to move forward and act in spite of fear, which is big on the list of regrets. Fear paralyzes.

I have heard claims that there are 365 "Do not be afraid" references in the Bible, which amounts to a daily reminder each day of the year. Stop and think about that.

Being skeptical about that number, David Lang from the Accordance Bible blog did a combined search in the Bible for "Do not be afraid" and similar phrases (such as "Do not fear," "Be not afraid," "Fear not") and found that "even with all these different variations" his search "only returned 119 occurrences—far less than the 365 claimed." (David acknowledged that when it comes to living fearlessly, "we don't need the Bible to say it 365 times in order to heed the message every day.")[62]

Even if it's "only" 119 times that the Bible tells us not to be afraid, that's a not so subtle hint that fear is not an option for us, in God's eyes.

Let me clarify. Fear is an emotion we can't control. God understands that we have fear. What he wants is courage. Courage is being able to move against that fear and not allow the emotion of fear to stop us from doing his will. He's testing our faith by our willingness to overcome fear and rely on him. That's the trust and reliance part of *believe*. If we want to grow our faith, we must lean heavily on those two: trust in, and rely on.

That means facing and braving the next wave, not spending maximum effort trying to avoid it. We tend to get in the habit of avoiding uncomfortable situations or tasks. We also talk ourselves out of taking risks. God wants us to grow our faith by learning to trust him in difficult circumstances. That means we have to learn to embrace them—to brave the next wave. *Rely on, trust in, and commit to.* That's living by believing.

The antidote to fear is love. A mother will run into a burning house to rescue her children because the love for her children overcomes the fear for her own safety. As we grow in our love, trust, and faith in the promises of Jesus and God, our fear diminishes. It's a giant anxiety and stress reliever.

> For God has not given us a spirit of fear and timidity, but of power, love, and self-discipline. (2 Timothy 1:7 NLT)

That's a verse everyone needs to memorize. I use this translation because it mentions both fear and timidity. That's not the spirit we have within us. We're not to be timid. When we get serious about our spiritual growth and our relationship with Jesus, we'll be asked to do things that make us uncomfortable or afraid. Count on it, bet on it, and don't be surprised by it.

Actually, that's a good indicator that you're hearing the voice of God or the Holy Spirit. If it makes you afraid or uncomfortable, pay attention. God wants to stretch and grow our faith. Being able to decipher the voice of the Holy Spirit and separate it from all the noise in our thinking is a valuable skill that everyone needs to develop.

One test that we can use to determine if we're hearing a spiritual whisper or the voice of God is to ask whether what we're hearing is consistent with God's Word. If you're hearing a voice telling you to divorce your wife, leave your children, and get on a bus to Hollywood so you can become an actor, you know that's not coming from God. God's will for our lives never contradicts God's Word.

God may be asking you to do something outside your comfort zone. He'll ask you to do something that requires faith. This is one of the primary ways he teaches us to learn to rely on and trust in him.

Fear may be your biggest obstacle. You begin to dread the building wave. You're tempted to just go under water and let it pass over you.

But there are two problems with not braving the wave. First, you could be missing the ride of your life. No guts, no glory. No one around to tell your story. Second, you miss out on the insights, revelations, and wisdom that come from getting closer to your authentic self. Remember, we're given a bold spirit. When you avoid that wave, you choose timidity, which is not in keeping with the spirit we were given. Our authentic selves.

There are many biblical examples of people having to move against their own fear. Moses, David, Peter, Paul, Abraham, and even Jesus in the garden of Gethsemane.

From my own experience, I can tell you that every great triumph or victory in my life had a requirement of moving against fear. I was scared to death. Starting a business. Making decisions that could have life and death consequences as a physician. I can remember the day I walked into my first Bible study. I was very uncomfortable, because I'm not Mr. Social. I'm kind of a loner and prefer just being at my kitchen table reading the Bible and studying by myself. But the Holy Spirit told me, "You need to join a small group Bible study." My response: "I really don't know very much, I won't add anything of value to the group. I'll just stay here by myself and keep reading the Bible. That's a good thing, isn't it?" Then here came the response: "You have no excuse, stop being afraid."

Well, I'm glad I did join a small group, because being in my small group is an important part of my spiritual journey. That's just a small example of our being asked on occasion to get out of our comfort zone. We're going to be asked to face our fears and to do assignments that stretch our faith. Steel yourself. Brave the wave. You won't regret it.

With regard to joining a Bible study or small group, this is another example of watching how Jesus did things. He put together a small group at the very beginning of his ministry. He chose his disciples right after being baptized:

> Now as Jesus was walking by the Sea of Galilee, He saw two brothers, Simon who was called Peter, and Andrew his brother, casting a net into the sea; for they were fishermen. And He said to them, "Follow Me, and I will make you fishers of men." Immediately they left their nets and followed Him. (Matthew 4:19-20 NASB)

Notice that they obeyed Jesus immediately. That's an important point, because delayed obedience is really disobedience.

God wants us in a small group studying and learning together. We're to be a part of the living body of Christ, which is the church. As we're moving along on this spiritual journey, God may ask us to join a small group. As we're going along, he may ask us to be a part of the living body of Christ, which is the church.

From the Bible and from NDEs we know that learning to love is the most important thing we should be doing in this life, and we can't learn to love and serve others alone in our kitchen studying the Bible by ourselves. Learning to love has the absolute requirement of interacting with other people. We must connect with others.

Remember, the church is the bride of Christ, and she isn't ugly. You may not be ready to join a local church, but keep in mind that God wants us to be in fellowship with other believers. It's easy to make an excuse by just bashing the church for being filled with hypocrites. That's a built-in excuse to ignore the church. We can all just sit back and criticize and make fun of and point out all the flaws of the Christian church. But remember, there are no statues put up for critics. No one remembers the famous critics of history.

Maybe we can make the church better by using our gifts and talents as part of the service. Jesus wants us to develop a relationship with other believers. We're on this planet to learn how to love. We start in the classroom of love, our families, and branch out from there. It's like concentric circles. Jesus and family in the middle. Then around that, extended family and friends. Then around that, spiritual family and friends.

I'm glad I joined that Bible study group because I've learned and shared with other believers, and it strengthens my faith. We'll be asked to do things that stretch our faith. Our faith will be tested, and God wants us to accept the challenge and move against that fear.

Strong faith is the faith that has been repeatedly tested through trials and storms. Jesus wants our faith strong, and we should desire that too, because there's real value in a strong faith.

Plus, we should remember this:

> Without faith it is impossible to please God, because anyone who comes to him must believe that he exists and that he rewards those who *earnestly* seek him. (Hebrews 11:6 NIV)

I emphasize *earnestly* there because it's defined as having "a sincere and intense conviction." Sincere and intense. Does that truly describe how you're seeking him?

Looking back to the list of regrets we discussed earlier, we can see that some people regret having not pursued their dreams and spirituality. They also mentioned how they wish they'd spent more time on life's biggest questions. In his book *The Rhythm of Life,* Matthew Kelly[63] has a very good breakdown of how we should approach these types of questions: *Who am I? Why am I here? What's most important? What's the least important?* That's a good breakdown of the going-off-to-college speech I give my own kids. If you spend time focusing on those four questions, you automatically are getting closer to your authentic self.

We can't ask ourselves who we are until we understand who made us. We're all children of God. He designed us and planned us and created us so he could love us and so we could learn to love him in return. That's the best way to define ourselves. We're each a child of God in the family of God. Jesus is our brother and best friend, and God is our Father. This means we have real value. We can't begin to discover our authentic selves until we understand that God created us. We identify ourselves in the context of family. We were created to be a part of his family.

For we are his workmanship, created in Christ Jesus for good works, which God prepared beforehand, that we should walk in them. (Ephesians 2:10 ESV)

This is another of those must-memorize verses, because it tells us who we are and why we're here. We're God's workmanship, created in Christ Jesus for good works, which he prepared beforehand. He knew what good works he wanted us to do before he created us. Be careful when other people give you their plan for *your* life. Whoever is telling you this didn't create you.

Notice that I'm not giving you a unique plan for your life; I'm outlining how to discover *God's* plan for your life. Other people can't possibly have any idea what God's plan and purpose is for you. People who are farther in their spiritual journey may be able to guide you, and God does speak through other people. You always have the Word to test what others are telling you and whether you're hearing God's voice in your own prayer or quiet time. We should test what we're hearing to see if it lines up with the truth and with what we know about Jesus and what he taught.

We also define ourselves in the context of Jesus, because we should view ourselves the way he sees us. We're humans created in Christ Jesus. God also created us to have a relationship with Jesus. We begin to discover who we truly are by developing that relationship. It's the best starting point for answering the question, "Who am I and why am I here?"

One fascinating idea is that God knew the whole plan before he made the world:

> Even before he made the world, God loved us and chose us in Christ to be holy and without fault in his eyes. God decided in advance to adopt us into his own family by bringing us to himself through Jesus Christ. This is what he wanted to do, and it gave him great pleasure. (Ephesians 1:4-5 NLT)

See the value in a relationship with Jesus? Jesus is our pathway to God and to salvation. We can't fulfill our destiny or reach full authenticity without coming into a relationship with Jesus. It allows us to come into a closer relationship with God. As Christians, we identify with being in the family.

> So that if I am delayed, you will know how everyone who belongs to God's family ought to behave. After all, the church of the living God is the strong foundation of truth. (1 Timothy 3:15 CEV)

We're members of the family of God. That's who we are as individuals. And we have a role to play in the family of God. We discover our role when we discover and fully realize our authentic selves.

That previous verse also identifies for us the strong foundation of truth. We talked about the "nones," and you may put yourself in the category of "no religious affiliation," and that's fine. The whole idea here is to value a relationship with Jesus first.

Begin to learn who he is through the Word and in prayer. He'll reveal himself as he promised. God's promises are reliable and trustworthy. They're the basis for our faith. As we go along and recognize who we are, and we begin to discover why we're here, it's a good idea to begin to value truth. If we don't value truth, we'll be vulnerable. Remember, Satan is the "father of all lies." So we need to seek and pursue truth. If you don't place value or emphasis on truth, our lives will be influenced by the world, by the devil, and by lies. Then we'll have a long list of regrets.

Remember, Jesus put it this way:

> Anyone who listens to my teaching and follows it is wise, like a person who builds a house on solid rock. Though the rain comes in torrents and the floodwaters rise and the winds beat against that house, it won't collapse because it is built on bedrock. But anyone who hears my teaching and doesn't obey it is foolish, like a person who builds a house on sand. When the rains and floods come and the winds beat against that house, it will collapse with a mighty crash. (Matthew 7:24-27 NLT)

Yes, I've mentioned this verse before, but I repeat it to make a point. No matter who you are, what you believe, what you value, how much money you make, or how smart you are, the waves and the storms are coming. If we believe Jesus, we start to pursue truth by reading, studying, and understanding his words and his teaching. We have the foundation for the waves and the floods.

Our relationship with Jesus is the basis for our desire to not only face the next wave, but ride it and learn from it so we can get closer to Jesus and thus to our authentic selves. Our lives, our marriages, our children, our families will all benefit from a solid foundation. Want a strong marriage? Put Jesus in the center. Want a strong family? Put Jesus in the center. Want a strong business? Put Jesus in the middle of that business and run that business with his teachings as the foundation. If you want to be in a better financial situation, understand that God controls the flow. I've noticed that money becomes more available when it becomes less important. Serve Jesus and money works for you.

Now we get to the questions of what's most important and what's least important. We've already discussed the value of relationships in this life. Learning and growing in the classroom and laboratory of love. When we talk about why we're here, we should try to think about what Jesus emphasized. Learning to love. Marriage, family life, friendships, and spiritual relationships are the most important pursuits of this life. Learning to love in each of these areas is what's most important.

By the way, when we're with our family members in Christ, those are spiritual relationships that last forever. We develop those when we belong to a local church or body of Christ. If you work for a company and you're at a big party, and the CEO brings his wife, it may be a good idea to meet her and get on her good side. Jesus gave his life for the church and we become a family of believers in the framework of the church. Spiritual family lasts forever. Learning to love God and learning to love and serve others is what's most important.

Remember, we're to love God with all our heart, mind, soul, and strength. There's effort and time involved. We also fulfill our purpose by loving and serving others within the power of the Holy Spirit and with the love of Jesus.

We discover and fully realize our authentic selves. As we grow in the knowledge of the truth, we begin to see fruit in our lives. We begin to experience love, joy, and peace. It takes time and patience, but the benefit to ourselves and those around us is observable, obvious, and tremendously valuable.

In the same way that we've talked about anger, pride, and the harm they do to those we love the most, when we get closer to our authentic selves we can also see love, patience, and kindness and the benefit they bring to those we love the most. If we can be more loving, patient, and kind to our husbands, wives, or significant others, they win and we win. It's the classroom and laboratory of love. In addition, our children see our love and learn to model that love when they begin their own relationships. We also grow in love because we see the positive response in our spouses and our children. If we can be more loving, merciful, and forgiving to our children, they benefit because they grow in their self-esteem. Simultaneously we grow more mature and become more like Jesus. Everyone wins.

The most difficult part in all this (and you will come across it) is when people are unloving, unresponsive, bitter, and angry. You may feel like that, or have a family member you love dearly who's very close to that description. Many times, it's because of unmet expectations or because of past hurts.

The most difficult thing in the world is to love the unloving. To be patient with the impatient. To be kind to the rude and hateful. I've been there; I bet you have too. It's trying, it's taxing, and it will test your faith. The jaw-droppers. Everyone knows one. Sometimes we may act like one. When we can be patient and kind to the rude and impatient, that's when we're most like Jesus. It's the toughest thing in this world to do.

Remember these words of Jesus:

Father, forgive them; for they do not know what they are doing. (Luke 23:34 NASB)

Remember that he was hanging on the cross in severe pain when he said that. The Christian life is a tough gig, but it's worth it.

23 - LOOKING FOR WOTS

We can learn a huge amount by what's not even mentioned on that list of regrets we looked at in the last chapter. We've talked about what's most important, but clearly the things that aren't even mentioned are the least important. More time watching television? Bigger house? More money? More things? More cars? There's a mention of travel, but that's more about experiencing life more fully.

I should stop here for a moment and digress. Here comes Lieutenant Colombo: "Just one more question before I go, ma'am; I apologize." When we look for value and what lasts in how we spend our time and money, there's research to support the notion that spending money on experiences rather than things seems to give us more satisfaction and happiness. In an article in *Forbes* magazine, the author writes,

> Recent research from San Francisco State University found that people who spent money on experiences rather than material items were happier and felt the money was better spent. The thrill of purchasing things fades quickly but the joy and memories of experiences, from epic adventures to minute encounters, can last a lifetime.[64]

We've talked about hope and eager expectation when it comes to vacations. One thing I notice is that when you have a nice week-long cruise planned, it tends to make life and the daily grind a little easier to endure. You have the eager expectation of enjoying yourself on a relaxing vacation with your family. For me, that anticipation starts about four to six weeks in advance of the trip. That's one of the added benefits of the vacation itself. It kind of makes me think about how we live our lives as believers. When we have faith and we're living our lives consistent with what Jesus had in mind and closer to our authentic selves, we live in anticipation of eternity. We get the added benefit of knowing we'll spend our eternity in heaven with Jesus. There's no better vacation than that.

Now, back to the list of regrets and what's least important. There are some themes to think about when we're looking at things or activities that are least important. Wasting time is one of them. Time squandered in chasing pursuits with limited value. Time wasted in worrying, time blown in caring about what other people think.

Time is clearly something that has real value. You only get a certain amount of time, and as we get older, time seems to be speeding up. I wish I would have known the things I know now twenty-five years ago. I can't do anything about the years when I was stumbling around lost like a zombie from *The Walking Dead*, but I've done something about the last ten years. Hopefully I can do something about the next ten, twenty, or thirty years, if God sees fit to give me that time.

There's something we all can be sure of: God is watching.

Time is a gift. Just like money, life, and the air we breathe. Health, family, and relationships are all gifts of God's grace. Time is something we can't go to the store and buy. Once this day is gone, it's gone forever. How much time are we wasting on things that aren't going to last? Money, houses, cars, or anything you can feel, touch, or count.

Could we use our time and money to gain things that last forever? What about love, peace, knowledge, our relationship with Jesus, and spiritual relationships with other believers? All those last forever. When we can see the value of those things, it will be reflected in our behavior and in our habits.

Is there a chance you could be wasting precious time on things or goals that don't have any real value?

Remember the mirror? It's a good idea to take it out and look honestly at ourselves. That's the first part of this journey. Everyone is flawed, so we shouldn't have any fear of being honest and seeing room for improvement. We're all WIPs—works in progress—and everyone (and that means *everyone*) has room for improvement. We're WIPs looking for WOTs (wastes of time).

One thing I've come to realize is that when I made the changes that emphasized spiritual values and fruit like love, joy, peace, kindness, and a strong loving relationship with Jesus, everyone around me was impacted in a positive way. Everyone. Spouse, children, family, and friends. There's the real value. It all starts in the classroom or laboratory of love. When you fill your heart with the love and light of Jesus, he touches people's hearts. It's his power and his love that change those around us.

There may be a few family members or coworkers or even people in your church who have bitterness or anger in their hearts. Jesus says, "Just keep loving them and trust in my love." John, the apostle of love, says this:

> We know how much God loves us, and we have put our trust in his love. God is love, and all who live in love live in God, and God lives in them. (1 John 4:16 NLT)

All we have is the now. The present. Yesterday is history, tomorrow's a mystery, today is a gift from God—which is why it's called the *present*. That statement is attributed to Eleanor Roosevelt or Alice Earle. Eleanor Roosevelt also said, "Great minds discuss ideas, average minds discuss events, small minds discuss people." Do we spend time talking about or watching other people's lives? We should remember that we aren't going to be shown anyone else's life unless we impacted their lives in a positive or negative way. We won't be asked about anyone else's life, anyone else's talents, passions, or purpose. We'll be asked about our own.

Remember what Jesus said to Howard Storm in his NDE when asked about our purpose:

> The world is like God's garden. And God made you and everyone else to bloom in that garden. And to be beautiful. And God made every one of you unique and special to be beautiful in your own way.

We can't bloom and be beautiful if we're focusing on and admiring the beautiful apple or peach tree across the dirt path from us, in someone else's garden. That's energy and resources we could be using to bear the fruit of love, joy, peace, and kindness.

We're here for a reason. We're to bloom in the full realization of our authentic selves. Everyone has a role, whether they realize it or not. Everyone. Everyone is valuable and is needed to play their part. If you don't play your part, it won't be played. We're all members of an orchestra. What if you're the one responsible for crashing the cymbals at the end of the song? No cymbal crash? Doesn't that change the song? Some people will argue that God is all powerful so if someone doesn't fulfill their purpose, he can just use someone else. That may be true, but it won't be fulfilled in the unique way that only you bring to the table. Your gifts and talents and personality are unique. How you go about fulfilling your purpose is unique and special also.

One important point is that when you begin to pursue your purpose and you do work you were created for, you help others—but really the one who benefits now and in eternity is you. You grow. You become fulfilled. You have joy. You impact everyone around you in a positive way. Plus, God promises a reward in eternity for us, but there are blessings he bestows on us while in this life too.

"We ourselves feel," Mother Theresa once said, "that what we are doing is just a drop in the ocean. But the ocean would be less because of that missing drop."

Remember, it's the little things that matter. We don't have to feel like we're going to change the entire world. From NDEs, we know that the small gestures of kindness or love are what matter:

> At the same time, all my life was instantly in front of me, and I was shown or made to understand what counted. I am not going to go into this any further, but believe me, what I had counted in life as unimportant was my salvation and what I thought was important was nil.... For instance, you may be at a stoplight and you're in a hurry and the lady in front of you, when the light turns green, doesn't take off, doesn't notice the light—and you get upset and start honking your horn and telling them to hurry up. Those are the little kind of things that are really important.[65]

> I relived those moments and felt not only what I had done but also the hurt I had caused. Some of the things I would have never imagined could have caused pain. I was surprised that some of the things I may have worried about, like shoplifting a chocolate as a child, were not there, whilst casual remarks which caused hurt unknown to me at the time were counted.[66]

Honking the horn at a green light at someone? I've done it. Everyone has. But it's those little things we don't even think about that matter most. Opening a door for someone. Being kind to someone, or giving an encouraging word to the checker at the grocery store who looks like he or she is having a hard day. Little acts of kindness and love go a long way. They can change the world. Our world, and that of our family and friends. That's what today is for. We can't do anything about yesterday, because it's history. We can live in the moment, love others, and bear fruit. We can develop the fruit of the Spirit. We can realize our authentic selves. We live in the now focusing on what we can do that has value, and examining our lives for any wasting of one of our most precious gifts, that of time.

We also know that tomorrow is in the unknown; only God knows what tomorrow will bring. That's his area. Whenever we try to predict or read the future, we're playing with fire. Prophecy and the future are God's business, not ours. Jesus spent significant effort and time fulfilling the Scriptures. Why? Because that was the proof that he was God's Son.

> Do not think that I have come to abolish the Law or the Prophets; I have not come to abolish them but to fulfill them. (Matthew 5:17 ESV)

That was the evidence. He foretold his death and resurrection. Plus, he fulfilled all the prophecy about his coming. The only impact we can have on our future is through the choices we make today. We can change the complexion of our future, and have an impact on our eternity, by how we choose to live our lives today. Our eternity is our responsibility. Our choices and our willingness to pursue our authentic self over the next twenty to thirty years will have a major impact on the next twenty to thirty billion years. Rejecting that idea could have serious consequences. I believe it's a hard, etched-in-granite fact. Your eternity is on you. No one else.

But that responsibility is reflected in how we *act* today. It's not reflected in sitting. Remember, the greatest regrets come from failing to act. We each have an eternity, no matter what you believe. We do have some responsibility when it comes to our spouse, significant others, or children. We'll be held accountable for those around us and whether we shared the gospel and the importance of a relationship with Jesus. We're responsible for sharing what we learn.

From my experience, spiritual issues and Jesus were for Sunday. That's a big mistake. Circumstances and opportunities to guide and talk about Jesus come up every day. There are lessons to be learned and spiritual principles that arise every day.

My children get frustrated with me, "Why does everything have to be a lesson?" Because life is a classroom, isn't it? Just like the family is the classroom of love. Our whole life is a test. We're constantly being tested. In *The Purpose Driven Life*, Rick Warren writes that life is a test and a trust. So if life is a test, everything is a lesson. And if life is also a trust, then we should be careful and use everything that God has entrusted to us in a way that's useful. He gives us a blessing, and then watches us to see what we do with it. We should be living our lives looking for the tests and looking to be trustworthy with our gifts and blessings. Both are everywhere.

My eternity, my responsibility

We should e-valu-ate our salvation. It's the most precious gift we have. It comes through our faith in Jesus. He's the most precious and valuable thing we own. We have the choice to go to heaven. We also choose exactly how close we want to be to Jesus. His desire is for us is to know him and love him. He has told us already and made it clear:

I am the way and the truth and the life. No one comes to the Father except through me. If you really know me, you will know my Father as well. (John 14:6 NIV)

Now *there* is some real value. Knowing Jesus. Any time spent getting to know Jesus and spending time loving and obeying and honoring him is always time well spent. Never wasted. Any mention in the hospice patient list about "I wish I'd spent less time in church, or reading the Bible, or with Jesus"? Nope. Not one mention. At the end of life, *all* you'll have is your relationship with Jesus.

Jesus calms the storms in our lives:

> Then he got into the boat and his disciples followed him. Suddenly a furious storm came up on the lake, so that the waves swept over the boat. But Jesus was sleeping. The disciples went and woke him, saying, "Lord, save us! We're going to drown!" He replied, "You of little faith, why are you so afraid?" Then he got up and rebuked the winds and the waves, and it was completely calm. The men were amazed and asked, "What kind of man is this? Even the winds and the waves obey him!" Matthew 8:23-27

We need Jesus in our boat. We need him in our marriages. We need him in our families. We need him at work. When we're afraid of that next wave, we can take comfort in the fact that even the waves obey him. So whatever happens when we decide to ride it, he is in control.

24 - CLIMBING THE LOVE LADDER

Spending time trying to conform to the way the world thinks is one big waste of time. I remember seeing a bumper sticker that was popular a while back: "He who dies with the most toys wins." Now we have an updated or modern version: "He who dies with the most toys wins, but he's still dead!"

Remember, it all starts in the way you think. Most great spiritual Christians and saints talk about detaching yourself "as radically as you can from the values of this world." We elevate our thinking to the higher values of the Spirit. Love, joy, peace, kindness, patience, and self-control.

> Do not conform yourselves to the standards of this world, but let God transform you inwardly by a complete change of your mind. Then you will be able to know the will of God. (Romans 12:2 GNT).

Look at that last line. There's true and real value in knowing the will of God for your life. We know that God wants all of us to grow in love and learn how to love in a selfless and more mature way. It's what I call the balloon ride. Jesus is in the basket of the balloon, he has a long rope ladder reaching down, and we are on the third rung from the bottom. The ladder is the *ladder of love*. The balloon is just cruising along. He's motioning to us, as if to say, "Climb up! come on!" But then we go lower and back to our old habits; we lower ourselves to the standard of the world, and it's like we run into some big cactus. Splinters in our butts. Then we try to climb higher.

That's the picture I get representing our spiritual growth. That rope ladder is long, and sometimes we climb a rung or two upward, then we go back down. Of course, we also have people on the ground, objects, houses, cars, money, and self-destructive habits, all beckoning for us to climb down. Jesus describes this:

> The seed falling among the thorns refers to someone who hears the word, but the worries of this life and the deceitfulness of wealth choke the word, making it unfruitful. (Matthew 13:22 NIV)

Notice he uses the word *deceitfulness* to describe wealth. As we've discussed, we know there's a lot of choking with regard to the Word, because studies show that only thirty percent of the population actually read the Bible regularly. Seventy percent ignore it. That's convincing evidence that there's a lot of choking of the Word going on in our society.

There's something inherently deceitful about wealth and materialism. We all get caught up in it. We're surrounded by it and engulfed in it and bombarded by the commercials and lifestyles of the rich and famous. It's inescapable. The allure is always there. We should focus and remember that it all rusts and fades and is only temporary. If we're wise, we focus on love, joy, peace, and goodness, which last forever.

Remember the time machine test. Most everything we're buying becomes junk in a very short time. Jesus says,

> Store up for yourselves treasures in heaven, where moths and rust do not destroy, and where thieves do not break in and steal. For where your treasure is, there your heart will be also. (Matthew 6:20 NIV)

Take the burning house test. Let's say you drive up your driveway and notice that your house or apartment is on fire. Your family is safe outside, and they're looking at you. "It started in the kitchen. I was making pancakes," says your son or daughter. You give a sigh of relief that everyone's safe. Then you have five minutes to run into the house to save one thing. You know that you won't be injured and you can run in safely and run out. So there is no risk of injury or death. What would that thing be?

There really is no right or wrong answer. I know exactly what I would run into a burning house for.

This is more of an exercise in self-awareness. Self-examination. You can't begin to make any type of changes in your life until you understand clearly what you value. Sometimes when I don't feel like going to a school function or family event because there's a good football game on, my wife just looks at me and says the magic words: "It's important." That's all I need to hear to shake up my value vision and know instantly that she's right.

As we grow in our spiritual journey, we begin to hear the whispers of the Holy Spirit telling us where to put our focus. Watching a sports event, reality show, or a movie is just entertainment. It's a pastime. So is social media. Something we do for enjoyment, like a hobby. We need those for balance in our lives, and there's absolutely nothing wrong with that. But they don't really serve a useful purpose or have any real value in the long term. They're kind of a mindless activity. We need those breaks for sure. They just shouldn't dominate our time or our lives.

Let's get back to that balloon ride. When we begin to slowly climb the ladder, we're starting to spend more time with Jesus. We begin to understand the value he brings to our lives. What's the payoff? Our love for him grows and our relationship with him is stronger. We develop the fruit of the Spirit the closer we get to Jesus. We experience his love more fully, and this allows us to express his love to others. (Remember, it's limitless.) We develop a more pure, mature, and higher form of love.

In the Greek language, there are four words for love. It's probably a good idea to understand the words for love and what they describe because we're in the love business. Business should be booming. As we continue to climb the love ladder that hangs from the basket of the balloon, we're getting closer to Christ and growing in the type of love we express.

On the bottom rungs is where *eros* is. This is erotic love. It's love based on body chemistry and self-satisfaction. It's a love that's more self-absorbed: "I love you because you make me happy." "I value you because of what you do for me." "I enjoy you for how you make me feel." See why it's kind of at the bottom?

As we climb up the ladder on the balloon ride, we can see the outline of Jesus, but not really his eyes or facial features. Then we get to *phileo,* or companion love. This is the love you share with a close friend you enjoy. You really have an affection for this person. It's a little more selfless, since it focuses on *our* happiness, not *my* happiness. It involves giving as well as receiving.

We climb a few more rungs and we can see the face of Jesus. He's saying something. We can't hear him. It's almost like he's whispering. We're at *storge*, which is familial love. It's a natural affection or obligation toward a husband, wife, or child. It's the burning house image. How do we know love conquers all fear? Who would be surprised if a father or mother ran into a burning house to rescue their children, knowing there was a major risk of death?

We keep climbing. We can see the eyes of Jesus and his smile, and he's whispering. We have to get so close to him and turn our head so our ear is right by his lips. That's where *agape* is. Sacrificial love. There's the payoff. Intimacy, friendship, and total focus on Jesus. We've climbed past our passion, past our friendships, past our families. We still love our friends and families, of course. But this is different.

Jesus says,

> Whoever has my commands and keeps them is the one
> who loves me. The one who loves me will be loved by

my Father, and I too will love them and *show myself to them*. (John 14:21 NIV)

He reveals himself to us in a personal way. We begin to get an *experience* of intimacy with him. No one knows how Jesus reveals himself to you, or me. No one. It's personal. Sacrificial love isn't easy, because it goes against every natural, instinctual urge we have. It's the highest form of love. It is God-given. It's the kind of love that's unavailable when we're hanging around on the bottom rungs, not able to see the face or hear the whispers of Jesus. It's the love that keeps loving, even when the loved person is being unkind, unloving, unworthy, unresponsive.

Unconditional love. No strings attached. Love is not a feeling. It's giving another person the thing they need most, even when they deserve it the least. It's an overwhelming concern for the well-being of others. This love's main concern is the good of the one being loved. It's godly love. It is oneness with God. We can't help being loving when we're one with God, because he is love. It isn't easy. Nothing of true lasting value is.

> If we accept human testimony, the testimony of God is surely greater. Now the testimony of God is this, that he has testified on behalf of his Son. Whoever believes in the Son of God has this testimony within himself. Whoever does not believe God has made him a liar by not believing the testimony God has given about his Son. And this is the testimony: God gave us eternal life, and this life is in his Son. Whoever possesses the Son has life; whoever does not possess the Son of God does not have life. (1 John 5:9-13 NIV)

One quick little point to make. If you think about it, the reason marriage is sacred and should be valued is that it's the only relationship with all four types of love in it: *eros, phileo, storge, agape*. (That's a very interesting point I heard expressed by Christian apologist Ravi Zacharias.) If you're married, go now and give your spouse a hug, and express your appreciation.

Jesus belongs to us when we surrender ourselves to him. When it comes to being "possessive," this is a time when that has a good connotation. Jesus wants us to be "possessive" when it comes to him.

Salvation is a gift. It's a gift we don't deserve. We've all sinned and don't deserve this wonderful mercy and grace.

It seems to me that there's controversy in the Christian faith about whether we can be confident that we're saved. Over my decade-long spiritual journey searching for truth, it just seems to me that God wants us to spend our time developing our relationship with Jesus and using the gifts and talents he has given us to serve others. We should be confident about our eternity and assume responsibility for it.

As we grow in love on this journey, he expects us to share the good news of salvation. You know you're growing in your relationship with Jesus when you just can't stop talking about him. You have a burning desire to share your experience. It's obvious that no one offers a better deal than Jesus.

Rick Warren describes it this way: "Our sins are forgiven, we have a purpose for living, and we have a home in heaven." That's not the big three, that's the *huge* three. Jesus offers all three. Sins forgiven? Check. Purpose for living? We find our purpose in our relationship with Jesus. Our hearts grow bigger to allow the love of Jesus to fill them up. Then we acquire love, joy, peace, kindness, gentleness, patience, goodness, and self-control. Having a home in heaven is the last part of it. This is important in how we live now, because it impacts our behavior with respect to how we view the world and the temptations of the world.

> Dear friends, I warn you as temporary residents and foreigners, to keep away from worldly desires that wage war against your very souls. (1 Peter 2:11 NLT)

We never become comfortable living in this world, because it's not our home. People who have NDEs frequently talk about feeling like they've gone home when they undergo an experience of heaven. It's like going off to battle in another country. We're in a war, and we fight to win the battle, but when the war is over, we get to go home. There's no place like home.

Thinking about eternity is useful when we face the inevitable trials and waves that are coming. Remember, these things are a reminder that we should never feel comfortable here on earth, because the earth is not our home. It's an uncomfortable and anxiety-producing place, because the devil roams the earth, and there's imperfection and disease and disasters and trouble. Just watch the news. This helps us think in terms of temporary versus eternal. Troubles and trials and sorrows and suffering are temporary. Heaven is eternal.

> So we fix our eyes not on what is seen but on what is unseen, since what is seen is temporary, but what is unseen is eternal. (2 Corinthians 4:18 NIV)

Why go over all this? Because if we're constantly unsure of our salvation, it's more difficult to think about our lives in a mental framework of temporary versus eternal. The confidence of eager expectation allows us to think in terms of the unseen and the spiritual.

Confidence in our salvation and the promise of heaven leads to peace and joy. Jesus spoke about peace and mentioned our joy many times. It seems to me that having peace and joy would be difficult if you're constantly wondering whether you're saved. This is my own opinion, though it's not like I have zero evidence to support this. The apostle Paul tells us,

> At one time, we too were foolish, disobedient, deceived and enslaved by all kinds of passions and pleasures. We lived in malice and envy, being hated and hating one another. But when the kindness and love of God our Savior appeared, he saved us, not because of righteous things we had done, but because of his mercy. He saved us through the washing of rebirth and renewal by the Holy Spirit, whom he poured out on us generously through Jesus Christ our Savior, so that, having been justified by his grace, we might become heirs having the hope of eternal life. This is a trustworthy saying. And I want you to stress these things, so that those who have trusted in God may be careful to devote themselves to doing what is good. These things are excellent and profitable for everyone. (Titus 3:3-7 NIV)

There's too much meat on this bone to just gloss over it. I want to focus on hope here, because the hope he's talking about has a different meaning. He's thinking of hope in the way we discussed earlier. It's eager expectation, not wishful thinking. It's like when you book a vacation or a cruise. When you get to the airport, you have eager expectation. When we go on a cruise, the funniest thing to me are the smiles of people going through the check-in process. Everyone's happy. You can't wipe the smiles off their faces. Including mine. It's *elpis*—eager expectation. When we're checking in, we aren't just wishfully thinking we're going to board the ship; we have full and eager expectation of boarding.

This is my own humble, non-biblical-scholar opinion, but that's a recurring theme that keeps coming across to me. We're to have confidence and fully expect to go to heaven when we have a loving, growing, thriving relationship with Jesus.

> So also Christ died once for all time as a sacrifice to take away the sins of many people. He will come again, not

to deal with our sins, but to bring salvation to all who are *eagerly waiting* for him. (Hebrews 9:28 NLT)

We rely on, commit to, and trust in Jesus. Look how Paul goes on and says, "This is a trustworthy saying and I want you to stress these things." Let's stop for a second here. The apostle Paul is probably in the top three greatest Christians of all time. He probably has his own floor in the Christianity hall of fame. Why do you think he says, "I want you to stress these things"? It's because having confidence in our salvation yields power, peace, and joy.

Here's another quote from Paul:

But let us who live in the light be clearheaded, protected by the armor of faith and love, and wearing as our helmet the confidence of our salvation. (1 Thessalonians 5:8 NLT)

Paul talks about the armor for battle in the Christian life, but can anyone imagine going into battle as a Roman soldier without a helmet? Think about that. *Confidence.* That's another essential that we need in our backpack, because Jesus is going to test our faith. Untested faith is unreliable faith. We need reliable and unshakable faith to do the things he has in mind for us.

Here's a quote from John Piper:

Jesus is precious because he removes our guilt. He is precious because he gives us eternal life. And he is precious because through him we become *authentic.* Jesus Christ is the most important man that ever lived. To know him is more valuable than knowing all the most famous and powerful people of history. To be known and loved by him is a greater honor than if all the heads of state were to bow in your presence. When this world is over and we all stand before the judgment seat of God, many of you will look back with shame and dismay at how small was the place granted to the Son of God in your daily lives: how seldom you spoke to him, how little of his Word you learned, how half-hearted your resolve to obey, how narrow the sphere of life in which you eagerly sought his lordship. And on that day, you will wonder no more why you were so unhappy in this life: unhappy at work, unhappy in school, unhappy at church, unhappy at home. It will all come clear: half-hearted allegiance to the lordship of Christ in the practical affairs of everyday life not only robs Jesus of the honor we owe him, but also robs us of joy and purpose.

When I first looked at that passage, it seemed a little rough. I don't want people to feel judged or brow-beaten. If you look at it closely, it's emphasizing the value and benefit Jesus brings to our lives. Notice that I highlighted *authentic*. Remember that we can't reach our full potential or get close to the full expression of our authentic selves without Jesus. It's through him that we get there.

It also points out a way to avoid the result of being unhappy at school, home, work, or even church. It's telling us that we can't reach fulfillment in this life at work at school or at home without the lordship of Jesus. We can realize true value in our lives when we give Jesus a larger role. When we speak, and listen to him. When we devote time to learning his Word and teachings. When we bring his principles and wisdom into our lives and into the lives of those around us. We realize the value of Jesus when we fully resolve to obey him and open the sphere of life where he's given the space to reign.

We were created to know and love God, and he made himself known and available to us through Jesus. When we seek his lordship, we get revelation, joy, and purpose. We get to joy and purpose when he's given room to operate in our hearts and in our lives.

It's important to understand how regal, majestic, powerful, and worthy of our worship Jesus is. He's the humble carpenter, but he's also coming as an all-powerful conquering King. He's a loving friend, but he's also Savior and Lord.

> Immediately after the tribulation of those days the sun will be darkened, and the moon will not give its light, and the stars will fall from heaven, and the powers of the heavens will be shaken. Then will appear in heaven the sign of the Son of Man, and then all the tribes of the earth will mourn, and they will see the Son of Man coming on the clouds of heaven with power and great glory. And he will send out his angels with a loud trumpet call, and they will gather his elect from the four winds, from one end of heaven to the other. (Matthew 24:29-31 ESV)

Jesus mentions "coming on the clouds of heaven with power and great glory." It's like he's telling us, "Hey, I love you and want to be your friend and grow in my relationship with you, but let's not forget the other part of who I am."

He deserves our worship and reverence and our obedience—and, most importantly for us, his rightful place in our lives. We should keep in mind that we're the ones who benefit from placing him there. He deserves the center spot where there's only one chair. We can't forget that it's a throne. Humans have made themselves king or made other humans king. There's only one *King*. Even Elvis said that.

25 - LOVING WITH EVERYTHING YOU HAVE

My whole exposure to faith was based on fear. If you commit this sin or fail to do something else, you'll be punished or possibly end up in hell. If you think about it, it kind of has its origin in human manipulation. Other people trying to control your behavior. Rules and regulations. That isn't what Jesus had in mind.

It's easy to see how people want to use the teachings of Jesus to control or manipulate. This reminds me of what I tell my own children. If they listen to my advice by studying and developing their minds, they'll have more knowledge, and knowledge brings wisdom and power. If they follow my advice and exercise and strengthen their bodies, they'll be healthier and have more energy.

There's no benefit for me other than knowing they're going down a wise path. If they follow my suggestions to avoid drug use or excessive drinking, no one comes out from behind the curtain and gives me a new car. No one comes around to offer me free lawn service. No one gives me a free lunch.

In the same way, if you begin to see and believe that there's value in a strong, growing relationship with Jesus, no one will ring your doorbell with a check from Publishers Clearing House. But you're the one who will benefit and win. Ultimately, *you* win, and so will everyone around you that you hold near and dear to your heart. Your work life, school life, worship life, home life, and marriage and family life will all feel the influence of the love and light of Jesus. Everyone wins.

It starts in the relationships closest to us. We already have a built-in sense of the value of those relationships. If we don't,

NDEs should help us to understand and see the real value in our closest relationships. That's my humble, non-pastor, satisfied-customer testimony. I've eaten at the restaurant, and the atmosphere and the food are wonderful. I've been on the awesome Caribbean cruise, and the beaches and the food and the activities were wonderful.

I'm not saying it's easy, free, and devoid of trouble, trials, or waves. Our faith will be tested, but it's easier to know, understand, and accept these trials because we *know* that God can see the end result. He's always looking to help us reach our full potential. Our authentic selves.

I remember eating at a restaurant in Mexico one time, and the waiter, after serving us food, stood about ten feet away from my wife and me, ready to respond if we needed him. He didn't move, but was far enough away so we could feel comfortable that he wasn't eavesdropping on our conversation. Now and then he checked to make sure we didn't need more water or any condiments. That was service. Most likely it was because there weren't many people in the restaurant, but that type of service is still rare. This is a testimony about that type of restaurant.

To simplify everything for us, Jesus tells us this:

> "You must love the LORD your God with all your heart, all your soul, and all your mind." This is the first and greatest commandment. A second is equally important: 'Love your neighbor as yourself.' The entire law and all the demands of the prophets are based on these two commandments." (Matthew 22:37-40 NLT)

Love God with all our hearts, minds, souls, strength, and love our neighbor as ourselves. It's simple but powerful.

Can we see the value in loving God the way Jesus had in mind? What does it mean to love God with *all* your heart, mind, soul, and strength? When we come to realize the value of loving God in this all-encompassing way, we spend time, effort, and energy on developing that love.

Loving God in this way is more involved and takes work. Love is an action. When we value our relationship with Jesus, we take it seriously. It takes effort, sweat, and time. How much do we value loving God and being loved by him? We can easily see it when we look at how we spend our time. How much time and effort are we giving to growing in love?

If we go about the business of loving God with all our minds, we should be using our minds and learning all we can. We should be actively seeking the truth. Remember, God has given you the power to solve most of your problems by giving you the capacity to think and reason. We were given a brain for a reason. The two most important pursuits in this life as described in NDEs are love and knowledge. There are many ways to solve your problems, but thinking your way out is a good start.

In *Life after Life*, Raymond Moody describes how in NDEs, the being of light "seems to stress the importance of two things in life: Learning to love other people and acquiring knowledge."[67] Those are the two things that we'll be able to take with us into the next life. Not toys. Plus, we'll continue to grow in love and continue to acquire knowledge in the next life.

If we go about the business of loving God with all our hearts, we come to realize that we must make room in our hearts for the love of Jesus. We clear out resentment, bitterness, and anger. This leaves more room for his love. When we realize that humans make mistakes, it becomes easier to forgive and forget things that people did or said to hurt us.

Sometimes we're walking around with guilt or an unforgiving attitude. It takes time to learn how to let go of anger and bitterness. It takes effort. When we hold onto anger and bitterness like a life preserver in an ocean coming at us wave after wave, there's no peace or joy. We need to let go of the life preserver and climb into the boat with Jesus. He may be reaching over to pull you in, but you must reach up to grab his hand. It's always there. And it's easier to ride the waves in a boat.

Anger and bitterness are not good friends because they interfere with the healing love of Jesus. If we have bitterness or anger, we must forgive the person or persons who hurt us. Remember, humans are human.

Forgiving others is nonnegotiable. Jesus tells us,

> You have heard that it was said to those of old, "You shall not murder; and whoever murders will be liable to judgment." But I say to you that everyone who is angry with his brother will be liable to judgment; whoever insults his brother will be liable to the council; and whoever says, "You fool!" will be liable to the hell of fire. So if you are offering your gift at the altar and there remember that your brother has something against you, leave your gift there before the altar and go. First be reconciled to your brother, and then come and offer your gift. (Matthew 5:21-24 ESV)

Any bitterness or anger? Forgive your brother, or if you were the one at fault, ask for forgiveness.

Some people have a hard time accepting responsibility if they hurt someone else. They're sometimes unable to recognize or accept blame. That's where we can see pride. Pride interferes with all relationships. Pride kills love.

There's no way for me to warn you strongly enough about the dangers of pride. I've experienced them first-hand. It was horrible. I've lived the destruction that follows pride, and it wasn't pretty. God allowed me to stumble, fall, and knock out some of my teeth. God allows that because he's the world's greatest dentist. He will fix your teeth while waiting for you to learn humility and gratitude.

I remember Hall of Fame linebacker Ray Lewis telling a story in an interview about being in jail, accused of being complicit in a murder. He heard a voice say, "Now do I have your attention?" That's when his life changed. If you aren't pursuing spiritual growth and a relationship with Jesus, God may be waiting for the perfect time to "get your attention."

When we can understand how people say things that are stupid, and how they sometimes say things they don't really understand or mean to say, we can learn to let go of bitterness.

I remember a parent with grown children bragging that he'd never said he was sorry to his children. Think about that. This person is saying he never did anything or said anything that resulted in hurting his children. Can any parent say that? Not me. I screw up all the time. If we say something or do something that hurts our children, we should just apologize. Simple. Not only that, apologize quickly. When we do, we acknowledge their pain and our responsibility in causing it. We teach them how to forgive by giving them an opportunity to do so. We also teach them that it's important to ask for forgiveness.

What did Jesus say about forgiving others?

> Peter came to him and asked, "Lord, how often should I forgive someone who sins against me? Seven times?" "No, not seven times," Jesus replied, "but seventy times seven!" (Matthew 18:21-22 NLT)

When we don't accept responsibility for our mistakes, we're teaching our own children to blame others and never accept responsibility for what we do. That's pride and immaturity.

Pride kills relationships. Period.

266

When we don't ask our kids for forgiveness, they don't learn to forgive others the way Jesus is explaining to us. We're modeling bad behavior. Jesus wants us to forgive "seventy times seven." Our children aren't stupid. They know when a parent screws up. Tell them the truth: you aren't perfect, but you're trying to be better. This helps them be free of anger and bitterness toward you. It also allows more love to enter their hearts.

If we're to love God with all our soul, then we come to realize and understand that we're spiritual beings guided by the Holy Spirit. We're fully capable of walking in the power of the Holy Spirit. We're guided by the whispers of the Holy Spirit. We work at getting in tune with the Holy Spirit.

The kind of love Jesus is talking about is an active love. When we value that kind of love, it shows in our lives. But it's developed over time and it takes the rest of our lives. I'm still working on it. God gives us guidance and his Word and other people, so there are many resources available to us.

Jesus wants us to love our neighbor as ourselves. He wants us to love and serve others the way we would love and serve him if he would come by our house for a visit. We love and serve him when we love and serve other people. This is most beautifully illustrated in these words of Jesus:

> But when I, the Messiah, shall come in my glory, and all the angels with me, then I shall sit upon my throne of glory. And all the nations shall be gathered before me. And I will separate the people as a shepherd separates the sheep from the goats, and place the sheep at my right hand, and the goats at my left.
>
> Then I, the King, shall say to those at my right, "Come, blessed of my Father, into the Kingdom prepared for you from the founding of the world. For I was hungry and you fed me; I was thirsty and you gave me water; I

was a stranger and you invited me into your homes; naked and you clothed me; sick and in prison, and you visited me."

Then these righteous ones will reply, "Sir, when did we ever see you hungry and feed you? Or thirsty and give you anything to drink? Or a stranger, and help you? Or naked, and clothe you? When did we ever see you sick or in prison, and visit you?"

And I, the King, will tell them, "When you did it to these my brothers, you were doing it to me!"

Then I will turn to those on my left and say, "Away with you, you cursed ones, into the eternal fire prepared for the devil and his demons. For I was hungry and you wouldn't feed me; thirsty, and you wouldn't give me anything to drink; a stranger, and you refused me hospitality; naked, and you wouldn't clothe me; sick, and in prison, and you didn't visit me."

Then they will reply, "Lord, when did we ever see you hungry or thirsty or a stranger or naked or sick or in prison, and not help you?"

And I will answer, "When you refused to help the least of these my brothers, you were refusing help to me."

And they shall go away into eternal punishment; but the righteous into everlasting life. (Matthew 25:31-46 TLB)

When we look at the emotion and strength of Jesus's words, it's obvious this is important to him. That's why we say that a nonserving Christian is a contradiction of terms. There should be no such thing.

When Christians act in ways that aren't consistent with the words of Jesus, it results in people feeling rejected and they become jaded. Here's an illustration from the life of Gandhi:

> While Gandhi was a practicing Hindu, Christianity intrigued him. In his reading of the Gospels, Gandhi was impressed by Jesus whom Christians worshiped and followed. He wanted to know more about this Jesus that Christians referred to as "the Christ, the Messiah." The Rev. Pattison tells the following story: One Sunday morning Gandhi decided that he would visit one of the Christian churches in Calcutta. Upon seeking entrance to the church sanctuary, he was stopped at the door by the ushers. He was told he was not welcome, nor would he be permitted to attend this particular church, as it was for high-caste Indians and whites only. He was neither high-caste nor white. Because of the rejection, the Mahatma turned his back on Christianity.[68]

We should be careful when we reject anyone. There's power in rejection. This rejection impacted Gandhi's entire life. What if you or I would have been there to explain the real nature of Jesus to Gandhi? Maybe Gandhi began to believe the lie that Christianity was meant only for the privileged. The mistake Gandhi made was losing the focus on Jesus. Maybe no one told him that Christianity is a relationship with Jesus. That is its essence. Jesus probably would have told him, "Don't worry about what those ushers told you; you're valuable, and I want you to get to know me and understand me more than your own desire for the same thing." The mistake those ushers made was that Jesus came for everyone.

Here's another example of humans being human and making mistakes. The ushers or church elders decided who was worthy of the message of Jesus. That's an example of humans playing God. Pride and stupidity.

There are countless examples of people doing things in the name of Christianity that have nothing to do with the teachings of Jesus. People are imperfect. We all say and do stupid things. Jesus didn't tell us that his grace, mercy, and salvation were available only to certain people or groups of people. Never. It's available to all.

That's why studying his words and the Word is so important. I'm not a biblical scholar, but I know that Jesus never said anything about his coming for only certain ethnicities or for the wealthy. That's not only ridiculous, it's just plain stupid. He did mention that he was here for the Jews first (Matthew 15:24), but he came for everyone. In the same way, we're to serve everyone. When we see someone in need, he expects us to help. Anyone who's hungry, thirsty, naked, a stranger, sick, or in prison. When we develop the "eyes of Christ," it's easier to see Jesus in people around us who are hungry, thirsty, sick, or in prison.

One thing I noticed is that it's easier to see spiritual and emotional needs in others when you grow in your relationship with Jesus. People have physical needs like food and water or clothing. As we begin to grow spiritually, we begin to see spiritual needs around us. Emotional needs around us. People in need of just a little affirmation or kindness just to get through their daily lives. They may have problems in their marriage, or have a teenager who feels isolated or unwanted in school. Some need comforting when sick.

"Be kind," Plato said, "for everyone you meet is fighting a hard battle." People need love, kindness, mercy, and patience. As we grow and get ever closer to our authentic selves, it's easier to see and recognize people who are feeling unloved and unappreciated. We should be generous with affirmation. We can learn to give complements freely.

Remember what NDEs teach us about the small things. If we're at a store and we see the clerk has a pretty blouse on, we should mention it. If we have that thought, we should just go ahead and say it. It's free and easy.

Think about what might have been if those ushers had given Gandhi some positive affirmation and welcomed him with open arms.

Being generous with positive affirmation really starts at home. We can tell our wives we love and appreciate them. No wife hates to hear that. You can tell your husband you appreciate his hard work and how he takes care of the family. No husband hates to hear that. We can tell our significant others how we love and appreciate them. We can tell our kids how special they are. I used to tell my son when he was younger that he was superman. I frequently tell him he's capable of many types of goals based on his many and varied gifts.

Those are the kinds of things we're more likely to see around us as we go through our lives. Those opportunities are everywhere, and as we grow closer to Jesus they're much easier to see.

If we're loving God and loving and serving our neighbor in the way Jesus had in mind, and we value those activities, they'll be manifested in our lives. If we're taking seriously his command to love God and others, there isn't much time or energy left to be thinking about or worrying about faith alone or faith and works. That's for the debaters and the arguers.

We have many doctrines and flavors of the Christian faith. Some estimate there are 30,000 denominations of Christianity. Ask yourself an honest question: Do you think that's what Jesus had in mind? My answer is no. That's just my humble opinion, and I'm just a layman. Flawed, but resolute. Imperfect, but willing to try. I'm a stumbling, bumbling, rumbling, tumbling sinner.

The apostle Paul encourages all of us:

> We have been beaten, been put in prison, faced angry mobs, worked to exhaustion, endured sleepless nights, and gone without food. We prove ourselves by our purity, our understanding, our patience, our kindness, by the Holy Spirit within us, and by our sincere love. We faithfully preach the truth. God's power is working in us. We use the weapons of righteousness in the right hand for attack and the left hand for defense. We serve God whether people honor us or despise us, whether they slander us or praise us. We are honest, but they call us impostors. We are ignored, even though we are well known. We live close to death, but we are still alive. We have been beaten, but we have not been killed. Our hearts ache, but we always have joy. We are poor, but we give spiritual riches to others. We own nothing, and yet we have everything. Oh, dear Corinthian friends! We have spoken honestly with you, and our hearts are open to you. There is no lack of love on our part, but you have withheld your love from us. I am asking you to respond as if you were my own children. Open your hearts to us! (2 Corinthians 6:5-13 NLT)

The Christian life is a tough gig. But we have each other. I think we get caught up in some of these arguments about faith and works and salvation being guaranteed and all the rest. Jesus wants us growing closer to him. Remember Howard Storm's NDE, and how Jesus (or a spiritual being) responded when asked to identify the "best" religion:

> The religion that brings you closest to God. Religions are a vehicle to take you to a destination. The purpose of religion is to help you have a personal relationship with God. Religion is only a means to find God. Religion is not the destination.

Jesus wants us spending our time loving and serving him and loving and serving others. We serve him by loving and serving others. That's it. That's the best use of our time. When we spend too much time debating and arguing, we waste it.

Think about this. The Old Testament has over six hundred rules and regulations.[69] But the New Testament simplifies everything. As we're going through our spiritual journey, learning and focusing on the words of Jesus will always guide us. His habits and how he acted will guide us. We never go off the path when we stick to that. But it's not a simple or easy walk. Jesus said,

> You can enter God's Kingdom only through the narrow gate. The highway to hell is broad, and its gate is wide for the many who choose that way. But the gateway to life is very narrow and the road is difficult, and only a few ever find it. (Matthew 7:13-14 NLT)

Man, I love that passage. Go back and read it again. That's why we focus on the words of Jesus. He's telling us that not many people are choosing to go the way he's showing us.

One thing I've noticed is that when you start to grow spiritually in the power of the Holy Spirit, you begin to see those around you more clearly. You can see how much emphasis our culture places on worldly values. We can see it in popular music or on social media. It's kind of like a cultural decay. A moral decay. Now there's internet bullying and "trolling." There's an obsession with celebrity, fame, and reality television. There's an obsession with money and material wealth. It's everywhere. But remember the words of Jesus: "The highway to hell is broad, and its gate is wide for the many who choose that way."

I'm not judging or condemning to hell everyone in our culture who's focused on fame or wealth. We've already said that we're not in the judging business, and no one gave us the keys to heaven with the power to condemn anyone to hell. But in order to try to change things for the better, we should be able to see the things around us that need changing. *We start with ourselves.* Just like the song "Man in the Mirror." It's the first tiny step to getting closer to our authentic selves. We start by looking at our own lives and changing the things that hinder us from reaching that goal. That's the one thing we have the absolute power to control.

We're all capable of self-examination. We're all capable of pursuing truth and growing in love and understanding. If you say you're incapable of loving more, that's a lie. Every single one of us can grow and learn to love more. Every single one of us can learn to be more kind and patient, and learn to put our focus on others while denying ourselves.

If we value our family and our closest relationships, we can take the lead and start with our own behavior. We can be more loving and kind and patient with those closest to us. We can point out the value of spiritual fruit like love and joy and peace, and how we can all be more kind.

This reminds me of an episode of *M*A*S*H*, the popular television show in the seventies and early eighties. In that episode, one of the characters told Hawkeye and BJ, "So you guys think you can change the world or what?" They responded, "No, just our little corner of it." So we may not be able to totally turn the world around, but we can grow, develop, and nurture love, peace, and kindness within our families and the people closest to us. As we begin to realize and see the value that Jesus brings into our lives, we can share him with those closest to us. We can change our little corner of the world. When we value our spiritual growth, and we value our relationship with Jesus, we accept our assignment and go about the business of serving and loving others. Then we're closer to our authentic selves.

Quick little digression. Hawkeye Pierce is one of the reasons I wanted to be a doctor. He was and is a role model that I aspire to being. He was flawed in many ways, but his love, concern, selfless attitude, and compassion for others was unrivaled. He drank too much and was always chasing around nurses, but somehow, we could always overlook those flaws. He had a true and tireless love and compassion for his patients. He had a palpably pure concern for others. Plus, he just didn't care what other people thought about him. He was just himself. A little crazy. Funny. Skillful, humble surgeon. Love that guy. When it comes to love and compassion as a doctor, I try to be like Hawkeye.

Getting back to that verse. Jesus says, "The gateway to life is narrow and the road is difficult, and only a few ever find it" (Matthew 7:14 NLT). You must find the gateway first. Jesus says he himself is the gate:

> All who came before me were thieves and robbers. But the true sheep did not listen to them. Yes, I am the gate. Those who come in through me will be saved. They will come and go freely and will find good pastures. The thief's purpose is to steal and kill and destroy. My purpose is to give them a rich and satisfying life. (John 10:8-10 NLT)

Boom. Let's stop here and read that over again. Too important. Look what Jesus is plainly saying. "My purpose is to give them a rich and satisfying life." It's not a secret, it's not hidden. He promises a "rich and satisfying life." There's real value there. We need to be honest with ourselves and ask: Do I have a rich and satisfying life? If not, why not?

Jesus promises a rich and satisfying life. He tells us that giving us that type of life is his purpose. We can trust and believe Jesus. He proved it to me. There was a before and after with me. He changed my life, my beliefs, my values, my vision, my spirit, my heart, my mind, my marriage, and my family. *Every single one* for the better. The keys to the fully loaded Benz were offered to me. But I had to reach for them. There's nowhere else you can get the type of rich and satisfying life other than through Jesus.

You know why Starbucks was so successful when it first opened in 1971? Because there was no other place that served coffee like that in the 1970s. You just couldn't find it anywhere else. That's always a good business idea or plan. Offer a valuable product or service that the customer can't get anywhere else no matter how hard they try. You'll succeed. That's what Jesus gives us when we develop a close personal relationship with him. You can't get what he offers you anywhere else, no matter how hard you try.

I'll tell you, as I'm going through all this working, trying, failing. and flailing, Jesus will inevitably give me some spiritual insight or a sign that's beautiful and wonderful, and it lets me know I'm not wasting my time. There's always encouragement, and he'll make his presence known. He also reveals a little more of himself, and I get closer to him with every new wave I choose to brave. It's always interesting and challenging, never boring.

Brave the wave. It's worth it.

Here's a promise from Jesus that we can trust:

> Whoever has my commandments and keeps them loves me. Whoever loves me will be loved by my Father, and I will love them and reveal myself to them. (John 14:21 CEB)

That, by itself, is enough for me. Totally worth it. Things change only if you know the promises of Jesus first. Many people aren't even aware of the parables and the principles behind them. The next step is to trust in the promises of Jesus, but you can't trust in them if you don't know them. That's one of the components of belief: *trust in, rely on, commit to*. That's the main reason I'm writing this book; I want others to feel the peace. I want others to get a glimpse of the spiritual side of our lives on this planet. To know the intimacy, closeness, and value of a relationship with Jesus. To feel his love. It's everywhere. It's available to all of us when we open our eyes and the eyes of our hearts.

26 - Relationships over Opinions

How much value do we place on the opinion of others or impressing other people? We know we're to love and serve others, but how much time, energy, money, and effort are we investing in trying to impress other people? We should look and be honest with ourselves.

Our time's better spent focusing on an audience of one. The question is: "What does Jesus think about what I'm trying to do?"

People who are trying to sell you something like a new car will show in their commercials how everyone stops what they're doing to turn and look at you driving by in that new car. You can tell what they're trying to sell because they keep cutting back to the person in the car just smiling and beaming, with an expression that seems to say, "Look at me! Everyone wants to be *me* in this new car!" Stop and ask yourself if there's any real value in having people envy you. There's also a very real and damaging danger. Pride. It's only natural to compare yourself to people around you, but it becomes dangerous when it becomes an all-consuming obsession that leads to pursuits of questionable value.

> We do not dare to classify or compare ourselves with some who commend themselves. When they measure themselves by themselves and compare themselves with themselves, they are not wise. (2 Corinthians 10:12 NIV)

We should ask ourselves what the payoff is when someone is envious of us. My simple answer would be pride. Pride is never useful. When and where is pride useful in what we're trying to do? Will it help us in reaching our authentic selves?

This screams for a list:

1. Pride puts the focus on ourselves.

2. It's quite the opposite of what Jesus had in mind.

3. It can lead to destruction (Proverbs 16:18), as you stumble and fall. (Remember the teeth?)

4. It destroys gratitude.

5. It emphasizes the fleshly or natural self.

6. It leads to entitlement.

7. It deemphasizes the spiritual side of who we are.

8. It interferes with our willingness to accept responsibility.

9. It hinders our ability to forgive others or ask for forgiveness.

It's obvious from this list that pride is something to be avoided on the journey toward our authentic selves. Pride kills love. Sometimes a list like this helps us to see the damage that something like pride does to our growth and our relationships.

When it comes to forgiving others, we know that's nonnegotiable, because Jesus tells us:

> If you forgive other people when they sin against you, your heavenly Father will also forgive you. But if you do not forgive others their sins, your Father will not forgive your sins. (Matthew 6:14-15 NLT)

Let's look at this. He emphasizes forgiving others when they sin against us, or else we won't be forgiven. Why do you think Jesus emphasizes that? He does so because it's *nonnegotiable*. There are no little openings for us to wiggle out of. We *must* forgive others. Period. It's tough sometimes, but there are no other options.

When we compare and focus on what we don't have, this leads to entitlement, envy, and frustration. Envy is an insult to God. You're telling him that he made a mistake with the blessings he gave you, because he gave more or something different to someone else. When we compare ourselves to others and feel like we're better than others, this can lead to pride. Pride places the focus on me, so I can't follow Jesus when my whole focus is on me. To be his follower we must deny ourselves first, then pick up the cross and follow Jesus.

When you "covet" or are envious of other people and want what they have, it interferes with our own gratitude. We can't be grateful or satisfied if we're constantly comparing what we have with what everyone around us has. We should be careful spending too much time and emphasis on what others have.

If we can learn to be content with what we have and be grateful for what we have, that leads to joy and peace. Think about where you are and what you're doing when you feel blessed. It may be spending time with family or doing something for others. Spend time in activities or places that give you the feelings of gratitude.

Each of us can find something to complain about. That's what children do.

Spend time being grateful. It brings peace and joy.

> Do nothing out of selfish ambition or vain conceit. Rather, in humility value others above yourselves, not looking to your own interests but each of you to the interests of the others. In your relationships with one another, have the same mindset as Christ Jesus: Who, being in very nature God, did not consider equality with God something to be used to his own advantage; rather, he made himself nothing by taking the very nature of a servant, being made in human likeness. And being found

in appearance as a man, he humbled himself by becoming obedient to death even death on a cross! Therefore, God exalted him to the highest place and gave him the name that is above every name, that at the name of Jesus every knee should bow, in heaven and on earth and under the earth and every tongue acknowledge that Jesus Christ is Lord, to the glory of God the Father. *Do everything without grumbling.*

Therefore, my dear friends, as you have always obeyed— not only in my presence, but now much more in my absence—continue to work out your salvation with fear and trembling, for it is God who works in you to will and to act in order to fulfill his good purpose.

Do everything without grumbling or arguing, so that you may become blameless and pure, "children of God without fault in a warped and crooked generation." Then you will shine among them like stars in the sky as you hold firmly to the word of life. (Philippians 2:1-18 NIV)

We've talked about what's easy, including sin and criticizing others. We learn about our unique talents by looking at what's easy for us compared to those around us. Here's another thing in life that's easy: whining, crying, complaining, and grumbling. Especially about how we don't have something, or the unfairness of our situation.

I remember talking to a patient once and whining and complaining that I had three jobs, including a business I was a part of. He said, "Wow, you're lucky. I've been looking for a job for over a year now, and I still haven't been hired." Boy, that got me. Do you see how it's all about mindset, and how we think about our situation?

If we look at the passage above from Philippians, it starts out by warning about "selfish ambition or vain conceit." Pride. Then

281

it points out humility and valuing others and the interests of others above our own. Humility is what we want. We want to try to be a humble servant like Jesus. And look at the payoff for him: "God exalted him to the highest place."

This is a tough one, but it goes on to mention doing everything "without grumbling." If we can whine or complain about how tough or bad we have it, it makes us feel better. But notice it goes on, telling us to "work out" our salvation "with fear and trembling," to fulfill God's good purpose for our lives. We're to take this spiritual journey seriously. We're to be humble. We're to avoid comparisons with others. We're to fulfill the purpose God had in mind for us before he created us.

If we're honest with ourselves, we come to realize that we're blessed to be alive. We may be blessed with good health or the love of family and friends. If we're believers, then we know we're loved and accepted by God who values every one of us. We're grateful for Jesus—who's our friend, and who's eager to love us and be loved by us. As we strive to grow in love, joy, and peace, it all starts from within. How we think. What we believe. What we value. When we begin to be content and grateful for our relationships, then we begin to value them.

The family unit is the place where we learn how to love and how we grow in maturity. It's the classroom of love. We began our understanding of love as babies in the classroom. We grew up in a family and learned what we know about love in that classroom. We may not have had a loving or close-knit family relationship as we were growing up. That doesn't mean we can't be loving to our spouses, significant others, and children. We can develop loving relationships with them. It can all be done through a growing, thriving relationship with Jesus. He has an inexhaustible supply of love, and when we ask Jesus to fill our hearts with his love, that's another undeniable prayer. He'll never withhold his love. It is inexhaustible.

When we value our marriage, our spouse, our significant others, and our families, it has an impact on our behavior. Our relationships are the most important things in this life. We should act in a way that reflects that. Remember the concentric circles.

One simple way to strengthen your own marriage is to ask yourself, "What can *I do* to make this marriage stronger? What changes can *I make* in my own behavior and attitude to strengthen this marriage?" I'm no marriage counselor, and my own marriage is far from perfect. From my own experience, and from the observation of marriages around me, I've seen that immaturity, selfishness, and pride are the most destructive forces in a relationship.

Think about this. If a husband wakes up every morning and says, "Honey, what can I do for you today?"—his focus is on the needs of the other person and off himself. And if a wife wakes up every morning and says, "Honey, how can I make this day easier for you?"—that's pure selflessness. And that is strength in a marriage. The focus, *from both sides*, is on the needs of the other person. Same thing with a significant other.

It's not one person doing most of the heavy lifting, which happens often. Marriage counselors will tell you that it's hard to improve a relationship when only one person is willing to look at themselves honestly and make changes for the benefit of the relationship. It's way easier when both partners are willing to work.

It's very similar to our relationship with Jesus. He has already done his part; he's just waiting for us to do ours. We just have to be willing to put in the effort.

What I tend to see in relationships that are having difficulty is finger-pointing about how the other person isn't doing something, or he or she is doing something that's bothersome and irritating. Lots of finger-pointing. Things change when people can be honest, mature and self-aware.

The components of a healthy thriving marriage are these:[70]

- love and commitment (at its core, love is deciding to be committed to another person)

- sexual faithfulness

- humility

- patience and forgiveness

- time

- honesty and trust

- communication

- selflessness

When we value our marriage, we value the laboratory of love and the family unit. The family is like a huge circus tent. Usually there are at least two huge poles in the middle holding everything up. The husband and the wife. If we focus on the marriage first, the family is strengthened. When *both* the husband and wife understand that the marriage is the foundation of the entire family, things are easier.

When we value our family, we value the classroom of love. It begins with a commitment to that other person. Just like we've been talking about with Jesus. We believe in Jesus. We rely on, trust in, and commit to Jesus. If we value our marriage, and we want to develop maturity and selflessness, we can begin looking at our own behavior and try to see areas in our lives where we're being selfish and immature.

Want to strengthen your marriage? Ask yourself, "What can I do to be more loving and giving in my marriage?" Start with you. Why? Because that's something you have control over. You can change your attitude and your behavior and become more self-aware.

I remember in my residency training how one of the other residents was always smiling and cheerful. We were getting slaughtered with work and taking care of sick and dying people with no sleep or rest. It was sheer drudgery and suffering. After one particularly hard day, as we were in the call room totally spent, I looked over at this resident and said, "Man, we're getting killed here, and we're totally exhausted, and every time I look at you, you're smiling. How can you stay so upbeat and positive when we're so miserable?"

"Brother," he answered, "the only thing I have control over is my attitude."

I've always remembered that, and I try to model it for my wife and family in difficult situations at home, or if something doesn't turn out exactly like we wanted.

Stay positive! If you're on a trip and things get sidetracked, call it an adventure! Model patience and love, and cover over every hurt with as much patience and love as possible.

It's extremely difficult to try to change another person, especially if they have their mind or values focused on other things. But if all they see in you is a selfless, loving person, it tends to bring out love from them. We can model the behavior, and we'll begin to see the results in our marriage and family.

When I began to see the family unit and my marriage as a classroom to learn love, I began to see how relationships and the family unit are an important starting point to developing our relationship with Jesus.

God is love. You want to develop love, kindness, gentleness, and patience? Begin practicing with your spouse, significant other, or your children. It's the classroom of love and spiritual fruit.

Here's an account that really drives home this message; it's from Howard Storm's NDE life review as described in *My Descent into Death:*

> The angels and Jesus shared their feelings of joy with me when love was expressed, and they shared their disappointment and sadness when we hurt one another. God had put my mother, father, sisters and me together to love and support one another in our life's journey to grow in love and spirit....
>
> In my life review, I had to turn away numerous times when I saw myself treating my children in unloving ways. The most unloving thing I did was to be at times so obsessed with my concerns that I was indifferent to their needs. I'm sorry for the occasions when I was impatient or cruel to my daughter and son. The most disturbing behaviors I witnessed in my life review were the times when I cared more about my career as an artist and college professor than about their need to be loved. The emotional abandonment of my children was devastating to review.[71]

Any of that sound familiar? Your spouse and family are gifts from God, and we're to develop the skill of loving by growing in love with them.

One simple thing to do in our marriage and with our children is a big part of communication: just *listen*. Stop and listen. If you're on your phone, put it down. Watching a television program? Everyone can pause a television program now, or record it. Listening is loving. In the movie *The Breakfast Club*, Emilio Estevez asks Ally Sheedy, "What do your parents do to you?" Ally got tears in her eyes and said, "They ignore me." We all need to be better listeners. Everyone.

Remember, love is an action. Talk is cheap. Here's my favorite line again: "Sorry, I can't hear what you're saying because your actions are screaming so loudly."

Listening is loving.

Notice that humility is on the list above of the components of a thriving marriage. Humility is the opposite of pride. Pride isn't listed. Pride is at the root of most arguments and disagreements. It also interferes with forgiveness, patience, and selflessness. You may hear someone complaining about how a spouse does this or that, "and it drives me crazy." We should ask that person, "Do you think there's anything *you* do that drives him (or her) crazy?"

When you can be self-aware, it's easy to see your own selfish and immature behavior. You can see the negative impact it has on your marriage and your family. That comes down to being honest with yourself.

I know that I'm kind of a loner and enjoy studying or doing projects by myself. I've been that way since I was a child. But I noticed that this was hurting my family, and it made my wife feel isolated and distant from me. I had to adjust my behavior and think about the family as a whole rather than my own selfish needs. Now I still get my alone time, but I wait until everyone's busy doing other things or out of the house. I also get up very early in the morning and spend time in the Word and with Jesus. It's one of the most valuable things I do, and it doesn't affect my family, because they're all asleep.

The love and the value we have for our marriages and our families are good anchoring points for developing our spiritual fruits. If you want to strengthen your marriage, put Jesus at the center of it. If you want to strengthen your family, put Jesus at the center of your family. Put him in your conversations. He wants to be at the center of our lives. As parents and spouses, we should point out circumstances to our children, spouses, or significant others where prayer, Bible study, or writing in a spiritual journal will help us get through a difficult time. If anyone in our family is having a difficult time, try to point out that God has a plan for our lives, and his plan is perfect. I point out that there may be something that God is trying to teach them, or he may want them to begin to learn to rely on him.

They need to understand that waves and difficult circumstances are inevitable. We should spend time and effort in helping them see the value and the potential growth that are available through braving the waves in their own life. We can point out that waves are thrilling and exciting, and can get them closer to their authentic self.

If there's a victory or something good happens, I always try to remind them that God wants us to experience victories and triumphs and blessings in this life as well as in eternity. He also wants us to remember to recognize where these gifts came from. These are graces and gifts from God. Our children need to learn to give God the credit. He deserves it. We should be thankful and grateful in all circumstances, good or bad. That's the kind of blessable attitude God is looking for.

When we learn to value our marriage and family, it's a good step toward growing in our relationship with Jesus. As we grow in love and patience, our families are the ones who benefit, because the love we give them helps them in their daily struggles. This is one of those situations where it's win-win. If my marriage grows stronger and more loving and exudes kindness and patience and gentleness, it has a direct impact on the whole family unit. It lends itself to greater self-esteem, confidence, and fearlessness in the children. They tend to become more confident and are more willing to try to reach their full potential. They get closer to their own authentic selves. They begin to understand that they'll be held accountable for their lives and their gifts.

Accountability not only helps children grow and mature as adults, but also helps develop a sense of responsibility. We'll be held accountable for what we did with our time and our talents. The inevitable storms and waves in our children's lives will become learning experiences, if we point out the opportunities they give every one of us for growth. No one has had smooth sailing. No one. It's easy to find events or circumstances that are hard or painful. Help your children begin to understand that loving God and learning to love and serve others are the most useful things we can do with our time here on earth. We model that in our actions and when we talk about spiritual principles.

At times there'll be frustration, because it feels like a waste of time guiding our children, and we can feel that some of these lessons are falling on deaf ears. But sometimes I can hear someone in my family talking to a friend on the phone and they're discussing spiritual principles. Sometimes I hear my wife talking to a friend and sharing the idea of how pride hurts relationships. Then I smile. Jesus will throw me a bone to let me know that it's not time wasted when I'm speaking the truth and sharing valuable principles.

We have to remember to keep on point and on message. We must have faith that it's getting through. When the whole family begins to see the value of spiritual fruit like love, joy, peace, kindness, and the value of a relationship with Jesus, everyone wins. Now and in eternity.

27 - ALL ARE WELCOME

W hen we share spiritual principles, it lends itself to the acquiring of wisdom. Thinking the way God thinks. Valuing the things that God values. When we value the things God values, it's a sign that we're growing in our spiritual life and becoming more mature. Jesus is most interested in people and bringing his lost children into the kingdom of God. Jesus sees everyone as lovable and forgivable. He says:

> What man of you, having a hundred sheep, if he has lost one of them, does not leave the ninety-nine in the open country, and go after the one that is lost, until he finds it? And when he has found it, he lays it on his shoulders, rejoicing. And when he comes home, he calls together his friends and his neighbors, saying to them, 'Rejoice with me, for I have found my sheep that was lost.' Just so, I tell you, there will be more joy in heaven over one sinner who repents than over ninety-nine righteous persons who need no repentance. (Luke 15:4-7 ESV)

Jesus wants his lost children found. Notice that he says there's more joy over the sinner who repents than the ninety-nine who need no repentance. He's pretty much telling us that when a sinner changes and renews his mind (repents) and comes to Jesus, the celebration in heaven is greater!

There must have been quite a party when I came to Jesus. That means no one has any excuse. There's no such thing as, "He can't possibly mean me, I've done too many bad things." *That* is the sinner he searches the hardest for. The one who knows they're a sinner and knows they need Jesus.

We've all sinned, and there are many examples of sinful people in the Bible who Jesus forgave, embraced, and loved. Mary Magdalene is a prime example. She was one of the most blessed people because she was one of the first people to encounter the resurrected Jesus. She had seven demons driven out of her (Luke 8:1-2).

Jesus will forgive, embrace, and love anyone and everyone. He aches for people to come to him, because his love is unquenchable. It's almost like it's pent up, waiting to burst out of his heart.

There's a trend here and in Europe of moving away from Jesus. When we come to realize how much Jesus wants people to come to him, we need to share it. That's part of our responsibility. He values the lost or he wouldn't have made the ultimate sacrifice on the cross for them. This quote from Saint John Vianney sums it up well: "Nothing afflicts the heart of Jesus so much as to see all his sufferings of no avail to so many." Jesus wants everyone to come to him. Once we see the light and can understand the value of loving Jesus and loving others, he wants us to share that newly found joy with others.

Knowledge has value. Especially knowledge of the truth. Which brings up one of the biggest obstacles to growth. There's a tremendous amount of ignorance out there, especially about biblical principles. I'm a prime example. The problem was, I didn't know what I didn't know. I wasn't even aware of my own ignorance.

How do we fight that? Simple. Value truth and knowledge. Especially spiritual or biblical principles. Start acquiring the wisdom of God. Think the way he thinks. We do that by spending time with Jesus in prayer and in the Word. When we develop our relationship to him, we learn to value what he values because we know it's important to him.

Imagine your wife has a hobby of gardening, and she plants beautiful flowers that are thriving. You drive up the driveway and see a deer eating her prize roses. Are you just going to saunter toward the house and wave at the deer as you walk by?

Pretend your husband loves golf and he has a prized set of golf clubs given to him for good performance at work. You drive up the driveway, and your kids are batting rocks with those clubs, as well as banging them on the driveway's concrete. Will you just casually stroll into the house whistling?

In both those situations, you'll instantly react. You'll scare away the deer from the roses, and you'll get those golf clubs out of your kids' hands. You love your wife, so you know how much she values those prize roses. You love your husband, and you know how much he loves those golf clubs.

Jesus loves lost people and desires that all of them come to the knowledge of the truth and turn toward him. We know that there's ignorance about this, because surveys tell us that many people don't refer to the Bible regularly.

We're here to learn. Wisdom is understanding that we'll gain for the rest of our lives. Spending time and energy on learning to love and acquiring knowledge, especially knowledge of the truth, is never a waste of time.

A humble, teachable attitude is always the best. We're here to learn how to love. Love God with everything that he has given us. Mind, heart, and soul. Plus, we learn to love and serve others. Learning these things isn't easy, because of a pervasive "I know that already" attitude. How can anyone learn anything when they already know everything?

Gaining more knowledge never hurts you. Lack of knowledge can do great damage. It can also lead to years of wasted time, energy, talent, or gifts.

Humility and the willingness to learn are helpful on this journey. Here's a great quote from Socrates: "I am the wisest man alive, for I know one thing: that I know nothing." Until we value truth and knowledge, we won't spend any time acquiring it.

One simple fact of life that probably every parent should teach their children is that to attain anything of value and any desirable goal requires three things; time, hard work, and discipline. Getting an education or a degree. Time, hard work, and discipline. Starting a business from scratch. Time, hard work, and discipline. Being a good parent or spouse. Time, hard work, and discipline. Learning how to paint, or sculpt, or play an instrument—they all require time, hard work, and discipline. I've always wanted to play the piano. I still don't know how. Why? Too much time, hard work, and discipline required.

At this point in my life, I value working on this book. I prefer to invest the time, hard work, and discipline on this. How about getting in better shape? Time, hard work, and discipline. Getting a degree, starting a business, being a good parent, learning to play an instrument, getting in shape are all worthy goals. None of them come easy or happen overnight. And none of them come close to the importance of our relationship with Jesus.

When we recognize the value of knowing, serving, and growing in the love of Jesus, that's when things change. We should try to remember that our relationship with Jesus, just like our spiritual relationship with other people in the family of God, is eternal. It's also absolutely required before we can get closer to our authentic selves and fulfill the plan God had in mind when he created us.

God's plan for every one of us has Jesus in the center of it— just as Jesus said:

> I am the vine; you are the branches. If you remain in me
> and I in you, you will bear much fruit; apart from me you
> can do nothing. (John 15:5 NIV)

Yes, this is the second time I've mentioned that verse. It's one of those verses everyone should memorize. And observe again that Jesus doesn't say, "Apart from me it may be a tad tougher to reach your goals." He doesn't say, "Apart from me it might take you a little longer to reach your goals." He doesn't say, "Apart from me, you'll have to work a little harder to get where you want to be in life." No, he says, "Apart from me you can do *nothing*." No thing. So we spend time and we develop disciplines that help grow and nurture our relationship with Jesus. We don't mind working toward a closer relationship with Jesus, because not only is it a worthy goal that brings value to our lives, it's *the* worthy and valuable goal.

Jesus understands that we're not perfect and that we're going to stumble. He allows us to be imperfect. We begin to spend time and effort and learn spiritual disciplines, and we realize that Jesus doesn't expect perfection. He asks for effort and time.

He's not looking for worthiness. He's more interested in willingness. He wants us to spend time with him. Spending time with Jesus is never wasted. That's a truth you should keep in your head, one that's worthy of stickiness.

Time is something we have limited amounts of. We're all given a set amount. No matter how much money you have, you can't buy more time, or get back the time you wasted on things of questionable value. As we've discussed, you can't do anything about yesterday. But you can do something about right now that will have a major impact on tomorrow. You can create value.

Because Jesus allows us to be imperfect, by extension we should allow others to be imperfect. It's totally within our power. It helps every relationship. One theme of this book is that people say and do stupid things, but that's more about learning to forgive. Also, placing too much emphasis and value on the opinions of people leads to a focus on worldly ideas. Worldly ideas focus on impressing others or trying to have what other people have. That leads to pride. That totally directs us to a false or socially constructed self.

If we can look at ourselves and think about the stupid things we've done or said, it's easier to allow others to make mistakes. It's easier to forgive them when they say things that hurt us. We can allow our spouse, our significant other, or our children to be imperfect for the simple reason that no one is perfect. Relationships become easier when we cut other people some slack. When a husband and wife cut each other a little slack and allow a little room for imperfection, the relationship gets easier. When we allow our children some room to make mistakes or to be teenagers or be themselves, the relationship becomes a little easier.

We can develop a classroom of love in any relationship, including with our closest friends. It's funny to me when members of my family say that someone they know is "so annoying." I think to myself, "Really? And *you* aren't?" It makes me think. Maybe we're *all* annoying in one way or another. We just have varying degrees of annoyance to people around us.

The attitude of being mature, self-aware, or patient applies to any kind of relationship. We allow imperfection, and we allow our friends or family to be annoying. The classroom or laboratory of love can be practiced with our closest friends or a significant other. It just takes another level of sacrifice and commitment when we get to marriage and children.

When we grow in our relationship with Jesus and begin to study the Word, we learn the mind of God. When we begin to understand how he thinks, we understand the things he values.

One thing that the Bible emphasizes, and that Jesus is constantly talking about, is faith:

> "You don't have enough faith," Jesus told them. "I tell you the truth, if you had faith even as small as a mustard seed, you could say to this mountain, 'Move from here to there,' and it would move. Nothing would be impossible." (Matthew 17:20 NLT)

Wherever we are in our spiritual journey, we can grow our faith. There's real value in faith, and it lasts forever. We should understand the value of our faith and develop and nurture its development. As we grow in our relationship with Jesus and value what he values, he may ask us to do certain things within the framework of our gifts or talents, but it will require a step or sometimes a leap of faith. It will require us to trust and turn. We brave the wave and turn to ride it.

Remember Peter stepping out of the boat to walk to Jesus on the water:

> About three o'clock in the morning Jesus came toward them, walking on the water. When the disciples saw him walking on the water, they were terrified. In their fear, they cried out, "It's a ghost!" But Jesus spoke to them at once. "Don't be afraid," he said. "Take courage. I am here!"
>
> Then Peter called to him, "Lord, if it's really you, tell me to come to you, walking on the water." "Yes, come," Jesus said. So Peter went over the side of the boat and walked on the water toward Jesus. But when he saw the strong wind and the waves, he was terrified and began to sink. "Save me, Lord!" he shouted. Jesus immediately reached out and grabbed him. "You have so little faith," Jesus said. "Why did you doubt me?" (Matthew 14:25-31 NLT)

Notice that when he saw "the strong wind and the waves," he began to sink. What happened? He took his eyes off Jesus. He focused on the waves.

That happens to me. When I take my eyes off Jesus, I tend to sink. As we're going along on this journey, Jesus may ask us to step out of the boat and walk toward him. Is he talking to *you* when he says, "Yes, come"? If you think about it, Jesus is talking to everyone. It's a good idea to keep your eyes on him. If you stop to think about it, Peter was probably the only other person to walk on water in the history of the world. But he had to get out of the boat.

Develop those spiritual disciplines. Daily quiet time with prayer and Bible reading. Maybe join a Bible study group. Start a spiritual journal. These don't have to all come at once, but they help on the bumpy road.

The apostle Paul spells it out clearly:

> Indeed, I count everything as loss because of the surpassing worth of knowing Christ Jesus my Lord. For his sake, I have suffered the loss of all things and count them as rubbish, in order that I may gain Christ. (Philippians 3:8 ESV)

Suffering the loss of all things is desirable if we gain Jesus. That's the reality of what happens to us when we die. We'll lose all the things we can see, feel, and count. All we have left is our relationship with Jesus and our faith. Real, true, and powerful value.

PART IV - TRUTH AND KNOWLEDGE

28 - ROOTS OF TRUTH

I quoted this earlier: "And those who were dancing were thought to be insane by those who could not hear the music." I mention it again because sometimes this is exactly how I feel. People around me who I care about most do not hear the music. It's frustrating.

Do *you* hear the music? Are *you* dancing?

Do you know what you don't know? Do you know truth?

We've talked about the journey and about beginning where we are. We've looked at how we think and how our thoughts influence our behavior. We've looked at what we believe and the beliefs that shape who we are. We've looked at what we value and how our lives are influenced by our values. The last thing I want to go over is what we know. *Knowledge.*

We can know many facts, but what if they aren't facts at all? A recurring theme in this book is truth. What do we know about truth? Truth is a constant in all the things we've talked about. We should think about and believe the truth.

Remember what Jesus said:

> I am the truth, the way and the life. No one comes to the father except through me. (John 14:6 NIV)

This comes back to the liar, lunatic, or Lord argument. If we think Jesus is telling the truth, we believe him. If we believe him, then we value what he's saying, and we know that we're on solid ground. We start with him. When we get to know him, we begin to learn and know truth and what's important.

What's the bottom line? We should spend time, energy, and effort in seeking, discovering, believing, and living truth. Why? Because what if we're spending time, effort, and energy on something that's a lie? What if someone sold you ten acres in the desert and told you there was gold on that property? They give you geology reports and soil reports and all the technical information. You spend time, money, and effort digging and trying to find that gold, and then after years and years of effort, you find out that the person was lying to you. Those reports were all fraudulent. You've just wasted time, money, and effort on something that wasn't even true. You were searching for treasure that didn't even exist.

That's the way I felt after I came to the knowledge of the truth. I'd wasted time, money and energy on things that had no value, or weren't even there. Digging and digging. I was believing a lie. I believed that objects or money could make me happy and have real value. They can't and they don't. Remember the twenty-year time machine test.

I came to realize that the most valuable diamond in the world is Jesus. We never waste time, energy, or money when we're seeking him and God's will for our lives. Once we seek truth, "things" begin to lose their appeal. We can see that they have no real or eternal value. When it comes to our spiritual growth and our eternity, nothing's more important.

> And now just as you trusted Christ to save you, trust him, too, for each day's problems; live in vital union with him. Let your roots grow down into him and draw up nourishment from him. See that you go on growing in the Lord, and become strong and vigorous in the truth you were taught. Let your lives overflow with joy and thanksgiving for all he has done. (Colossians 2:6-7 NLT)

We have choices. We know that people who've been through a near-death experience are sometimes given the choice to stay in the afterlife or go back to earth to finish tasks and continue to learn to love and acquire knowledge. When it comes to truth, we've used the Bible as our primary source. But I've used NDEs as another source for further affirming what the Bible teaches us. I've been referencing these near-death experiences because they're fascinating. Who doesn't want to know what happens to them after they die? Another reason is the impact they have on people after they go through these experiences. People's lives change when they see and understand the truth.

We know that people who have NDEs no longer fear death. Those who've had an NDE after a suicide attempt also rarely ever try to commit suicide again. Dr. Jeffrey Long in "Evidence of the Afterlife" writes:

> Many different after-effects of near-death experiences have been described in prior studies. One of the earliest studies found that NDErs described more self-confidence, a stronger sense of spirituality, a reduced interest in material gain or status, and a greater appreciation of life. Later research found a myriad of after-effects, including a belief in the sacredness of life, a sense of God's presence, and an awareness of meaning and purpose in life. Near-death experiencers often become increasingly aware of the needs of others and are willing to reach out to them. They may seek to live life more fully and joyfully. Near-death experiencers usually undergo not just one after-effect but many.[72]

Notice that there isn't just one after-effect; there are many. Why? Very few things or experiences change *everything* in your entire life. NDEs do, and Jesus does. People who've undergone these experiences have changes that affect every single aspect of their lives. Coming to the knowledge of the truth of salvation and to a thriving growing relationship with Jesus does the same thing.

My whole reason for including and using these experiences is they're not meant to be a secret; they're meant for all of us. Why would some of the people who underwent these experiences be told to go back and tell others?

These experiences didn't become common knowledge or widely known until the mid-1970s with the release of *Life after Life* by Raymond Moody. In *Lessons from the Light*, Dr. Kenneth Ring says this:

> Through these testimonies, we can see how it is not only possible for persons open to NDEs to learn from them, but to internalize their essential insights and make them their own. In this way, such persons become like NDErs themselves and come to see the world with NDE-mediated vision. And in doing so, these individuals have clearly come to exemplify the proposition enunciated by Steve at the beginning of this chapter: "It is possible to gain all the knowledge a person learns when they die, without dying. You don't have to die to get there."[73]

This has been my experience. It has been shaped by a closer personal relationship with Jesus, but has been fertilized, expanded, and grown by looking at these experiences and the study of the Word. If we can accept Jesus as the truth, and believe the Word as the truth, and believe what these NDErs are trying to tell us, this is a powerful trifecta that can have a profound impact on the very lives that we lead today.

Remember: *personal, powerful,* and *practical.* All three can lead to major positive changes.

One thing I can attest to is "NDE-mediated vision." The one thing I would add is that our "spiritual vision" is enhanced. The "eyes of our hearts" are opened when we become more in tune with our spirits. Primarily in the power of the Holy Spirit while developing a close intimate relationship with Jesus.

Someone may ask, "How do you know you have this vision?" I remember when I was in my mid-twenties and I went to the wedding of a friend. He'd dated around and finally found the girl he wanted to marry. I asked him, "How did you know she was the one?" He said, "You just know." I've heard answers like this: "If you have to ask yourself if she's the one, she ain't the one." My friend was right. When I got married there were no nerves or jitters. This truth reverberates in our interactions with others, especially those closest to us in a powerful and beneficial way. We become beacons of love, light, and truth. Isn't that what Jesus said?

> You are the light of the world. A city set on a hill cannot be hidden. Nor do people light a lamp and put it under a basket, but on a stand, and it gives light to all in the house. In the same way, let your light shine before others, so that they may see your good works and give glory to your Father who is in heaven. (Matthew 5:13-16 ESV)

And he mentions about our eye being the lamp of the body, and how our vision influences our spiritual health:

> Your eye is the lamp of your body. When your eyes are healthy, your whole body is full of light. But when they are unhealthy, your body is also full of darkness. See to it then, that the light within you is not darkness. Therefore, if your whole body is full of light, and no part of it dark, it will be just as full of light as when a lamp shines its light on you. (Luke 11:34-36)

This is a call to acquire spiritual vision. You may have light within you that is darkness, light that is based on lies. Like a false light of shiny, blingy, material wealth. How much value is there in "bling"?

True light is from Jesus and the truth that he speaks. He shows us values that are higher and above what the world values. The same values that the majority of NDErs talk about and tend to gravitate toward after their experiences. True light.

After these experiences, people have major life changes in the areas listed here:[74]

- appreciation for life—increased sense of gratitude
- self-acceptance—greater self-worth and self-acceptance
- concern for others (the most striking and consistent change)
- reverence for life—appreciation for the planet and nature
- antimaterialism—acquisition of things seen as pointless and empty
- anticompetitiveness—impressing others not important
- spirituality—a more universal sense of the spiritual
- greater quest and thirst for knowledge
- sense of purpose—more meaning and sacred purpose in life
- the disappearance of any fear of death—such fear completely gone
- certainty of life after death
- belief in God—deep inner certitude that God exists

Look at this list carefully. We already know that people who've had NDEs understand the importance of love and relationships. These are extra after-effects of their experiences.

One could easily argue that every one of those changes occurs to some degree by accepting and growing in our relationship with Jesus. When we grow in our love for Jesus and we know and understand how he thinks and what he values, we gain an appreciation for life, and we have greater self-worth, more concern for others, and less materialism. And we aren't concerned with comparing and competing. Our eyes become healthy and our bodies become full of light. We get in tune with our spirits and desire to learn and know more. We grasp that we all have a purpose that impacts our lives here and in eternity.

It's uncanny how the same things happen when we get closer and closer to our authentic selves. If we spend time studying the NDE phenomenon, it serves to reinforce all these major life changes. These changes are all for the better. They narrow the gap between where we are and where God had in mind for us to be. Our authentic selves. These changes have an impact on us and those around us as we grow in the laboratory of love.

This is just like the apostle Paul and Jesus's half-brother James. Their lives changed after they saw the resurrected Jesus. They understood the truth of Christ. His resurrection proved that he'd been telling the truth when he predicted his death and resurrection.

They were willing to die for him, as others were. The Christian movement started right after the resurrection of Jesus, and it grew rapidly. It's interesting that New Testament historians use this very point to prove the validity of the writings in the gospels. Paul changed from a persecutor and executioner of Christians to one of Christianity's biggest proponents.

If we look at the studies of near-death experiences, people's lives change. Often very dramatically. That gives us further evidence that what they experienced really occurred. People's lives don't change based on a fabrication or something they made up. People don't change careers and everything about their lives based on some lie they invented. Ask yourself, "Are people willing to die for something they know to be untrue?" Remember, a conviction is something we're willing to live or die for.

There's truth and value in studying what these experiences tell us. If we study these experiences, they reveal truths we may not have seen before. They can help us to change our lives for the better. We don't have to die to get the benefit of these very experiences.

One of the most interesting accounts of an NDE was given by a person named Tom in Dr. Kenneth Ring's book *Lessons from the Light*:

> As a youth, Tom had an uncontrollable temper, and one day, as he explained to us, it really got him into trouble. He had been driving his hotrod pickup truck through town when a pedestrian darted out and almost collided with Tom. Tom, rather than being relieved that no accident had occurred, found himself incensed that this man had almost damaged his beautiful truck, of which he was inordinately proud. Angry words were exchanged, soon followed by blows, and Tom eventually pummeled his victim into unconsciousness and left him lying in the middle of the street.[75]

Here's where it gets interesting, as Tom has a "life review" during his NDE:

> Years later, during his NDE, Tom was forced [notice here he didn't have much of a choice] to relive the scene, and like others we have talked about, he found himself doing so from a dual perspective. One part of himself, he said, seemed to be high up in a building overlooking the street, from which perch he simply witnessed, like an elevated spectator, the fight taking place below. But another part of Tom was actually involved in the fight again. However, this time, in the life review, he found

himself in the place of the other party and experienced each distinct blow he had inflicted on this man—thirty-two in all, he said—before collapsing unconscious on the pavement.

This is the part that had an impact on me, reported in Tom's words:

> I also experienced seeing my own fist coming directly into my face. And I felt the indignation, the rage, the embarrassment, the frustration, the physical pain. I felt my teeth going through my lower lip—in other words, I was in that man's eyes. I was in that man's body. I experienced everything of that interrelationship between Tom and that man that day. I experienced unbelievable things about that man that are of a very personal, confidential, and private nature.

This is a graphic example, but there are numerous accounts of reliving situations where the NDEr could feel the pain they caused others, or—thankfully—the love they freely gave to others.

This may be a good time to reflect on times we inflicted pain on others, or when we freely gave love to others. It makes me stop and think a little more when I get into an argument with those closest to me or say sarcastic or mean things to those I love the most. Remember the argument I had with my daughter?

NDEs teach us very important lessons. Every interaction matters. Every smile we show to others matters. Every smirk or snide remark we give to someone matters. Every kind word or kind deed done out of a loving heart matters. When we understand these truths, it has an impact on our interactions. Do we all become saints suddenly? Do we become Mother Theresa overnight? *No.* In *Evidence of the Afterlife*, Dr. Long tells us of studies showing that "it takes as long as seven years or more for a person who has a near-death experience to fully integrate into their life the changes that resulted from the experience."[76] If the people who almost died take seven years to fully change, don't expect major changes in your life in a few days. It takes time, discipline, and effort.

Remember: "As a dog returns to its vomit, so fools repeat their folly" (Proverbs 26:11 NIV). This fool repeats his folly too many times to count. We get tired and cranky, or we get easily offended and let our pride get the best of us. It happens all the time.

The point is that we don't need to die to learn from this account and be more cognizant of our behavior around other people, whether strangers or family or friends.

Love, joy, peace, kindness, gentleness patience. The thing I hear the most as I read through accounts like this is the voice of Jesus echoing in my head:

> Do to others as you would have them do to you. (Luke 6:31 NLT)

He spoke the truth, and accounts like the one outlined above confirm exactly what Jesus said. It will have a positive impact on us individually if we can look at our own lives and think about the times we did or said things that hurt other people. We can't do anything about those instances in the past, but we can try to be more loving, kind, and gentle in the future, to the benefit not only of others but of ourselves as well. That's truth.

Let me digress for a second. These are the kinds of things I think about. These are the kinds of questions I always ask myself. It seems to me that when we discuss heaven or hell or evil, there's always one name that comes up: Hitler. The embodiment of evil. Responsible for so much suffering. Joseph Stalin reportedly murdered twenty million people. Mao Zedong was reportedly responsible for the murder of forty-five million people.[77]

Now think about the life review that this fellow Tom just described. Is it possible that Hitler would have to relive, one by one, the murder of six million people? Would he feel—millions of times—all the physical punishment, the terror, and the choking sensation of being killed by lethal gas? Think about that. Would that not be considered justice?

Would it be the same for Stalin and Mao Zedong? Imagine having to relive, one by one, the murder of forty-five million people, and experiencing each one individually as if you're the person being murdered. You know what I would call that? *Hell.*

29 - ALLOWING AN EXPERIENCE

Listen to this exchange between Jesus and the man with the power to crucify him:

> Then Pilate said to him, "So you are a king?"
>
> Jesus answered, "You say that I am a king. For this purpose, I was born and for this purpose I have come into the world—to bear witness to the truth. Everyone who is of the truth listens to my voice."
>
> Pilate said to him, "What is truth?" (John 18:37-38 ESV)

Two things. First, Jesus tells us one of the reasons for his very existence: to "bear witness to the truth." If we're "of the truth," we listen to his voice.

And second, Pilate asks, "What is truth?" We should be seeking truth actively and with vigor. Start with the words of Jesus. We look at near-death experiences and what they teach us, but they're confirming what Jesus already taught two thousand years ago:

> Do to others as you would have them do to you. (Luke 6:31 NLT)

There are many books documenting these near-death experiences. Sure, some of those authors are just trying to make a buck. But there are many people who just want to share their story.

Dr. Mary Neal is an orthopedic surgeon who underwent a near-death experience, and in her book *To Heaven and Back* she says, "They told me a little bit about this mandate to share my experience with other people."[78] She reports that she didn't want to write a book and was reluctant to speak about her experience. She put off writing the book for ten years. She and her husband are both doctors, and they don't need the money.

Skeptics say that these experiences can be explained by low oxygen or a dying brain or something called REM intrusion. As Dr. Long says in *Evidence of the Afterlife,*

> Over 20 different "explanations" of the near-death experience have been suggested by skeptics over the years. If there were one or even several "explanations" of NDEs that were widely accepted as plausible by the skeptics, there would not be so many different "explanations." The existence of so many "explanations" suggests that there are no "explanations" of NDEs that the skeptics agree on as plausible.[79]

One thing I've noticed is that sometimes people don't want to accept the most logical and simple answer. They'll go down fighting, dying, and arguing, because they won't accept a simple truth that's staring them in the face. There are twenty different explanations of why near-death experiences occur. If you have twenty, you have none. Or is it that maybe, just maybe, these accounts are true, accurate, and real? Wow. What a concept.

One interesting facet of NDEs is that people say these experiences are not like memory, which fades and gets fuzzy. The experiences are more real, and the clarity of the details are retained even thirty or forty years later. This all goes back to what we think, believe, or know about God and his Son Jesus. Could it be possible that maybe they're trying to get our attention? Just like he told us in the parable of the lost sheep:

> Suppose one of you has a hundred sheep and loses one of them. Doesn't he leave the ninety-nine in the open country and go after the lost sheep until he finds it? And when he finds it, he joyfully puts it on his shoulders and

goes home. Then he calls his friends and neighbors together and says, 'Rejoice with me; I have found my lost sheep.' I tell you that in the same way there will be more rejoicing in heaven over one sinner who repents than over ninety-nine righteous persons who do not need to repent. (Luke 15:4-7 NLT)

Is it so silly to think that God our Father allows people to go through these experiences of his love for their own benefit, but also for ours? God reveals himself to us in a myriad of ways. The Word. Pain. Blessings and triumphs. Circumstances. Other people. Impressions. The promptings or whispers of the Holy Spirit. Maybe he's revealing himself through NDEs because much of the population ignores the Bible. Just a guess.

These revelations are for our benefit. Yours and mine. Remember that the one constant people describe is the overwhelming, indescribable love of God. God is love.

The apostle John told us that two thousand years ago:

Beloved, do not believe every spirit, but test the spirits to see whether they are from God, for many false prophets have gone out into the world. By this you know the Spirit of God: every spirit that confesses that Jesus Christ has come in the flesh is from God, and every spirit that does not confess Jesus is not from God. This is the spirit of the antichrist, which you heard was coming and now is in the world already. Little children, you are from God and have overcome them, for he who is in you is greater than he who is in the world. They are from the world; therefore, they speak from the world, and the world listens to them. We are from God. Whoever knows God listens to us; whoever is not from God does not listen to us. By this we know the Spirit of truth and the spirit of error.

Beloved, let us love one another, for love is from God, and whoever loves has been born of God and knows God. Anyone who does not love does not know God, because God is love. In this the love of God was made manifest among us, that God sent his only Son into the world, so that we might live through him. In this is love, not that we have loved God but that he loved us and sent his Son to be the propitiation for our sins. Beloved, if God so loved us, we also ought to love one another. No one has ever seen God; if we love one another, God abides in us and his love is perfected in us. (1 John 4:1-12 ESV)

You may be asking yourself, "If it's all written down here for everyone to see, why do people have these experiences?" My non-biblical-scholar layman opinion thinks there are two reasons. For one, most people don't bother reading the Bible. Or they may have learned lessons, parables, or truth, but as we grow older we tend to ignore those lessons. We get caught up in the daily activities of life, work, and family responsibilities.

The second reason is that there's a growing devaluing of truth in our society. There's a movement away from truth and toward "tolerance."

European countries in general have seen substantial declines, but it is the Netherlands leading the way. The Catholic Church predicts that two-thirds of its churches will be retired from holy service within a decade and seven hundred Protestant churches are expected to be decommissioned within four years. While the U.S. has avoided a similar wave of church closings for now, recent trends lead religious researchers to say the country could face the same problem in coming years. Every piece of social data suggests that those who favor faith over fact-based evidence will become the minority in this country by or before the end of this century. In fact, the number of Americans who do not believe in a deity doubled in the last decade of the previous century according to both the census of 2004 and the American Religious Identification Survey (ARIS) of 2008, with religious nonbelief in the U.S. rising from 8.2 percent in 1990 to 14.2 percent in 2001. In 2013, that number is now above 16 percent.[80]

These are the trends. It looks like people are ignoring the bride of Christ. There are more "nones," and it's a growing category here in the United States, while Europe is closing churches or turning them into nightclubs. As we can clearly see, the trend is to move away from even believing in God.

From what we know, believe, and understand, it seems obvious that Jesus is doing everything he can to bring more people to the knowledge of the truth. He wants to find his lost sheep. That's part of our purpose as we begin to see with the eyes of Christ. As he reveals more of himself to each of us, and as we grow in our spiritual vision, our common task is to try to get people to see and understand the unbelievable deal Jesus offers, which we can't get anywhere else. Nowhere.

We can understand about learning to love, and that our relationships are the most important activities we can be engaged in. Instead of digging for the fool's gold buried in the desert, we should be pursuing knowledge and truth. We can choose to believe the Word of God, or we can choose to ignore it. This is where truth and knowledge come together. We have a responsibility to pursue truth and knowledge. We were given a brain and reason. The more you seek truth or answers, the more you'll be given.

Is not wisdom found among the aged? Does not long life bring understanding? (Job 12:12 NIV)

This is a good reminder to find a spiritual mentor who's further along in his or her journey than you are. It's helpful to have someone to guide you. It's also good to have a reference person who helps break down Scripture, because some passages won't make sense to you. We have the advantage of Google, so we can look up commentaries by different pastors or biblical teachers.

Reading the Bible, asking questions, and looking for answers will open God's Word. The Bible will start to come alive and speak to you personally. It's important, when seeking truth, to have a humble, teachable, fertile, hungry mind. This is one time when hunger is a good thing. As Lee McIntyre says in his 2015 book *Respecting Truth: Willful Ignorance in the Internet Age*, "The real enemy of truth is not ignorance, doubt, or even disbelief. It is false knowledge."[81]

Is there any value in truth? Do people really care about the truth in our modern society?

If we don't seek the truth, we waste time, money, energy, and effort on lies. On "false knowledge." We may be believing a total lie about ourselves. Let me give you a personal example.

Most people who are scientifically minded and believe in the pursuit of science have taken evolution for granted. We evolved from lower species over many billions of years through a process known as natural selection. For me, I reconciled these "facts" with my faith by saying, "Well, God intervened in every step of the process, and that's how he created man." Evolution isn't an area of great interest for me, but when I was doing research for this book, I began to look at some of the problems associated with this theory. The problem lies with the very beginning of life.

I don't want to get too technical on this, because that's when people start nodding off. But in their documentary series *Unlocking the Mystery of Life*, researchers Stephen Meyer, Michael Behe, and William Dembski[82] concluded that the theory of evolution as proposed by Charles Darwin falls apart when you get to the origin of the human cell. The bottom line is that the odds of chemicals, amino acids, and complex proteins coming together randomly to form the first cell are so astronomically high, that it would take a miracle for it to occur. Sound familiar? The best description I've ever heard is that it would be like a tornado going through a junk yard and ending up with a 747 jet airliner. Think about that one for a second. You need an intelligent designer. You need God.

So the fully authoritative theory of evolution is an example of "false knowledge" with regard to the origin of the cell. It is a reasonable theory when it comes to evolving and adaptation within a species. That's why we need to ask questions, seek truth, and spend time acquiring useful and truthful knowledge. We could be basing our entire life or worldview on a lie. There are serious repercussions to that decision.

Where can we go to seek the truth? We've been using the Bible as a source for truth, and that's a great place to start. We can find some truth in science. For instance, no one disputes that cigarette smoking is related to lung cancer, heart disease, and early death. No one disputes that fact. But things change all the time regarding science.

From surveys conducted in the United States, we find that most Americans believe truth is "relative to the person and their situation"; moral truth is relative, never absolute. This is the "What's true for you may not be true for me" approach. Tolerance is more valued than the pursuit of truth. Everyone has their beliefs, and what's true for one person may not be true for another. It's all relative.

People committed to truth don't get much attention in a society that devalues truth. So why should we spend time seeking truth? Because our spiritual lives and our eternity depend on it. Knowledge and truth are vitally important.

30 - THE WILL AND THE WORD

When we seek truth, we're living above the world. The truth is that Satan roams the earth because we live in a fallen world. If we don't seek truth, we'll be overtaken by lies.

When we seek truth, we're more in tune with the spiritual sides of ourselves. Remember, we're spirits living in a physical body. If we don't seek truth, Satan will fill our minds and our hearts with lies. When Satan speaks, he's lying. As Jesus said in John 8:43, "There is no truth in him." He's the father of lies, and he has power in this world. Satan hates you and he hates me. He loves it when there are arguments, anger, and pride in a family. He loves it when we do or say hateful things to each other.

I remember watching a speaker talking about demons and how they try to disrupt our lives, and he said something very interesting. He said that demons torment people, and their goal is to get a person to commit suicide.

Most people who are clinically depressed feel hopeless, helpless, and worthless. All lies. Whenever a negative thought or idea like that comes into our minds or our children's minds, we need to remember and point out that those thoughts are never from God. God wants us to have biblical hope. If we remember the Bible, we have hope—eager expectation, *elpis*. We wear the helmet of salvation, and we're confident in salvation. That by itself brings joy.

We already know Jesus wants us to have joy:

> I have told you these things so that you will be filled with my joy. Yes, your joy will overflow! (John 15:11 NLT)

Jesus wants our joy to overflow. He wants us confident and filled with joy! That's why they call it *the good news.*

We already know we aren't worthless. We're all valuable, lovable, forgivable, and acceptable. The cross proves our value. We know we aren't helpless because we have the power of the Holy Spirit living in us. We can live, work, and call on the power of God when we're aligned with his will and purpose.

You may be believing a lie. That leads to all sorts of behavior that's totally destructive and a waste of time. You may be telling yourself, "If I drive this car, or have this house, or make this much money, then I'll truly be happy." You can see all that in today's advertising. If I had this, or drove that, I'd be happy. If I lived in this neighborhood, I'd be satisfied and fulfilled.

I saw a movie that portrayed living in the "wrong" New York City neighborhood as a nightmare. It's not just about believing a lie, it's about *living* a lie.

Ask yourself: Am I living a lie? I was.

Look at these two short passages:

> While he [Jesus] was still speaking to the people, behold, his mother and his brothers stood outside, asking to speak to him. But to the man who told him he replied, "Who is my mother, and who are my brothers?" And stretching out his hand toward his disciples, he said, "Here are my mother and my brothers! For whoever does the will of my Father in heaven is my brother and sister and mother." (Matthew 12:46-50 ESV)

> Then Jesus' mother and brothers came to see him, but they couldn't get to him because of the crowd. Someone told Jesus, "Your mother and your brothers are outside, and they want to see you." Jesus replied, "My mother and

my brothers are all those who hear God's word and obey it." (Luke 8:21 ESV)

Both these passages convey the importance of God's will and of hearing and obeying God's Word. These two actions signify belonging to the true family of Jesus. Who doesn't want to be a brother or sister or mother of Jesus? We should want to be a true member in the family of God, and we should want to be called a brother or sister of Jesus. We've talked a lot about the value of our personal relationship with Jesus, and you really can't get any closer than brother or sister or mother.

Notice in these passages that Jesus doesn't say, "Oh, my mother and brothers have come; tell them I'll be right out!" Instead he stops and says, "Look at these people already here— *they* are my brothers and sisters." That's one of my favorite things about how Jesus teaches. He does the opposite of what anyone expects.

Think about that in your own life when you're listening for the voice of Jesus. Many times, he will ask you to do something that's outside what you would think or expect. If that was *my* mom waiting outside, I'd be thinking I'd better get up and go greet her, or there'd be trouble. Jesus is making a very important point: we must do the will of the Father.

The Lord's Prayer says, "Thy will be done on earth, as it is in heaven." In heaven, God's will is constantly being done. All the time, 24/7. Jesus told us that.

I once heard a pastor say, "The majority of the time on earth, God's will is being ignored." I'm not sure that's true, because it's hard to find a survey involving thousands of people that asks, "Are you seeking God's will for your life?" We do have the survey results showing that only about twenty-five to thirty percent of the American population reads the Bible regularly. We know that God's will for us as a group and as individuals is in the Word. So maybe there's something to that statement. It kind of just makes me stop and think.

The one thing we can do is spend time and effort in finding God's will for our lives. Jesus said,

> Very truly I tell you, whoever believes in me will do the works I have been doing, and they will do even greater things than these, because I am going to the Father. (John 14:12 NLT)

Two things in this passage. First, this is another of those "very truly" mentions, which should always send us a signal: "Stop and listen up to what I'm telling you." It's an elbow in the ribs to get our attention. Not to hurt us, but to wake us up.

Second, here's another example of never going wrong when we emulate Jesus. When we believe in him, we do the things he did. He fed the hungry, cared for the sick, and loved and served others. He spent a quiet time in prayer with God the Father. He spoke about the good news. He spent his life serving, loving, and giving. When we live by believing in Jesus, we do the works he did. In this way, we can discover and realize our authentic selves.

God has a will for all his children as a group, and he also has an individual will for each of us to complete. We're to come to the knowledge of the truth and accept Jesus as our personal Savior. He also has an individual will for each of us that's personal and powerful. When we seek God's will for our lives, we get "hope and a future":

> "For I know the plans I have for you," declares the LORD, "plans to prosper you and not to harm you, plans to give you hope and a future." (Jeremiah 29:11 NIV)

There again we see hope. Eager expectation. This is God's promise to each of us.

God's will is in his Word. When we don't bother reading the Bible, or we don't spend any time learning God's will for our lives, we're saying: "Uh, God? Yeah, I know you're all-powerful and all-knowing, and you created me with specific talents and gifts, but honestly, I have a better plan for my life than yours. You see, I kind of know me better than you do. So, uh, thanks but no thanks."

The way I look at it, there are many roads we can take when it comes to our career or who we'll marry or what goals we choose to focus on, worldly or spiritual. The important point to remember is that God knows the outcome of every single decision we make. There could be a hundred different paths. He knows exactly what's at the end of the road for each one. He won't interfere with our free will. Ever. There can be no real love without free will. He wants real love. He wants us to choose to come to him. It's our choice. But he knows the outcome, and he also knows what's best for us. What he's planning is "to prosper you and not harm you," and "to give you hope and a future." Doesn't that sound like a good deal to you?

We know that God isn't moved or motivated by our complaining or self-pity. Self-pity is not an option for us. It's looking at ourselves as pitiful or weak. We're to be confident and feel strong in the power of the Holy Spirit.

> For God has not given us a spirit of fear and timidity, but of power, love, and self-discipline. (1 Timothy 1:7 NLT)

Notice that he speaks of God giving us a "spirit"—a spirit not of fear and timidity, but a *spirit* of power, love, and self-discipline We were all given a spirit. Whether we have fear and timidity, or whether we have power, love, and self-discipline, it's something that's happening in our spirit.

Self-pity is dangerous because it comes from not believing the truth that God gave us a spirit of power, love, and self-discipline.

Self-pity also doesn't bring anything to the table as far as finding our authentic selves. So get self-pity out of your backpack.

When we feel sorry for ourselves, it's the "I don't have any control" myth. It's wallowing in self-deception. I've heard people say that if a bowl of chocolate candy is in front of them, they have no power to resist it. The biggest liar I know is me. The biggest lies we tell are the ones we tell ourselves.

When we accept God's Word and seek his truth, we *know* we have power and self-discipline, and we have total control over what we eat or drink. No one is putting a gun to our heads and making us eat the chocolate or order that third margarita or glass of wine at happy hour.

God doesn't want us feeling sorry for ourselves, because he knows we're just lying to ourselves. It's destructive. No one did anything great or did anything of value or importance while feeling sorry for themselves.

The opposite is taking too much credit for the grace and gifts we've received. If we're good at something or we've received blessings, spiritual insight, or discernment, the first thing we should do is thank God. Don't go down the "I deserve it" road. I deserve a kick in the butt, that's it. Anything else I get is a gift and blessing from a gracious, merciful, and loving God. Sometimes I feel like he made a mistake with all that he has given me, and then I realize that he doesn't make mistakes. It makes me love him that much more.

That reminds me of what Howard Storm described in *My Descent into Death*, as he was being carried by Jesus to a place that was away from the hell he'd experienced after he'd rejected faith and all religion:

> I felt like garbage, filthy rags in the presence of the Holy One. My friend carrying me, Jesus, my best friend, was

aware of my fear and reluctance and shame. I thought to myself, "I'm scum that belongs back down in the sewer. They've made a terrible mistake. I don't belong here." For the first time, he spoke. He spoke directly to my mind in his young male voice. "We don't make mistakes, and you do belong here."[83]

Howard Storm's NDE was very detailed and included a glimpse of hell. It's fascinating reading. The point is, when we get blessed or we're given a profound spiritual insight, we should be grateful and give God all the credit. No one else deserves it.

God isn't moved or motivated by our whining, complaining, or self-pity. What is he motivated by? Our faith, love, and obedience. There's another huge three.

Sounds like we need another list to kind of keep in order some of the things we've talked about.

Three biggest temptations:

- pride of life
- lust of the flesh
- lust of the eyes

Three biggest obstacles to Jesus:

- the world
- Satan
- the flesh (our natural selves)

Three huge benefits Jesus brings:

- sins forgiven
- purpose for living

- home in heaven

Three ways to please God:

- faith
- love
- obedience

If you memorize those lists, we're pretty much done. See ya!

Yeah, right. That's just outlining the issues. We already know about the supreme importance of loving God with mind, heart, and spirit. Faith is a central part of our growth and maturation:

> Then Jesus got into the boat and started across the lake with his disciples. Suddenly, a fierce storm struck the lake, with waves breaking into the boat. But Jesus was sleeping. The disciples went and woke him up, shouting, "Lord, save us! We're going to drown!" Jesus responded, "Why are you afraid? You have so little faith!" Then he got up and rebuked the wind and waves, and suddenly there was a great calm. The disciples were amazed. "Who is this man?" they asked. "Even the winds and waves obey him!" (Matthew 8:23-27 NLT)

> When Jesus returned to Capernaum, a Roman officer came and pleaded with him, "Lord, my young servant lies in bed, paralyzed and in terrible pain." Jesus said, "I will come and heal him." But the officer said, "Lord, I am not worthy to have you come into my home. Just say the word from where you are, and my servant will be healed. I know this because I am under the authority of my superior officers, and I have authority over my soldiers. I only need to say, 'Go,' and they go, or 'Come,' and they come. And if I say to my slaves, 'Do this,' they do it." When Jesus heard this, he was amazed. Turning to those

who were following him, he said, "I tell you the truth, I haven't seen faith like this in all Israel!" Then Jesus said to the Roman officer, "Go back home. Because you believed, it has happened." (Matthew 8:5-10,13 NLT)

I know we've gone over this verse before, but I use it again to point out the contrast. Jesus was amazed at the faith of the Roman officer and frustrated with the faith of his disciples. Faith comes first, then the miracle. Because we believe, then the miracle happens. Faith moves and motivates God to act.

One way to know whether you're being given a God-sized goal is the fact that there's no way you'll be able to complete it in your own power. Writing a book and getting it noticed among the one million books published every year is a good example. The odds are a million to one.

This is another warning from the management: faith is of significant value and power only when it has been tested. As you go further along on this road, there'll be more revelation and discernment, but there will also be significant trials and waves— to build, strengthen, and sharpen our faith. Plus, they build up our perseverance.

> Nothing in this world can take the place of persistence. Talent will not: nothing is more common than unsuccessful men with talent. Genius will not; unrewarded genius is almost a proverb. Education will not: the world is full of educated derelicts. Persistence and determination alone are omnipotent. (Calvin Coolidge)

Remember, no matter who you are, what you believe, how much money you make, or what kind of job you have, there'll be trials, storms, and waves coming at you one after another. If you think about it, life is just a series of hills and valleys. The spiritual life is no different except for one important difference: in a spiritual triumph, you get to a higher hill. You can see more, and you're closer to Jesus. You have more of the spiritual fruit we're after: love, joy, peace, kindness, gentleness, and patience.

If you don't understand the value of the things we can't see or count, you just keep walking like a zombie or rolling along like a pinball in a machine, bouncing off those bumpers with a ding-ding here and a ding-ding there. (Kind of reminds me of Old McDonald's farm.)

Here's another verse that tells us we should have eager expectation of our salvation:

> Now we live with great expectation, and we have a priceless inheritance—an inheritance that is kept in heaven for you, pure and undefiled, beyond the reach of change and decay. And through your faith, God is protecting you by his power until you receive this salvation, which is ready to be revealed on the last day for all to see. So be truly glad. There is wonderful joy ahead, even though you have to endure many trials for a little while. These trials will show that your faith is genuine. It is being tested as fire tests and purifies gold—though your faith is far more precious than mere gold. So when your faith remains strong through many trials, it will bring you much praise and glory and honor on the day when Jesus Christ is revealed to the whole world. (1 Peter 7:3-7 NIV)

Notice the first line. Peter is saying we live with great expectation, hope, and confidence in the inheritance of our salvation. Also, notice that he says, "you *have to* endure many trials for a little while." There are no other options.

That is why looking for the next wave and having a good attitude helps us build joy and peace. We know the wave is coming, but we know that the ride is thrilling, and at the end we're closer to authenticity and to Jesus. The most valuable diamond in the world.

We should brave the wave. This is absolutely essential to reach the full realization of our authentic selves. The wave allows us to discover and develop who we were created to be. We don't need to be fearful, because God is protecting us by his unlimited power until we receive the inheritance. He tells us there's joy ahead, but also "many trials." All these trials help us learn to trust Jesus in our pain. We trust that he'll strengthen and prepare us for what's ahead. These "trials of fire" test and purify our faith. The praise and glory are just icing, because the real value lies in our growth and maturation and the increasing strength of our faith.

But make no mistake; the praise, glory, and honor are reserved for those who accept Jesus. We must be honest with ourselves. When we don't believe, when we choose to reject Jesus, there's no faith to strengthen. It doesn't exist. This belief is defined by relying on, trusting in, and committing to Jesus. As believers, this strengthening of our faith gives us the valuable currency we need to persevere and to focus on our purpose. We're not just existing. We're trying to reach our full potential by completing our tasks.

Saint Augustine wrote, "Faith is to believe what you do not see. The reward of this faith is to see what you believe."

31 - THE POWER OF OBEDIENCE

We know truth is valuable. We understand the supreme importance of love and our relationships. We know the value of faith as we begin to grow closer to our authentic selves. We know that whining, complaining, and self-pity will not get God's attention. Faith, love, and obedience do.

Obedience is the other factor that Jesus speaks about in the verses about being a brother or sister of Jesus. He says we must "hear the word and then obey it." Jesus tells us plainly that if we love him, we obey his commandments. When we have true intimacy and love for Jesus, we value what he values, and we try to live in a way that reflects his love.

No one's saying it's easy. We're going to stumble, bumble, rumble, and tumble. But we know he'll be there to pick us up and love us and cheer us on. If you're a mom or dad at a baseball or soccer game, and one of your kids stumbles and falls while he's running, what do you do? Do you turn around and go get another soda or hot dog at the concession stand? No. You stay right there and cheer him on and encourage him.

Jesus, who has an indescribable love for all of us, does the same thing. He tells us he won't leave us, and he gives us the Holy Spirit, who will lead us "into all truth." He knows we'll stumble and fall. He'll be there to pick us up and encourage us. But he wants obedience as proof of our love, our trust, and our faith. If the love and light of Jesus is in our hearts, it shines through. We reflect his love. Sometimes we're asked to do things that don't make sense, and we don't understand them, but we're to have faith and to obey. There are many examples in the Bible where God gives instructions that didn't make sense, but when faith and obedience were employed, God acted.

One of the ways we know God is involved in our guidance is that faith is absolutely required, and we know we can't complete a task without his power. Obedience releases God's power.

That's what happened at Jericho:

> Now the gates of Jericho were securely barred because of the Israelites. No one went out and no one came in. Then the Lord said to Joshua, "See, I have delivered Jericho into your hands, along with its king and its fighting men. March around the city once with all the armed men. Do this for six days. Have seven priests carry trumpets of rams' horns in front of the ark. On the seventh day, march around the city seven times, with the priests blowing the trumpets. When you hear them sound a long blast on the trumpets, have the whole army give a loud shout; then the wall of the city will collapse and the army will go up, everyone straight in." (Joshua 6:1-5 NLT)

The walls of this mighty city of Jericho would fall with some trumpet blasts and loud shouting. Kind of an unusual request, don't you think? But that's exactly what happened. Obedience to the details are what allowed this miracle to occur.

When God asks us to do something out of the ordinary, he'll always supply us with what we need to carry it out. We have access to his power and guidance, especially when it comes to work that's done for the kingdom of God.

One crucial principle that needs to be mentioned is that pursuing your purpose is never a waste of time. We have a promise. I can tell you from experience that not everything you're going to attempt will be successful. You may fail in your pursuits. But there's always something good that comes from those efforts.

I myself was pursuing something I thought was for the kingdom. It lined up perfectly with my talent and my passion, so in my mind it was a no-brainer. I was using my passion, resources, and talent to serve others in a way that emphasized spiritual growth and a reliance on Jesus. There was no way it was going to fail.

I spent money, time, energy, and lots of effort, but it was a total failure and a major disaster. I was angry, I was frustrated, and I felt betrayed. After all, I was doing this work for Jesus.

After a major pity party, the conversation went something like this. "Look, I've done all this work, expending time and energy, not to mention all the money I lost. And it failed! I feel like I was tricked and hoodwinked. I'm embarrassed, frustrated, and angry that you would do this to me!" That's almost word for word what I wrote in my spiritual journal. Can you see how angry I was?

As tears streamed down my face, the response came ever so slightly, so quietly, almost like I had to get closer to hear: "Are you closer to me because of this effort?"

My response: "Well, uh, yes. Yes, I am."

Then I heard, "Can you see me, hear me, and feel my love more strongly now?"

My response: "Well, of course I do."

His response: "Now you understand."

The realization came that I was closer to the most valuable diamond in the world. Money, time, sweat, and effort were all irrelevant. Revelations like these come when you least expect them. I was ashamed and embarrassed because I'd missed the whole point.

Here's one of my favorite quotes from Saint Padre Pio: "There is no flowering of the soul to the beauty of its perfection except at the price of pain." That's a topic for another book. Pain and suffering are part of this journey. True spiritual growth that is valuable, strong, and lasting comes at a price. We can't grow in our relationship with Jesus on a beach in the Caribbean with a margarita in our hands.

Look at Romans 8:28: "In all things, God works for the good of those who love him, who have been called according to his purpose." As usual, I was thinking or seeing from my perspective, the human perspective. Human vision. But we need the eyes of Christ. The real value was the major growth in my personal relationship with Jesus. It grew by leaps and bounds. There is the treasure. There is the most valuable diamond in the world.

By the way, if you're wondering about the financial costs, the money I invested in this effort was returned to me tripled. Serve Jesus, money works for you.

We should remember that we're vehicles and conduits of God's power and love. When our hearts are filled with the love of Jesus, we have more spiritual fruit in addition to love—such as peace, kindness, and patience. When God blesses us with material wealth, talents, and gifts that we can use to serve others, we're actively involved and partnering with God in blessing other people. The kicker is that when we serve and give of our time, money, and energy to others, we're also blessed. Now and in eternity.

We also should realize that it's an honor and a privilege to serve others in the power and love of Jesus. Being a vessel that can be used for God's purposes is the highest use of our time, energy, and resources. Many times, we mistakenly think we're doing something for God when we're the ones truly being blessed. It's living in a way that's fruitful and pleasing to God. It allows us to know we aren't wasting the gifts, time, physical health, and energy that God has graciously bestowed on us. We get fulfillment, peace, joy, and a large bucket of gratitude. Therein lies true happiness and joy.

> If you love me, obey my commandments. And I will ask the Father, and he will give you another Advocate, who will never leave you. He is the Holy Spirit, who leads into all truth. The world cannot receive him, because it isn't looking for him and doesn't recognize him. But you know him, because he lives with you now and later will be in you. (John 14:15-17 NIV)

We've talked about faith, love, and obedience, and they're all woven together. As our faith is tested by trials, we continue trusting God, and as he gets us through each test, our love for him grows. We choose to be obedient. When we're obedient, we're telling God, "Look, I don't understand exactly how doing this task or project will help you or me, but I'm going to trust that you love me. I'm going to have faith that in the end, somehow, and in some way, I'll grow from this experience, and there'll be some benefit to other people. Plus, I'll get some benefit—like spiritual maturation, discernment, or wisdom. This all fits within your plan and your will for my life. What's the next step?"

One very useful idea—one that you should do everything in your power to make sticky—is that God isn't going to immediately reveal the finish line of any big task or project that he calls you to. He'll reveal only the next step. We'll occasionally get impressions or visions, but most of the time he'll reveal only the next step. Sometimes you'll be led into a trial or test. You may think that you've failed, or that something didn't work out right, and you may think, "Oh, I made a mistake. He didn't want me to go that way." In reality, it was the right step. He was preparing you for the next series of steps that go in a totally different direction.

That was what happened to me. He promises that he'll guide us, but he doesn't promise that everything will work out exactly like we wanted. That's why spending time in prayer and in the Word is so important. We're on a set course, but we need navigation and course correction. We need to keep checking our GPS.

Exploring God's Word and listening for God's voice will give us clues as to what God has in mind for our lives. Prayer and the Word also help us see how he wants us to use our gifts and talents as we seek our purpose. As we go along, we develop an attitude of immediate obedience. When we're in tune with our spirits and the voice of the Holy Spirit, we begin to hear the promptings and the whispers which are the guidance.

Remember, Jesus told us the Holy Spirit leads us "into all truth." It takes time and effort to learn to recognize and distinguish the voice of Jesus or the Holy Spirit. There's no Twitter or Instagram account you can go to. We learn to get in the Word because that's the primary way God speaks to us. We listen to gifted Bible teachers or pastors to help us on the path. We can start by keeping a spiritual journal and writing down what God has revealed to us as individuals and what we've prayed to him with dates and times. It's a great reference to go back and review what we've learned.

One critical aspect of obedience is that when we act out of love and faith, we're granted access to God's power and grace. But our actions must be consistent with his will for our lives. When we focus on his will and spend time in the Word, we are not only focusing on his will for all of us but also his will for each of us. We should remember that when God grants us a vision for our lives, he is giving us an impression of what is *possible*. He is not showing us the future. If he was showing us the future, we would be prophets. Remember that he only shows us the next step, but occasionally he will give us a vision that is within the realm of possibility if we are willing to spend the time and effort to carry it to completion. Consistency with his will must be the essential component to this act of obedience. Whenever we spend time, energy, and effort to do or complete a task that's more for our own benefit to the exclusion of others, we're on our own.

In my own study of these principles, one phrase has especially grabbed my attention, a phrase associated with implementing our purpose and the motives behind our pursuit of purpose. That phrase is *purity of intent*. As we grow in our love for Jesus, we choose goals that benefit others and please him. He can see the real intent in our hearts. Is there greed, envy, pride, or selfish ambition involved in any goal you're focused on? We should examine our thoughts carefully. Are you working on a goal that you believe is within God's will for your life? Who benefits the most? You or others? If there's any hint of selfish ambition in a task or goal that you think is God's will for your life, don't be surprised if you're having trouble getting it off the ground.

Let's briefly go back to NDEs to illustrate this point. In Dr. Kenneth Ring's book *Lessons from the Light*, we learn from a woman named Peggy:

> In examining the lives of the NDErs we have met in this chapter, do you not feel that all of them, to various degrees, have been aided to live more *authentic lives*, much more in keeping with their previously dormant gifts and propensities, and emboldened to throw off the social shackles, where necessary, that previously constrained them? The Light told Peggy, in effect, that she should "follow her love" and that yielding herself to it was, in fact, to do the most unselfish and constructive thing in the world. The Light seems to be telling us, each of us, that we have a unique gift, an offering to make to the world, and that our happiness and the world's happiness are both served when we live in such a way as to realize that gift, which is no less than our purpose in life.[84]

TBH. That's a Twitter term, if you aren't familiar with it. *To be honest*—that's exactly what we all should do. Live more authentic lives. Use dormant gifts and propensities. We should look for and remove whatever "social shackles" have constrained us and forced us to live out a false or inauthentic life.

The whole premise of this book is that we don't need to nearly die to accomplish that. We develop our gifts to bloom brightly in the garden, as Jesus told Howard Storm. We make our offering to the world for the benefit of others, not our own.

Jesus tells his disciples to *follow* him:

> If any of you wants to be my follower, you must turn from your selfish ways, take up your cross, and follow me. (Matthew 16:24 NLT)

I saw a bumper sticker the other day with this message: *Jesus said "Follow me."* This probably refers to when he was recruiting the disciples Peter and Andrew (Matthew 4:19). Later in Matthew, Jesus says that if anyone wants to be his follower, they first must deny themselves and turn from their selfish ways. So really, there are some prerequisites to following Jesus.

It's like in high school, when we take algebra before we get to calculus. Once we turn from our selfish ways, then we can pick up the cross. We pick up the cross and carry some of the burden with him if we're to partner with him. He promises to lighten our load, but we all have a load. It's always way better to follow and fail rather than fail to follow.

From your backpack for the journey, get rid of any selfish ambition. If you're going on a journey through the desert, bringing along a soft, cozy, comfortable recliner strapped to your back won't help you. Selfish ambition on a spiritual journey is worthless. We can follow him when we dump selfish ambition and pick up our load. The reason I emphasize this is that we should always check ourselves for selfish ambition, greed, envy, or pride whenever we're trying to be obedient.

Jesus knows our hearts better than we do. We can't hide pride, greed, or envy. We need purity of intent if we want to succeed in doing something valuable for the benefit of others or the kingdom.

I've heard it said that a preacher can preach sermons for forty years and be serving his own pride and ego the whole time. It's the kind of pride and ego the Pharisees had, and it's what Jesus despised. Look at the emotion in his words when he's criticizing the Pharisees.

God hates pride. Serving our own pride and selfish ambition will never unlock the power, grace, or guidance of God.

32 - Experience Joy and Peace

I want to point out a big truth that we see when Jesus is praying one of his last prayers in the garden of Gethsemane—before being crucified, when he knows he's going to die:

> I am coming to you now, but I say these things while I am still in the world, so that they may have the full measure of my joy within them. I have given them your word and the world has hated them, for they are not of the world any more than I am of the world. My prayer is not that you take them out of the world but that you protect them from the evil one. They are not of the world, even as I am not of it. Sanctify them by the truth; your word is truth. As you sent me into the world, I have sent them into the world. For them I sanctify myself, that they too may be truly sanctified. (John 17:13-19 NIV)

First, he says he wants "the full measure of my joy" to be within us. He's telling us all these things so that we may have joy and peace. He then says that we're not to be "of the world any more than I am of the world," so we're to shun worldly values or ideas. Remember that with faith, we value and believe what we *do*, not what we see. Love, kindness, goodness, and patience.

We see here also that Jesus is praying that we be "sanctified." That means being set apart or purified or made holy. Really, it means to become more like Jesus. That's the simplest way to explain or to manifest this process. We're to be like Jesus. That's it. But we can't become like Jesus without the truth, and without the Word.

Even more important is that salvation and truth are totally intertwined, as far as their value to us. John Piper sums it up like this:

> So since we are saved by grace through faith in the finished work of Jesus, not by our own works, this implies that taking truth seriously is inseparable from saving faith. *No love for truth, no saving faith.* Passing this passion on to the next generation is very important. Very important.[85]

Love for truth and saving faith are inextricable, linked, fused. *Inextricable* means "incapable of being untied or disentangled." No love for truth, no saving faith. It makes sense. Jesus already told us that he is truth. How can we expect salvation without love for Jesus?

That's a powerful idea that everyone should think about. It was the question I asked myself at the very beginning of my own journey: Do I love Jesus? I mean, like a spouse, child, parent or sibling. It goes back to that cafeteria-style way of going through life. We want to skip the salad and the vegetables, but we'll take the meat and the dessert.

Remember what Jesus says:

> I am the truth the way and the life. No one comes to the Father except through me. (John 14:6 NIV)

Further in his sermon, Piper makes another important point that's something I wish I'd known before, and have now come to realize about the experience of Jesus. The point is this: the experience of the Holy Spirit is real and valuable. Piper says,

> Our children do not need to be able to explain this when they're young. They need to *experience* this. We can't make them experience it, and we should not try to rush it or coerce it. It's a supernatural work of God. And without

it, the compliance of our children will prove fruitless in their adult years.

In my own life, it was about rules and regulations, and the Bible was only a book of rules and regulations.

All that wasn't true; it's all about a relationship with Jesus and an experience of Jesus. It's also about an experience with the Holy Spirit.

Let me tell you a story to illustrate. A few years ago, I was on a tour in Italy on a big bus with my family on the Amalfi Coast. It was a bright, sunny, beautiful day, and we were on a very narrow winding road that this bus could barely fit on. Our tour guide had a thick Italian accent, but I could still understand all the history he was giving us about ancient Rome and how the wealthy Romans would go and visit this coast on summer getaways.

We began to pull up to a small town where we were going to stop for about an hour and a half. So he told us about some of the things we could do in this town. He mentioned a church there that's about a thousand years old. My ears perked up a bit. I love old historic sites. I looked over at my wife and kind of lifted my eyebrows, like, "That sounds interesting."

The guide also mentioned places where we could get lunch or snacks, and then he said, "Oh, and the apostle Andrew is buried in a shrine at this old church." I said to myself, "Come again? The apostle Andrew is buried at this old church? The guy who hung around with Jesus for, like, three years?" For me, it doesn't get any better than that. Old historical church, plus one of the people who sat and ate and talked to Jesus being buried there—wow, I couldn't contain myself. I felt like a four-year-old going to Disneyland for the first time.

Remember that Andrew and Peter were brothers, and the first men chosen by Jesus to be apostles:

> One day as Jesus was walking along the shore of the Sea
> of Galilee, he saw two brothers—Simon, also called
> Peter, and Andrew—throwing a net into the water, for
> they fished for a living. Jesus called out to them, "Come,
> follow me, and I will show you how to fish for people!"
> And they left their nets at once and followed him.
> (Matthew 4:18-20 NLT)

I remember watching a television show on a sports channel
about New England Patriots owner Robert Kraft taking a group
of former NFL players to Jerusalem. Some of them had the
experience of being baptized in the River Jordan, just as Jesus was.
They commented that there was something different, unique, and
powerful about that experience.

I've also heard descriptions of special places on earth—like
Jerusalem, for instance—where there's a unique and unusual
spiritual presence or power. These special places are described as
being where heaven and earth seem to come together.

For me personally, I felt something unusual and unique being
in the shrine dedicated to the apostle Andrew. His remains are
buried under an altar at that shrine. That experience was a totally
unexpected gift. It was a spiritual high or triumph that I'd never
felt before. It had an effect that stayed with me. Something unique,
special, and powerful happened.

I'm not saying you must travel all over the world to experience
the Holy Spirit. You can have an intimate experience with Jesus at
your kitchen table praying and reading the Bible. I have. I'm just
sharing this story with you to illustrate the experience of Jesus and
the Holy Spirit.

In our own lives, seeking a relationship and seeking truth
should always come first. As John Piper mentioned, it's a
supernatural work of God, an experience that he allows.

In the same way, we should emphasize a relationship with Jesus and the truth of the Word to our children. Hopefully, God will grant some measure of experience. Something that's supernatural or spiritual. Kind of like the gift I received. (Now I want to go to Jerusalem.)

Everything *starts* at salvation. We accept Jesus, believe him, rely on him, and commit to him. One very important point is that as we grow closer to Jesus and our love for him grows, we begin to acquire discernment. Spiritual discernment is not only exciting, it's extremely important in our study of the Word. The Bible begins to come alive. You can read a verse one way for years, and then out of the blue you see it differently, and it becomes more clear.

It also helps when you're listening to pastors or reading spiritual books. You begin to see things more clearly and begin to be able to separate what is true from what is noise. This is so very important. You'll hear so many thoughts and ideas, and your own mind will be filled with waves of noise. We need to be able to hear the voice of Jesus in our own minds or speaking through other people. I pray that he's speaking to you through me.

You need to be able to tease out truth from lies. Especially if you actively spend time reading and learning spiritual truths. The world throws so much at us, and we should filter out the noise and listen for the whispers of Jesus. We have the Bible to use and test any message we're receiving. As we've mentioned, *God's will never contradicts God's Word.*

The Holy Spirit helps us with this. It takes time and effort to be able to filter out truth and discard garbage. Lies thrive in a world that devalues truth. They're everywhere. Also, there's so much willful deception. People know they're lying, and they justify it by saying they're just making a living. Some people think that lying is just a normal way to go about business. But Jesus said,

> For you are the children of your father the devil, and you love to do the evil things he does. He was a murderer from the beginning. He has always hated the truth, because there is no truth in him. When he lies, it is consistent with his character; for he is a liar and the father of lies. (John 8:44 NLT)

Satan is interested in two things: hate and lies. He loves it when we hate each other. He also spreads lies and deceit. The best deception that Satan ever pulled off is convincing so many people that he doesn't exist, and that there's no hell.

We fight Satan with love and truth. That's why they're so important. Remember that the laboratory of love and the classroom of love should be awash in love and truth.

Christians are accused of being exclusive. The view that our only path to God is through Jesus is not very popular in Western society. People have a view of pluralism. The world argues that there are many paths to God, that Christianity, Buddhism, Islam, Hinduism and more all lead to heaven. In pluralism, we all meet at the same point.

That's where we get to the crux of the matter. Isn't it interesting that the definition of the word *crux* is the most important or decisive point? Its origin is from the word *cross*. It tends to answer this whole issue. The whole point *is* the cross. You want truth. Look at the cross.

Today, tolerance is more important than truth. The world says we should accept that what's true for you may not be true for me, but they both work. But as Ravi Zacharias writes, "Truth by definition is exclusive. If truth were all-inclusive, nothing would be false."[86] The truth about truth is that by its very nature it excludes other ideas that don't jibe with reality.

In truth, Christianity is all-inclusive. Everyone is welcome. The Spirit is available to all. Jesus says,

> I have come to call not those who *think* they are righteous, but those who *know* they are sinners and need to repent. (Luke 5:32 NLT)

That's us, folks—sinners who need to repent. That's many, many people. Some people know that. Others *think* they're righteous. But no one is righteous.

We really should invest energy and effort in finding truth. Tolerance is important and essential for being able to put up with obnoxious and rude people. Jaw-droppers. But when it comes to truth, we should be determined and serious.

Jesus said, "I am the truth." We should start and end with him. Our eternity depends on it.

33 -PERSONAL HAPPINESS

s we're going along, you may be saying, "Yeah, yeah, this truth and knowledge thing is great and all, but I got my own problems right now. My marriage is in trouble. I'm unemployed. I just got diagnosed with cancer. I'm having a real tough time raising these teenagers. I don't have enough money to pay my bills. I'm in an abusive relationship. I'm in a depression that has lasted for years."

Where the heck do we start? With a list.

Here's a list of the top ten things people want more of (according to a survey of seven hundred people):[87]

1. happiness
2. money
3. freedom
4. peace
5. joy
6. balance
7. fulfillment
8. confidence
9. stability
10. passion

I bet your own top three are on this list.

This isn't a scientific study, but a survey. It's here to give us an idea of what people would like more of in their lives. If we closely scrutinize this list, it's clearly a list of *wants*. It clearly is a list of values, because why would you want *more* of something you don't value. Like pain.

It's not a list of needs. The essentials are water, shelter, food. If you watch any of those survival shows, they seem to always build a shelter first, then start looking for water. I like to watch those shows in case I accidentally get stranded in the Serengeti in my underwear with only a knife and some toothpicks.

It's not a bad thing to aspire to have more peace or joy. That's what this book is about. We need to understand that we don't want to transform our wants and turn them into needs: "If I get a higher paying job, I'll have more peace and happiness." Your disposition shouldn't be tied to a want.

Remember, we live in a world of lies. Everyone's selling something and trying to convince you that you'll be happy if you have it—drive a certain car, wear a certain dress, live in a certain part of town, own a certain size house.

It's interesting that there's only one thing on that top-ten list that you can measure: money. Jesus talked a lot about money. Sixteen of the thirty-eight parables were about money. It's a very good indicator of where we are in our spiritual growth and what we value in our own lives. Going over your bank statements over the past three to six months will give you a good indicator of what you value in your own life. Take out the monthly mortgage, car payments, food, and necessities, and see what you spend your discretionary money on. Actions don't lie. You want truth? There it is.

It goes back to the idea of choice. Where do we spend our *extra* time and money? What we see is that once the basics are taken care of, having more money doesn't contribute to a significant amount of happiness.

In their book *Happiness*, psychologists Ed Diener and Robert Biswas-Diener write,

It seems natural to assume that rich people will be happier than others, but money is only one part of psychological wealth, so the picture is complicated.... Rich people and nations are happier than their poor counterparts; don't let anyone tell you differently.[88]

What these authors are saying is that once shelter and basic needs are met, any extra disposable income doesn't contribute significantly to the feelings of well-being or happiness.

What's the real truth about money? One of the most important things I learned is that none of the money you have—not a cent—actually belongs to you. It belongs to God. He's just letting you borrow it for now.

How you use your money is a good indicator of your own spiritual journey. It's like a mile marker on a long walk or bike ride.

When you're responsible with money, that's when you get more. God knows he can trust you, and you won't waste it. Remember the parable of the talents? God knows your heart better than you do.

Don't get me wrong, we all have our bills to pay, but as you grow in your relationship with Jesus, you'll find yourself not wanting to spend your discretionary income on things that have no value. Jesus says we should spend our money on bringing others to the knowledge of the truth:

Here's the lesson: Use your worldly resources to benefit others and make friends. Then, when your earthly possessions are gone, they will welcome you to an eternal home. (Luke 16:9 NLT)

If we use our gifts, talents, and treasure wisely, God will give us more. Seems to me that we should be spending time, energy, and effort figuring out what he wants us to do with the treasure, talent, and abilities we already have. We spend so much time, effort, and energy on getting more, we're ignoring what we already have.

Remember, it's the little things in this life that matter. A kind word or small gesture of love or patience. Don't be discouraged if you're offering only small amounts to help the poor or others who are less fortunate than you. What matters is the love given with the offering.

> Jesus sat down near the collection box in the Temple and watched as the crowds dropped in their money. Many rich people put in large amounts. Then a poor widow came and dropped in two small coins. Jesus called his disciples to him and said, "I tell you the truth, this poor widow has given more than all the others who are making contributions. For they gave a tiny part of their surplus, but she, poor as she is, has given everything she had to live on." (Mark 12:41-44 NLT)

We should focus on using the gifts that we already have. God takes care of the "giving more" department. He has total control over how much money he allows every one of us to have. He uses it to test us and to test our faith.

When you value Jesus, and he becomes the true value in your life, money works *for* you. Trust me, I've seen it. It's the basic principle of reaping and sowing. It's been around for two thousand years:

> Remember this: Whoever sows sparingly will also reap sparingly, and whoever sows generously will also reap generously. (2 Corinthians 9:6 ESV).

Want more money? *Give* more away to those who truly need it. Remember what Prince said: "Money is best spent on those who need it most." Be generous. God wants us to be generous because he is generous.

We're to be generous with true spiritual riches also. Be generous with love, kindness, and patience. Give more love, receive more. Show more kindness and patience, receive more.

The only thing we truly get to keep are the things we give away to others. You begin to value love, joy, peace, and kindness. True spiritual riches. You begin to live above worldly concerns. Sure, you have to pay your mortgage or rent or whatever. We all should pay our bills. But as we grow closer to our authentic selves, we spend less and less time thinking about money. Money just isn't that important.

In their book *Your Money or Your Life*, authors Vicki Robin and Joe Dominguez[89] describe a fulfillment curve: once you get beyond basic needs and to a certain level of spending, there's a peak of fulfillment; once you get to overspending, fulfillment drops. Extra wealth seems to have a negative effect on our fulfillment.

In *Your Money: The Missing Manual*, J. D. Roth writes,

> Psychologists call this vicious cycle the hedonic treadmill, though you probably know it as the "rat race." People on the hedonic treadmill think they'd be happy if they just had a little more money. But when they get more money, they discover something else they want. Because they're never content with what they have, they can never have enough.[90]

Remember, on a treadmill you aren't going anywhere.

I heard a comment the other day from an athlete who was being compared to another athlete, and he said, "I have what he will never have. Enough." I know exactly what he's talking about. It's the idea of being satisfied. Being fulfilled with what you have at this current moment. It lends itself to two things in life. Peace and joy. Yes, there are friends and colleagues of mine who have bigger homes or nicer cars, or who go on more expensive vacations, but I'm happy with where I am at this moment in all those areas.

Most Americans are stuck on this treadmill. J. D. Roth writes further,

> According to the U.S. Census Bureau, in 1967 the median American household income was $38,771 (adjusted for inflation). Back then, less than one-fifth of U.S. families had color TVs and only one in twenty-five had cable. Compare that with 2007, when the median household income was $50,233 and nearly everyone had a widescreen color TV and cable. Americans now own twice as many cars as they did in 1967, and we have computers, iPods, and cellphones. Life is good, right? But despite our increased incomes and material wealth, we're no happier than we were in the 60s.[91]

Does that sound like you?

People get a small high from buying something new. A sense of happiness or fulfillment. The problem is, it's only temporary. Once they get it, they move on to something else. How do we get off this fast-moving, hedonic treadmill? By recognizing the truth. Change the way you think about "stuff."

If we look again at that top-ten list of wants, there seems to be a relationship and interaction between many of these values. Money, happiness, freedom, fulfillment, stability, and maybe even confidence. I'm not saying that money gives everyone more happiness, freedom, or fulfillment, but these values and their interaction probably deserve some study. I mean, that's five out of the top ten. Doesn't that make sense?

So where do we go? If we're trying to see with the eyes of Christ, we go to the source. Jesus says,

You are truly my disciples if you remain faithful to my teachings. And you will know the truth, and the truth will set you free. (John 8:32 NLT)

Freedom. When we jump off that hedonic treadmill, Jesus will be there to catch us. Then we'll be truly free.

What about happiness? This one is very subjective. What's a useful definition of happiness that applies to everyone? Is there such a thing as a happiness set-point?

A study published in the *Journal of Personality and Social Psychology*[92] found that people who had won the lottery were not much happier than everyone else. They also found that people who'd endured devastating injuries such as paralysis were not as unhappy as the researchers had expected. Their conclusion was that there's a happiness set-point. We get a little bump in happiness, then we come back to our set-point. We get a little down or depressed based on circumstances at work or home, then we come back to our set-point.

There's some research to indicate that certain events in life have an impact on our ability to feel happy. The death of a child or repeating bouts of unemployment tend to lower the happiness set-point.[93] The interesting thing here is that there's also other research that indicates our own ability to increase our happiness set-point. The German Socio-Economic Panel is a survey of approximately eleven thousand private households in Germany from 1984 to 2015. This survey has the most data on happiness and satisfaction in the world. Studies using data from this survey indicate that the one thing associated with life satisfaction and long-term happiness was a commitment to and pursuit of altruistic goals. Helping others.

In another study,[94] Sonja Lyubomirsky and other researchers found that simple acts of kindness toward other people increased a person's happiness. We're hard-wired to help others. You want to be happy? Help other people. You want satisfaction in your life? Commit to helping others. Want to get closer to your authentic self? Serve others.

We should look at how God wants us to use our gifts and talents in helping others. Sounds like we're hard-wired to get fulfillment and good positive feelings of joy and peace by helping other people within the framework of who we were created to be. Our authentic selves. Our pursuit of God's truth and knowledge brings confidence, freedom, peace, and stability.

If we think about passion, that's something innate within us. Do we really need more passion? Have you discovered the passion that lies deep in your own true, authentic self? Do you know what you're passionate about? We already have the passion within us that's God-given; we should discover and uncover it.

Let's revise that list of what people want—or what *you* want. Try adding these items to it:

- coming to the knowledge of truth through Jesus
- obedience (critical for access to God's power)
- learning to value spiritual riches rather than worldly values
- love (wow, isn't that the most valuable?)
- faith (the most valuable of all besides love)
- more opportunities to help others with our gifts and talents

Don't forget simple acts of kindness. Try an experiment. Be kind to one person every day. If you think something nice about someone at the grocery store, or at work, or at a restaurant, just give the compliment. This is especially powerful in the classroom of love.

In the movie *The Shack*, one of the characters says, "A simple act of kindness can change the world." What if that's true? You want to change the world? Remember the drop of water in the ocean? If it's missing, the ocean is different. It's not the size of the act that matters, it's the amount of love that goes into the act.

Remember also that people who undergo NDEs always comment about being shocked when they undergo their "life review," and they're shown small acts of kindness and love they showed to others. To the NDEr, those acts at the time seemed insignificant, and they totally forgot about them. In actuality, those are the acts deemed most important and significant. Those were the kinds of actions that were stressed, and that's how we're to love and care for one another. The little things are most important. Jesus said, "and if you give even a cup of cold water to one of the least of my followers, you will surely be rewarded." (Matthew 10:42 NLT)

Be kind to one person every day. Family, friend, or stranger. Give a compliment. Most of the time people respond: "Thanks, you just made my day!" And what did it cost you? Nothing. Talk about easy! There it is. Very little time energy or effort required. It's just as easy to give a compliment as it is to give a criticism. The difference is that you get the satisfaction of making others feel a little better about themselves. Plus, you're better because you're becoming more selfless. When you give, you deny yourself. Giving includes a compliment. And most importantly for all of us, by giving you've made the world a better place. So make it a habit, and I guarantee that you'll have more happiness and satisfaction in your life. You may also get closer to your authentic self.

This may be a good time to honestly examine ourselves if we have a difficult time giving someone else a compliment. Do we tend to be critical, especially around our families? Are you one of those hypercritical people? Those attitudes totally wreck and destroy the laboratory or classroom of love.

We're to encourage and lift up each other. The concept of doing something positive for each other or for one another is mentioned fifty-nine times in the New Testament.[95] Stop and think about that. How many times does it need to be mentioned before we truly understand that this approach to life is important? That's an important question. Help, encourage, pray for, care for, love, and lift up one another. That's the job of each of the family members in the classroom of love.

A psychologist at the *Psychology Today* website writes this:

> As Oscar Wilde put it, "Criticism is the only reliable form of autobiography." It tells you more about the psychology of the criticizer than the people he or she criticizes. Astute professionals can formulate a viable diagnostic hypothesis just from hearing someone criticize.

> Criticism is the first of John Gottman's famous Four Horsemen of the Apocalypse, which predict divorce with more than 90% accuracy. In my clinical experience it is the most predictive of disaster in love relationships, as the other three tend to follow from it—stonewalling, defensive, and contemptuous partners almost invariably feel criticized.[96]

Look, if we're to learn how to love, and if we value our closest relationships, we must come to understand that being hypercritical is poison to a loving relationship. Remember, it says more about the person who's constantly criticizing others than about whoever's being criticized. It's always easier to point out other people's flaws than our own. It's uncomfortable to look at ourselves honestly. This point is important, because we're here to learn how to love. Being overly critical with our children, spouse, or significant other is a sure way to destroy or hurt relationships, rather than strengthening or improving them. Be on the lookout for criticism.

There'll be skeptics and critics who'll say, "Are you sure that serving others will really make me happy?" The data is there. It's looking right at you. Jesus said it two thousand years ago:

> For even the Son of Man came not to be served, but to serve, and to give his life as a ransom for many. (Mark 10:45 ESV)

He's saying to us, "Look guys, I'm the Son of Man, and even I am serving others. You need to also."

We know about service and happiness. We know that being on the "hedonic treadmill" doesn't improve our happiness.

There's also something else that has a major impact on happiness, peace, and joy. It's gratitude. The attitude of gratitude. Marriages where husbands or wives express gratitude to each other are more satisfying. This comes down to discipline in our thinking. We tend to point out flaws or faults in our spouses more readily than appreciate the good qualities. It's the hypercritical response: "Let me help you by pointing out what's wrong with your behavior."

It's much more helpful to look at ourselves and see where we can improve. Especially if you're a "glass half empty" type of person. If you're constantly looking at what's wrong with a spouse or child, it gives you a negative mindset. It creates a negative atmosphere in the household.

Discipline your mind and thoughts to appreciate the positive. It's way easier to be a critic and point out flaws, but everyone has positive attributes. Find them—in your spouse and children, in your friends and family—and point them out. Tell them you're grateful for them and appreciate them and love them. Your feelings will change.

Dr. Sarah Algoe writes,

> Feelings of gratitude and generosity are helpful in solidifying our relationships with people we care about, and benefit the one giving as well as the one on the receiving end.[97]

Notice that this also benefits the one who's showing or expressing the gratitude. Our feelings of gratitude are beneficial to *us*. If we start the day with prayer and being grateful for all the blessings we've received, our day begins the exact right way.

That's why the cross is so important. It reminds us of the cost of our salvation, and it tills the soil of our minds and our hearts to be generous with gratitude and compliments. It's free and easy.

Yes, that's another thing that's easy. Remember the others: sin, being a critic, and using the gift or talent you were born or blessed with. It's also easy to express gratitude. Not only that, it doesn't cost you a penny.

If you have a hard time being grateful or giving compliments, you need to be honest with yourself. There may be some things you're carrying around in that backpack of yours that are hindering your own growth and ability to reach your authentic self.

We should be developing our self-esteem as we're seeing with the "eyes of Christ." We're valuable, lovable, acceptable, and forgivable.

We should all give compliments. Tell your family that you appreciate and value them. It will make them feel better about themselves, and you'll feel better. Why wouldn't you? You married a wonderful person. You have the gift of a unique and beautiful child. You were given great parents.

Now here come the critics and naysayers: "Well that sounds all squishy and sweet and all, but you don't know *my* spouse, *my* children, *my* mother or father." True. There's always a Debbie Downer, isn't there? But do you think it's possible that any of those representative members of my own family are perfect? How about highly unlikely or impossible?

And what about me? Far from perfect. WIP, work in progress. Long way to go.

If you've been following along through all this, you know and remember what we've been talking about. No one's perfect. That doesn't mean we shouldn't be grateful and appreciate our family members. They're a gift from God, and we should always remember that. Everyone knows it's impossible for any of those people in your family or my family to be perfect. They all have flaws, and we could spend days pointing them out.

But how much value is there in pointing out flaws in others? Our time would be better spent in looking at how to improve ourselves. When we focus on the positive and appreciate each other, we lift each other up. Remember those fifty-nine "one anothers" in the New Testament. Encourage one another. Love one another. Support one another. Pray for each other. Forgive one another. These aren't written in there as filler to take up space. They're mentioned for a reason, and we should all take them seriously.

Stop and think: what if just twenty percent more of the population started doing that on a regular basis?

> For God chose to save us through our Lord Jesus Christ, not to pour out his anger on us. Christ died for us so that, whether we are dead or alive when he returns, we can live with him forever. So encourage each other and build each other up, just as you are already doing. (1 Thessalonians 5:9-11 NLT)

That's our responsibility as members of the lab or classroom of love.

I remember telling a friend to give compliments to everyone and be kind and grateful. He said, "What if they don't deserve it?" There's that *deserve* idea again. Who gets to decide what anyone "deserves"? You? Me?

I've said this before, and I'll say it again: love is not a feeling. Love is giving someone what they need most when they deserve it least. That's the kind of love Jesus gave every one of us. We're not in the judging business with the power to decide who "deserves" anything. No one gave anyone that job title.

Notice Paul's phrase in that last quoted passage: "just as you are already doing." We're the role models, and we're to model that behavior. That's what Jesus had in mind. How have you been doing so far?

When we talk about joining a small group, the whole idea is to pick each other up and encourage and support each other. That's our responsibility. It's on us. The truth is that you're already part of a small group: your own built-in family. The laboratory of love. The classroom of love.

34 - THE POWER AND PEACE OF GRATITUDE

W hen we express our thanks and gratitude to Jesus our Savior, it makes him feel good. We never go wrong in doing that. Never. We show our appreciation for what he has done for us. We owe him everything. He owes us nothing.

I want to point out a verse that kind of got my attention when I read it, because it sounds kind of rough:

> Will any one of you who has a servant plowing or keeping sheep say to him when he has come in from the field, "Come at once and recline at table"? Will he not rather say to him, "Prepare supper for me, and dress properly, and serve me while I eat and drink, and afterward you will eat and drink"? Does he thank the servant because he did what was commanded? So you also, when you have done all that you were commanded, say, "We are unworthy servants; we have only done what was our duty." (Luke 17:7 ESV)

This verse is pointing out that no matter what we do for the kingdom of God, and no matter what we do for Jesus, he never owes us anything. He has already given us everything, and there's nothing we can do to make things "even." There's no "Okay, now we're even." Christ paid a debt he didn't owe because we owe a debt that we'll never be able to pay.

When you or I do something for someone else, we might expect something in return. That's like looking for fairness. "Fair is a place where they judge pigs," says sports commentator Stephen A. Smith; "don't go looking for fair." He's right, because if you spend your time looking for what's fair, you'll be

360

disappointed. Especially in marriage and family life. If you're looking to keep score, you already lost.

We "deserve" nothing, if you think about it.

We know that in general, people who have a sense of gratitude are much happier. The recognition of our blessings every day is a great starting point for each day. This is a basic spiritual principle that we really need to understand and wrap our heads around. Gratitude versus entitlement.

A sense of entitlement for the wealthy or the poor is a bad idea. The "I deserve it" thought or focus in our lives most often leads us to dangerous areas. Usually sin. It's wrapped in pride and selfishness. Neither is great for our spiritual growth. When we focus on our self and the things we "deserve," it often leads to trouble. To be a follower of Jesus, the first step is to "deny" the self.

> Then Jesus told his disciples, "If anyone wants to follow me, he must deny himself, pick up his cross, and follow me continuously." (Matthew 16:24 ISV)

I like this version because of the word *continuously*. This is a continuous process. Deny the self *daily*. Follow Jesus *daily*. Express gratitude *daily*. The verse about the master and servant kind of always bothered me a little. For four or five days, it stuck in my mind. It always seemed a little cold or distant. Then I was shown something else so that I could see things a little more clearly. How did that happen? Revelation. It's what we've been talking about:

> Those who accept my commandments and obey them are the ones who love me. And because they love me, my Father will love them. And I will love them and reveal myself to each of them. (John 14:21 NLT)

Here's the message he revealed to me:

> I no longer call you servants, because a servant does not know his master's business. Instead, I have called you friends, for everything that I learned from my Father I have made known to you. (John 15:15 NIV)

We *know* the master's business. We're in the love business. Business should be booming. Jesus reveals things to us when we have a personal relationship with him. He has made known to us everything he learned from the Father. It's all there in the Word. We're in the family business, but unlike Michael Corleone in *The Godfather*, this is personal *and* it's business.

As we learn the truth about happiness and satisfaction, we discover that things which are simple and free are what make us most satisfied and fulfilled.

In his book *100 Simple Secrets of the Best Half of Life*, David Niven writes, "People who could identify a goal they were pursuing were nineteen percent more likely to feel satisfied with their lives and twenty-six percent more likely to feel positive about themselves."[98]

This is what I call the bumping along factor. If you're living with no set goals, you're just bumping along or coasting. It's the zombie "walking dead"—no direction, groaning and muttering walk. There's no driving force or engine trying to get you anywhere, because you have no idea where you're going. Your boat is kind of tied to the pier.

Life gets more interesting and exciting when we set out to sea. It's scary, but you can't get to a nice island if you stay tied to a pier.

It's also especially helpful for teenagers and young people. If they're goal-oriented, they aren't as likely to get distracted by behavior that hinders them, such as drug use, alcohol, or risky sexual behavior. They're too busy trying to reach their goal.

If you look around at friends and family, it's not very difficult to find people bumping along. But resist the urge to start criticizing people for having no goals. That leads to pride. Just make a mental note.

It's possible to turn it into a lesson for your children. You can say: "You know kids, I wonder just how happy Aunt Penelope is. She goes to work driving that taxi in the morning and working at that video store in the afternoon. She seems obsessed with Uber and Netflix and the impact they'll have on her two jobs. She comes home and watches reality shows on television until she falls asleep on her couch next to her empty twelve-pack of Keystone Light. It doesn't seem like she has any direction in her life." You can gently point out that maybe if she were involved with some group or other activity that involved people, she might be more fulfilled.

If you can look at your own life with the eyes of Christ, you can figure out if you're a coaster or a climber. We talked about the balloon ride and how we're climbing up the rungs of the ladder. I understand this one because I was bumping along myself. Just getting up, going to work, getting in a routine, with no real goal. Coasting. I can tell you this: climbing is way more interesting. It's more difficult and more challenging, but the reward, my own personal growth in Christ, is priceless. It's exciting. There are failures and disappointments, but there are triumphs and spiritual revelations that are extraordinary. Absolutely mesmerizing.

Remember what Jesus said about a "rich and satisfying life"? He wasn't kidding.

We each have a purpose. God has a plan for our lives. He has a dream for our lives. Whatever you can come up with, more than likely his dream is bigger and better than what you can think up on your own. Discovering and fully realizing our authentic selves is exciting and worthwhile. There's value in discovering and pursuing your own purpose. Find your passion and your purpose. You won't regret it.

Here we go with another digression. It's another list, a list of our responsibilities. Sometimes it's helpful to stop and think about it. We really are responsible for some very important tasks. Whose responsibility is it to point out our responsibilities? The church? What if you don't even go to church? We each have a part to play in the song.

1. It's our responsibility to know and understand the breadth, width, depth, and vastness of the love that God and Jesus have for us. Just because it's beyond our comprehension doesn't give us a pass.

> And may you have the power to understand, as all God's people should, how wide, how long, how high, and how deep his love is. May you experience the love of Christ, though it is too great to understand fully. Then you will be made complete with all the fullness of life and power that comes from God. (Ephesians 3:18-19 NLT)

Notice the benefit of understanding this love. We'll be made complete with the fullness of life and power. Our authentic selves perhaps? Power comes from the experience of the love of Jesus.

2. Your salvation is your responsibility. Your eternity is your responsibility. No one's going to work those out for you.

> For no one can lay any foundation other than the one already laid, which is Jesus Christ. If anyone builds on this foundation using gold, silver, costly stones, wood, hay or straw, their work will be shown for what it is, because the Day will bring it to light. It will be revealed with fire, and the fire will test the quality of each person's work. If what has been built survives, the builder will receive a reward. If it is burned up, the builder will suffer

loss but yet will be saved—even though only as one escaping through the flames. (1 Corinthians 3:11-15 NIV)

We've spent plenty of time on the idea of relying on and committing to Jesus. This is about eternal rewards and what we build on the foundation, which is Jesus. Our salvation and our rewards are our responsibility, but we have total power to choose what we do with that responsibility. We can build or bounce off the pinball machine bumpers. It's our choice to either ride the wave or bounce off the bumper. We can climb the ladder of love, or we can cave in to the allure and deceit of earthly goals.

3. Discovering our God-given passions, talents, and gifts is our responsibility. It's on us to find these gifts and use them in a way that's consistent with our authentic selves. The self that God had in mind when he created us.

God saved you by his grace when you believed. And you can't take credit for this; it is a gift from God. Salvation is not a reward for the good things we have done, so none of us can boast about it. For we are God's masterpiece. He has created us anew in Christ Jesus, so we can do the good things he planned for us long ago. (Ephesians 2:8-10 NLT)

Even if we came to Christ only recently, we're already created anew. Discovering our passions and talents—and then using them to do the good things God planned for us a long time ago—is our responsibility.

4. The classroom and laboratory of love is our responsibility. We're held responsible to love and guide our families to be more loving and giving. You may be the father, mother, or even a sibling or child in the family. If you're the only one who understands this responsibility, you must lead.

If I speak in the tongues of men or of angels, but do not have love, I am only a resounding gong or a clanging cymbal. If I have the gift of prophecy and can fathom all mysteries and all knowledge, and if I have a faith that can move mountains, but do not have love, I am nothing. If I give all I possess to the poor and give over my body to hardship that I may boast, but do not have love, I gain nothing. (1 Corinthians 13:1-3 NIV)

We can have faith, knowledge, wisdom, and good works, but without love, they mean nothing. We're responsible to learn how to love in the laboratory of love, and to teach those closest to us the same thing.

Once we understand our individual responsibilities, we can understand the truth about our part in all this. We now know that we're responsible, but it's also important to understand that we're response-*able*: we're able to respond to this truth. There must be *action*. Bearing fruit is an action. Discovering and fully realizing our authentic selves will require time, effort, hard work, and discipline.

That was a long digression. Back to happiness.

One last but very important principle for happiness is that you need friends. Remember Aunt Penelope? A study done looking at on-line versus real live friends yielded these results:

First, the number of real-life friends is positively correlated with subjective well-being even after controlling for income, demographic variables and personality differences. Doubling the number of friends in real life has an equivalent effect on well-being as a fifty percent increase in income. Second, the size of on-line networks is largely uncorrelated with subjective well-being. Third, we find that real-life friends are much more important for people who are single, divorced, separated or widowed than they are for people who are married or living with a partner.[99]

This makes a lot of sense. Again, we learn from Jesus's teachings and behavior. He was always around people.

> As Jesus went on from there, he saw a man named Matthew sitting at the tax collector's booth. "Follow me," he told him, and Matthew got up and followed him. While Jesus was having dinner at Matthew's house, many tax collectors and sinners came and ate with him and his disciples. When the Pharisees saw this, they asked his disciples, "Why does your teacher eat with tax collectors and sinners?" On hearing this, Jesus said, "It is not the healthy who need a doctor, but the sick. But go and learn what this means: 'I desire mercy, not sacrifice.' For I have not come to call the righteous, but sinners." (Matthew 9:9-13 NIV)

There's much to be learned from this verse. First, Jesus was always around people. All kinds of people. He healed them, taught them, and ate with them. That's what we're supposed to do. This one is a little tough for me personally because I'm not Mr. Social. Jesus says that's irrelevant. His two big commandments are love God and love others. You can't love others if you don't want to be around people.

It took me about a year to join a Bible study small group. It was very tough that first day walking into a room with a group of men I didn't know and sitting down. But Jesus isn't interested in our own personal little anxieties and hang-ups. He said, "Sorry dude, you have no excuse and no options. You want to get closer to me, you must join a small group. End of story." That went on for about a year. I'm glad I did.

Jesus wants us to grow together. We're to help each other in our spiritual growth. We're to support each other. We're to share our experiences, pain, and suffering as well as our triumphs and victories.

The second thing to learn from the verse above is that Jesus came for *all* sinners. We all have sinned. No one's perfect. He came for everyone. That voice in your head says, "Your sins are different; there's no way he can forgive you." But that voice is lying. He came for you too.

What's true about peace? Well, the following passage says that the peace we get from a relationship with Jesus surpasses all understanding:

> Let your reasonableness be known to everyone. The Lord is at hand; do not be anxious about anything, but in everything by prayer and supplication with thanksgiving let your requests be made known to God. And the peace of God, which surpasses all understanding, will guard your hearts and your minds in Christ Jesus. (Philippians 4:5-7 ESV)

That always grabbed me. *Beyond our understanding.* Notice that we give thanks before we let our requests be known. Gratitude first.

Peace is still one of my goals. This is the peace of knowing and loving Jesus. It truly does surpass all understanding. The Eagles wrote a song called "Peaceful Easy Feeling." Peace isn't easy. Peace isn't free. In that verse from Philippians, Paul says we're not to be anxious about anything. Easier said than done. There's an environment of anxiety and stress in the world all around us.

Let me give you a typical conversation at work that happens so often it's mind boggling. It usually starts by my saying, "Well, Mr. Thomas, we've received all your results, including the CT scans and all the blood work. Everything looks really good. I'm not sure why you're having the dizziness and the tingling-all-over feeling, but it looks like there's nothing dangerous going on here." The patient looks down and seems disappointed. Slowly he looks up and asks—wait for it— "Doc, do you think it could be stress?"

Boom. There it is. Stress and anxiety.

> More than one in five American adults took medications for psychiatric disorders such as anxiety and depression in 2010, according to new research by Medco Health Solutions, Inc. Titled America's State of Mind, the report released this November by the pharmacy benefit manager was based on its prescription medication database of 2.5 million insured Americans.[100]

What these trends do not reveal is that those are the people who went to a doctor and got a prescription. Think about the number of people who didn't go see a physician, but instead have a few glasses of wine in the evening or a six pack of beer to "take the edge off."

As I've mentioned, my own journey started with frustration and anxiety. We all have stress. What's important to emphasize is that there are ways to deal with stress that are healthy and useful. There are ways to deal with our anxiety that help us grow to become better parents, wives, husbands, or children. If we can learn to depend and trust in Jesus, this helps us deal with the daily stress that we all have. When we can model a more peaceful and gentle approach to stress in our own families, the whole family benefits. There's no doubt that there's more peace when we get closer to Jesus.

> Therefore, I tell you, do not worry about your life, what you will eat or drink; or about your body, what you will wear. Is not life more than food, and the body more than clothes? Look at the birds of the air; they do not sow or reap or store away in barns, and yet your heavenly Father

feeds them. Are you not much more valuable than they? Can any one of you by worrying add a single hour to your life? And why do you worry about clothes? See how the flowers of the field grow. They do not labor or spin. Yet I tell you that not even Solomon in all his splendor was dressed like one of these. If that is how God clothes the grass of the field, which is here today and tomorrow is thrown into the fire, will he not much more clothe you—you of little faith? So do not worry, saying, 'What shall we eat?' or 'What shall we drink?' or 'What shall we wear?' For the pagans run after all these things, and your heavenly Father knows that you need them. But seek first his kingdom and his righteousness, and all these things will be given to you as well. Therefore, do not worry about tomorrow, for tomorrow will worry about itself. Each day has enough trouble of its own. (Matthew 6:25-34 NIV)

Look closely at how Jesus tells us how to solve this problem of worry and anxiety. "Seek first his kingdom." What is the kingdom of God? It's his reign, his governance, and his sovereignty. *Sovereignty* means ruling without any other influence. The kingdom is wherever God is king. It's the earth, heaven, the universe. Everything. God is sovereign. He controls everything. When people ask about tragedies and suffering, those are things he allows. We don't understand the whys or the how. That's his business. This is the beginning of learning how to deal with stress and worry.

Notice that Jesus mentions the birds of the air, and how God cares for them, and then says plainly, "Are you not much more valuable than they?" He says it in a way that reminds me of the guy behind the counter at a New York deli with a Brooklyn accent: "What are you, stupid or what?"

Here's where faith comes in, and belief. Jesus is telling us that God cares. He cares about every one of us. When we worry and are anxious, we're telling Jesus, "I don't believe you." One of the consistent things I've heard from multiple pastors and authors is that the surest sign of a lack of faith is one thing only: worry. Hey, it's still a struggle for me.

The surest way to relieve stress and anxiety is to get closer to Jesus. He's the Prince of Peace. Remember, I was looking for a new fuel pump, but I got the fully loaded Benz. Believing, understanding, and having faith that God is sovereign and in control of *everything* brings peace. It makes the waves, storms, and revolving door of Goliaths bearable.

We know we can win because we're precious and valuable to him:

> And we know that in all things God works for the good of those who love him, who have been called according to his purpose. (Romans 8:28 NIV)

When our focus is on loving him, having faith, obeying him, and seeking the purpose and plan that *he* has for us, things change. We taste peace.

Acquiring faith, confidence, peace, and joy is a process. We learn them by going through storms, waves, unexpected bumps, and difficult circumstances. We learn real love by showing love to the seemingly unlovable. The jaw-droppers come to mind. We learn peace in the midst of trials and storms. *Un*peaceful situations. Those storms are going to come whether we're growing in the Lord or not. They'll come whether we're rich or poor, employed or retired, walking like a zombie or pursuing goals. The difference is that if we learn to trust Jesus when the wave is coming, and we trust in his love, he'll take us on the ride of our lives, and we'll end up closer to who we were created to be—our authentic self.

He wants us to depend on him. Run to him in our times of trouble. Lean on him. When we step onto the water like Peter, we keep our eyes on Jesus. Then when he gets us through a tough time and gives us insight and understanding of the why and the how, we acquire peace.

> Peace I leave with you; My peace I give to you; not as the world gives do I give to you. Do not let your heart be troubled, nor let it be fearful. (John 14:27-28 NASB)

That's a promise. Notice, though, that we can't get peace when we look to what "the world" gives. If we keep focusing on the lower rungs of that ladder of love, we just keep bumping into cactus. That's looking for what the world gives. Pursuing worldly goals brings stress, worry, and anxiety. If you're spending time, effort, and energy on worldly goals or what the world thinks is important, you don't need to look for stress, worry, and anxiety, they *will find you.*

Jesus is talking about a higher level of love, understanding, and purpose. This is where we're closer to reaching and realizing our authentic selves. The self that we were created to be is where that peace lives.

I've gotten closer to that peace. It's available to everyone.

35 - CONFIDENTLY FACING GOLIATH

There are battles and waves that we've already survived that we can learn from. We can think about times when God bailed us out of some tough situation. We won that battle. We can begin to think like David when he was facing Goliath:

> "Your servant has struck down both lions and bears, and this uncircumcised Philistine shall be like one of them, for he has defied the armies of the living God." And David said, "The LORD who delivered me from the paw of the lion and from the paw of the bear will deliver me from the hand of this Philistine." And Saul said to David, "Go, and the LORD be with you!" (1 Samuel 17:36-37 ESV)

We've all faced our Goliaths. The key for David was remembering how he'd killed the lion and the bear with the help of the Lord.

Stop and think right now. How many jams have you gotten through? Can you stop and see how the Lord worked in your life? As you grow spiritually, you begin to see circumstances where you were rescued, but at the time you didn't even realize it.

Everyone has had battles with lions and bears and we came out winning. Dorothy did, in *The Wizard of Oz*: "Lions and tigers and bears, oh, my!" She was afraid of a lion, but the Cowardly Lion became her ally to help defeat the Wicked Witch.

Some of those lions we're afraid of or that we defeated can become our allies if we can remember that we won the battle. Sure, we've all had our defeats, but there are victories in our lives also. Stop and take a moment to think about it. Pray about it. God will show you how he rescued you. You can go ahead and thank him now. There were probably dangers you were protected from that you weren't even aware of.

We'll face a revolving door of Goliaths. Sometimes they get bigger and bigger. But we have victories in our past that remind us that God is with us. He's all-powerful, and he's for us. We're never alone.

Some of these waves and Goliaths are of our own creation. These include self-destructive behaviors. Habits and actions that hurt us and those around us. You may want to look in that backpack and see if there are habits like excessive alcohol, drug addiction, or pornography. Things like gossip, laziness, pride, lust, overeating, and not taking care of our bodies. These are of the flesh, the opposite of the spirit.

> But, I say, walk by the Spirit, and you will not gratify the desires of the flesh. For the desires of the flesh are against the Spirit, and the desires of the Spirit are against the flesh, for these are opposed to each other, to keep you from doing the things you want to do. But if you are led by the Spirit, you are not under the law. Now the works of the flesh are evident: sexual immorality, impurity, sensuality, idolatry, sorcery, enmity, strife, jealousy, fits of anger, rivalries, dissensions, divisions, envy, drunkenness, orgies, and things like these. (Galatians 5:16-21 ESV)

These are all extra burdens that we carry with us. They all tend to interfere with our relationships. You may be walking around with a backpack full of huge Goliaths on this journey. It's hard to get very far walking around with three Shaquille O'Neals on your back. I mention alcohol and drug addiction, pride, laziness, anger, lust and sexual immorality specifically because they're the biggest problems we face in our own relationships, and they're the most common.

This is where brutal honesty with ourselves is critical. If we can't be honest with ourselves, nothing will improve, and we can't get closer to our authentic selves. If we value our relationships with our families and with Jesus, we should look at these habits. These habits interfere with our relationship with Jesus, so they interfere with our love, joy, and peace. These habits can destroy our relationships with our spouse, children, parents, siblings, and friends.

It's like being in a small pleasure boat with your family out in the ocean. Suddenly you take out a hand-operated drill and start drilling in the bottom of the boat. Water starts coming in. Your family screams, "Hey, Dad! What are you doing?" Your response: "Oh, don't mind me, this is no big deal. Relax and enjoy the beautiful view."

That was me. Drilling holes in the bottom of the boat. You may have some habits that cause you to drill holes in your family boat. Criticism, unkind remarks, sarcasm, or any of the habits mentioned above. Things change when we begin to value Jesus and our relationship with him. When he reveals more and more of himself, and we experience true intimacy with him, those self-destructive habits become less important. They become less important when we realize that our relationships are the most valuable things we have. But those destructive habits move us away from our authentic selves and our families. The laboratory or classroom of love. When we value our families, we do what we can to get rid of those destructive habits. I'm not a big Tony Robbins disciple, but what he says about change is true: "Change happens when the pain of staying the same is greater than the pain of change."

If you're in pain at this very moment, there's hope. If you can begin to see the value of learning to love Jesus, things will change for the better.

The thing that's different and most important is that with Jesus, the pain of change brings love, joy, peace, kindness, self-discipline, and eternal salvation. Plus, the ability to fully realize who you were created to be, your authentic self. There's discomfort or pain, because we get comfortable in our self-destructive habits. Sometimes they're difficult to break because those patterns of behavior have been around for years. But the payoff is beyond anything you've experienced without him. The payoff is beyond what anyone or anything can give you. Only Jesus can. I've experienced it. The great restaurant with the great food.

Remember the classroom of love, the laboratory of love, involving the relationships closest to us. Self-destructive habits can be difficult to kill, but if we succeed, who benefits the most? We do and the people we love the most do. Everyone wins.

Self-destructive habits hinder the true expression of our authentic selves because we can't reflect the love of Jesus. We were all created to reflect his overwhelming love. We're like mirrors. When we engage in selfish, prideful, relationship-killing behavior, the mirror gets caked with mud.

When an engagement ring gets cleaned by a jeweler, it sparkles and shines more brilliantly. We're all like diamonds that sparkle and give light. We can't sparkle when we're engaging in self-destructive habits that hinder our authenticity and our capacity to love others. Some of those habits have been nurtured and supported for decades, so they're big bears or lions.

But we know we're not alone in the battle:

> Teach these new disciples to obey all the commands I have given you. And be sure of this: I am with you always, even to the end of the age. (Matthew 28:20 NLT)

He's commanding us to "be sure of this." We've defeated the lion and the bear. He was with us then, he's with us now, and he'll be with us the next time Goliath walks through that revolving door.

We don't have a right to know and understand everything. God's ways and his plan aren't always clear to us. Sometimes things happen that we don't understand and we get frustrated. The best attitude is accepting that he'll share his plan when he's good and ready.

I remember a time when I was in a crisis getting a business off the ground, and I called my mom. It was like I was a twelve-year-old boy again with the whining and complaining: "Mom, I'm not sure this thing is going to work. We still don't have enough cash flow to cover our overhead, and this isn't looking good. I'm really scared we're going to have to borrow more money." Mom listened, and her only response was to quote our heavenly Father's words: "Be still, and know that I am God" (Psalm 46:10).

Sometimes we should just be still and trust in his love. God can do anything. That doesn't mean *I* can do anything. If I have a strong desire to be an opera singer, but no talent for singing, then it just ain't happening. God can and will do anything that's consistent with his will and plan for our lives. We have access to his power when our goals bring us closer to our authentic selves while reflecting the love of Jesus.

The one critical point or idea to remember is that it's *his* plan for us that he'll support, not our plan. Sometimes he has every intention of giving us what we want, but he's waiting for us to be more mature or to reach a higher level of spiritual understanding. He's waiting until we're ready. We think he's denying our prayer; in reality, he's waiting for us to grow up. Maturity is one of his desires for us.

One crystal clear sign of maturity is thinking of others before we think of ourselves. Another is seeing *everyone* the way Jesus sees them. Lovable, valuable, forgivable, acceptable. Everyone.

One of the things I notice about unbelievers is they always ask the same question: "If God is so loving, and he loves us, how does he allow suffering and pain in the world?" If you listen closely, there's always, without question, a tinge of anger in their voice or their demeanor. Always. The Bible doesn't have any verses that promise understanding of everything as it occurs. Remember Proverbs 3:5:

> Trust in the Lord with all your heart; lean not on your own understanding.

We're to seek understanding. It takes some work. We must drill for it. Sometimes God makes us wait for it. My favorite definition of wisdom is that it's thinking the way God thinks. Another good one: wisdom is the combination of knowledge and obedience. You don't become wise until you act on what you know. You work at it. There's no instant wisdom or instant understanding. God says,

> Call to me and I will answer you and tell you great and unsearchable things you do not know. (Jeremiah 33:3)

We don't get understanding by sitting on the couch watching football, eating chips, and having a beer. I've tried that route to understanding. It doesn't work. No revelations for me sitting on the couch.

Many times, the most significant revelations come through pain. From braving the wave, turning to face the shore, and anticipating the ride. If we can learn to trust and turn, that brings joy and peace.

God speaks to us through his Word, through circumstances, and through gifted teachers who really touch our hearts. He uses people around us like our family. We should be willing to listen for his voice. One thing I've noticed, as I get closer to Jesus, is the ability to see the hand of God in everyday circumstances. That's the point. He's everywhere *all* the time. He's easier to perceive when we have our eyes, ears, and hearts open to him.

In the parable of the sower (Matthew 13:3-23), Jesus explains what happens to the Word when we're consumed with the worries of this life.

> The seed falling among the thorns refers to someone who hears the word, but the worries of this life and the deceitfulness of wealth choke the word, making it unfruitful. But the seed falling on good soil refers to someone who hears the word and understands it. This is the one who produces a crop, yielding a hundred, sixty or thirty times what was sown.

Life is coming at us very fast. Work, bills, kids, soccer, baseball, dance recitals, piano lessons. The worries of this life. We can't ignore them, right? One solution is to compartmentalize them.

Develop the habit of a quiet time. Early morning or late at night when everyone's asleep. You and Jesus. No interruptions, no cell phones, no laptops, no social media. In the Word and in prayer. We talked about destructive habits and how they interfere with our ability to reflect light. Quiet time in the Word and prayer are good spiritual habits that are allies in our battle against that revolving door of Goliaths. Those habits reinforce our faith and give us the ability to trust and turn, to brave the wave. A quiet time shines up the mirror and takes off some of that mud so we can reflect the love of Jesus. These spiritual habits give us confidence and direction. These habits help in discovering and fully realizing our authentic selves. Life-changing.

Full understanding of everything in our lives isn't something we deserve. We've gone over the danger of entitlement. You may be saying, "Yeah, yeah you mentioned that already." Yes, but it's important because the attitude of entitlement is the opposite of humility and gratitude. It's pride, it's selfishness, and it lends itself to being ungrateful. Huge inhibitors to authenticity. We're not entitled to anything. Anything we have is a gift from God that we don't deserve. Intellectual entitlement is the attitude that we have a "right" to know and understand *everything*. It's prideful and arrogant.

Do you let your children in on your important business decisions? Do we let our teenage daughter in on our biggest financial decisions? Why would we? She doesn't need to know. Likewise, God doesn't owe us an explanation for how or why he does things. We're to have faith and trust in him. He's all-knowing; we aren't. As he tells us through Isaiah the prophet:

> "For My thoughts are not your thoughts, nor are your ways My ways," says the Lord. "For as the heavens are higher than the earth, so are My ways higher than your ways, and my thoughts than your thoughts." (Isaiah 55:8-9 GNT).

He knows what's best for us, even when we don't understand it. He'll reveal secrets to us personally when he knows we're taking our spiritual growth seriously. That's the basis of faith. But—there's always a but—the more time you spend with Jesus and reading the Word, the more things you'll see. The more time you spend developing the habit of faith and obedience, the more he'll reveal himself to you. You'll experience the presence of Jesus and the Holy Spirit. Everything will begin to make more sense to you.

In my own life, I notice that the time gets shorter and shorter between when a circumstance occurs and when I gain understanding of it. We know and understand that any time, money, or effort expended to further the gospel and bring others to Jesus and all that he offers is never wasted. Never. But any effort for the kingdom of God done in partnership with Jesus is an honor and a privilege. Jesus says,

> You do not realize now what I am doing, but later you will understand. (John 13:7 NIV)

There's always a light at the end of the tunnel with Jesus. Always. If you stop and think about events in your own life and begin to see with the "eyes of Christ," you can start to slowly see the hand of God in your own life. He bailed you out of some situation somewhere.

As I've mentioned, there were at least three episodes where I could have easily been killed. No question about it. There are probably things that happened where he protected me and I wasn't even aware of the danger. Why was I protected or saved? Because he had a plan for me. He knows the plan, and he could see I was going to come back home again. He already knew it. He allowed me to stumble, fall, skin my knee, knock out a few teeth and slam my head on the pavement. Sometimes he allows things to happen to kind of shake us up a bit.

You get to a point in your life when you see the benefits and you become grateful for your pain. Usually that's where the real growth happens and the real diamond gets revealed. Remember, a diamond isn't formed until it's exposed to tremendous pressure. The diamond is Jesus and our relationship to him. But our lives begin to sparkle and shine when we allow his love and light into our hearts.

The hard part in all this is that once we begin to grow our faith and try to pursue our purpose or try to share our faith, we should be prepared for rejection, criticism, and mocking. The Christian life is a tough gig. Not only should we not judge or criticize, but once we pursue our purpose and live the life God had in mind, that's when we'll be rejected, criticized, and ridiculed. Hey, don't start a pity party. We're in good company. Jesus was rejected and did nothing but heal the sick and feed the hungry. They crucified him. The apostles and all the great Christians of the past were rejected and criticized, and many were martyred for their faith.

This is where we begin to look at ourselves regarding the opinions of other people. This is a major idea that we should begin to evaluate in ourselves. Everyone's different when it comes to processing what other people think about us as individuals. Some of us couldn't care less about what other people think or say about us. I'm probably a little too far in this camp, as my wife and kids will attest to. Some of us are marginally affected by the opinion of other people. Some people are living in an environment that's limited or constrained by thoughts about what other people will think or say about them. We've already talked about the "social shackles" that interfere with our fully realizing our authentic selves. I'll admit I get passionate about this one, because I see family and friends all around me who are engrossed and controlled by the opinions of people around them. It's frustrating to me because I can see the power this has over people, and that's not what God had in mind for us. This is the epitome of living a lie. It's living within the framework of a false or inauthentic self.

> For we speak as messengers approved by God to be entrusted with the Good News. Our purpose is to please God, not people. He alone examines the motives of our hearts. (1 Thessalonians 2:4 NLT)

That's a good summation of what our lives should be focused on. We live to please an audience of one.

We've already talked about what we believe about ourselves. We can't trust the negative things people say about us, because humans are human, and we all say stupid things and do stupid things. We all do. So why are we so worried about the opinions of humans?

Now of course there are exceptions. If you're in prison wrongly accused of murder and you've hired a good lawyer, his opinion on how to proceed is important. If you're having chest pain and the heart surgeon says you need an operation because you have an aneurysm and you'll die if you don't have the procedure, that's different. In these cases, we defer to experience. Experience matters.

Be honest with yourself. How many times have you said to yourself, "How could I have been so stupid?" Or this one: "How could I have done something so stupid?" You can rest assured, everyone has asked that about themselves. People who say they haven't, are lying. We can also be sure that Jesus has never said that. His opinion is probably the most important.

The smartest thing we can do is to seek the opinion of Jesus. Make that idea sticky. We already know what he thinks about us and how he sees us. We're valuable and acceptable. Lovable and forgivable. It's the truth, so we believe.

When we begin to think and see like Jesus, then we get something that we all need. Wisdom.

> Jesus said to his disciples, "Would anyone light a lamp and then put it under a basket or under a bed? Of course not! A lamp is placed on a stand, where its light will shine. For everything that is hidden will eventually be brought into the open, and every secret will be brought to light. Anyone with ears to hear should listen and understand." Then he added, "Pay close attention to what you hear. The closer you listen, the more understanding you will be given—and you will receive even more. To those who listen to my teaching, more understanding will be given. But for those who are not listening, even what little understanding they have will be taken away from them." (Mark 4:21-25 NLT)

EPILOGUE

My first instinct when I was writing this book was to use a pen name. One reason was because I work in the medical field. If you work in that area, you know that faith and medicine are not bosom buddies. Another reason was because my family wasn't interested in people asking if their husband/dad wrote a book. The one thing that I read about when it came to Christian readers is they need to be able to trust the author. Connect. How can they connect with someone using a pen name? When it comes to critiques about what I am writing about, I am prepared. "I wrote about what I was inspired or compelled to write about. Period." Well now I am compelled to use my real name. That makes me a little uncomfortable. That is how I know that the spiritual prompting is real and valid. It makes sense. We all need to connect. Honestly, for this first book, I want to focus on the message and take the focus off the messenger. "I'm a finger pointing at the moon. Don't look at me, look at the moon." No one's sure where this comes from, but you get the point. Jesus is the moon.

As I was writing this book, early every morning before touching a key on my laptop, I read the Bible, prayed, meditated, and asked for guidance. These were the main points of emphasis that I was consistently inspired to write about. There were many, but these were the most consistent. Time for one last list:

- We should all endeavor to understand and experience the vastness and indescribable nature of the love of God and Jesus for every one of us.

- Jesus yearns and aches for us to come to him and get to know him. Our past and the amount and perceived nature of our sins is irrelevant to him.

- People aren't worthless or without hope. We all have value. Anger or bitterness never leave space for the love of Jesus.

- We should allow for imperfections in the church. They're institutions run by people.

- Everything begins in the classroom of love. The family. All those relationships are easier when we allow people, especially those close to us, to be imperfect.

We're all in this thing together. We're to help, encourage, and pick each other up. We start with our families and those closest to us. We all need each other, and when we act to help and love each other in meaningful ways, this makes Jesus smile.

I know I need help with this book. If you were moved or inspired by this book and it helped to open your eyes, please share. Share with those closest to you. My whole motivation to write it, honestly, was that I felt that many years of insight, learning, and experience would be wasted if I didn't share it. I truly believe it could have a major impact on every one of your relationships for the better.

I've finished my second book on passion, power and purpose. My third book deals with pain and the role it plays in our lives and in our growth, a huge topic. Those are the second and third books in the Authentic Self series. They are both in the editing process. By the grace of God, there'll be an interest.

I also hope and pray that some of these ideas and stories had an impact on your heart. Maybe they opened the eyes of your heart. It will all be worth it if others begin to see more love, joy, peace, gentleness, patience, and kindness in your interactions and relationships. Keep looking for your authentic self.

CONNECT

Life is about relationships. Life is about connecting with others. The New Testament uses the phrase "each other" or "one another" fifty-nine times. I know that I have been repeatedly emphasizing my lack of expertise on biblical doctrine and theology, but there are some things that I am definitely an expert on. I know this because I have been called as an expert witness in jury trials. So, there must be something to this. I have been thinking about what I can give or offer of value that would be useful or practical. Well, practicing medicine for thirty years does brings a few valuable nuggets of useful or practical knowledge when it comes to health. I hope to write on those subjects in the future. From a personal or selfish standpoint, most of my interest with regard to health involves exercise physiology, weight loss, and nutrition. The book is coming. Right now though, I want to get this book out and finish up the book on passion, power and energy, and my third book on the role of pain in our growth. I hope that people will find the ideas and stories in my upcoming books to be entertaining, thought provoking and helpful.

I have put together a pdf file to download and it's an article on the most important physical symptoms (head to toe) that should prompt you to make an appointment with your doctor. I have included a link below so that you can download it. This will also take you to my website and my blog which will hopefully add some useful information about my upcoming books. I have about ninety blog posts that are waiting to be posted on many and varied topics. I will also post articles on recent topics in health care that people are interested in on my blog. If you have any suggestions, by all means, please share. I would love to hear them. As I mentioned, I'm most interested in exercise physiology and nutrition, so there will be a smattering of those types of articles.

I want to thank you personally for downloading/buying this book. I hope you visit the website and I look forward to connecting with you. www.bravethewave.org

We all have a choice. We can choose to brave the wave and ride, or we can do everything in our power to avoid stressful or uncomfortable situations. We hide. I say,

WE RIDE!

Brave the Wave

With Love,

Johnny Cavazos MD

bravethewaveweride@gmail.com

NOTES

1 https://www.cbsnew.com/news/survey- more-americans-unhappy-at-work/.

2 Raymond Moody, *Life After Life*, special ed. (San Francisco: HarperOne, 2015), 54-55.

3 Moody, *Life After Life,* 57.

4 Kenneth Ring, *Lessons from the Light* (Needham, MA: Moment Point Press, 2006), 50.

5 Howard Storm, *My Descent into Death: My Second Chance at Life* (New York: Doubleday, 2005).

6 https://religionnews.com/2013/04/04poll- Americans-love-the-Bible-but-don't-read-it-Much.

7 Greg Behrendt and Liz Tuccillo, *He's Just Not That Into You* (New York: Simon & Schuster, 2009), 94.

8 Ring, *Lessons from the Light*, 18.

9 Matthew Kelly, *Rediscover Jesus: An Invitation* (New York: Beacon, 2015), 28.

10 https://www.thebalance.com/most-powerful-words-in-advertising-38708.

11 https://www.cnsnews.com/blog/michael-w-chapman/alice-cooper-christian-world-belongs-satan

12 [http://purposedriven.com/day29/]

13 Ring, *Lessons from the Light*, 187.

14 Ring, *Lessons from the Light*, 188.

15 Ring, *Lessons from the Light*, 46.

16 https://www.nderf.org/Experiences/1jim_f_nde.html.

17 https://www.nderf.org/Experiences/1darlene_k_nde.html.

18 Moody, *Life after Life*, 56.

19 Moody, *Life after Life*, 88.

20 C. S. Lewis, *Mere Christianity*, revised ed. (San Francisco: HarperOne, 2015), 55.

21 http://www.georgewashington.org/death.jsp.

22 https://sites.fas.harvard.edu/~hpcws/asreview.htm.

[23] Ring, *Lessons from the Light*, 56.

[24] Ring, *Lessons from the Light*, 61.

[25] Ring, *Lessons from the Light*, 62.

[26] Ring, *Lessons from the Light*, 173.

[27] http://www.phatmass.com/phorum/topic/118767-what39s-the-church39s-position/.

[28] https://www.baylor.edu/mediacommunications/news.php?action=story&story=145864.

[29] https://www.thoughtco.com/what-is-a-talent-700699.

[30] Moody, *Life after Life*, 59.

[31] Moody, *Life after Life*, 75.

[32] https://www.youtube.com/watch?v=RwOWYtXKV6g&t=168s.

[33] Ring, *Lessons from the Light*, 50.

[34] Ring, *Lessons from the Light*, 50.

[35] Ring, *Lessons from the Light*, 54.

[36] John Burke, *Imagine Heaven: Near-Death Experiences, God's Promises, and the Exhilarating Future That Awaits You* (Grand Rapids: Baker, 2015), 241.

[37] Burke, *Imagine Heaven*, 251.

[38] Gary Habermas and Michael R. Licona, *The Case for the Resurrection of Jesus* (Grand Rapids: Kregel, 2004).

[39] "How (and Why) Athletes Go Broke" in *Sports Illustrated*, March 23, 2009.

[40] Moody, *Life after Life*, 50.

[41] https://www.payscale.com/career-news/2014/01/5-reasons-people-hate-their-jobs.

[42] http://religion.blogs.cnn.com/2011/03/20/finding-faith-amid-disaster/.

[43] http://www.independent.co.uk/news/people/stephen-fry-explains-what-he-would-say-if-he-was-confronted-by-god-10015360.html.

[44] Moody, *Life after Life*, 46-47.

[45] https://www.desiringgod.org/messages/do-not-love-the-world.

[46] Jeffrey Long, *Evidence of the Afterlife: The Science of Near-Death Experiences*, reprint ed. (San Francisco: HarperOne, 2011), 61.

[47] Long, *Evidence of the Afterlife*, 77.

48 Long, *Evidence of the Afterlife*, 16.

49 http://www.pewforum.org/2015/11/03/u-s-public-becoming-less-religious/.

50 http://www.pewresearch.org/fact-tank/2016/08/24/why-americas-nones-left-religion behind/.

51 Lee Strobel, *The Case for Christ,* updated and expanded ed. (Grand Rapids: Zondervan, 2016).

52 Storm, *My Descent into Death*, 73.

53 http://www.pewresearch.org/fact-tank/2016/08/24/why-americas-nones-left-religion-behind/.

54 http://www.newsweek.com/newsweek-poll-90-believe-god-97611.

55 https://www.desiringgod.org/messages/what-does-it-mean-to-receive-the-holy-spirit.

56 https://www.stevenaitchison.co.uk/7-ways-to-be-more-spiritual-without-being-religious/.

57 Robert Kiyosaki, *Rich Dad, Poor Dad*, updated ed. (New York: Warner, 2017).

58 https://www.socialmediatoday.com/marketing/how-much-time-do-people-spend-social-Media-info graphic.

59 Matthew Kelly, *Resisting Happiness*, second ed. (New York: Beacon, 2016).

60 Mark Batterson, *Chase the Lion* (Colorado Springs: Multnomah, 2016), 127.

61 Stephen King, *On Writing* (New York: Scribner, 2010).

62 https://www.accordancebible.com/A-Do-Not-Be-Afraid-For-Every-Day-Of-The-Year.

63 Matthew Kelly, *The Rhythm of Life* (New York: Beacon, 2015).

64 Ilya Pozin, "The Secret to Happiness? Spend Money on Experiences, Not Things"; https://www.forbes.com/sites/ilyapozin/2016/03/03/the-secret-to-happiness-spend-money-on-experiences-not-things/#53d33f3a39a6.

65 Ring, *Lessons from the Light*, 156.

66 *Imagine Heaven*, 245.

67 Moody, *Life after Life*, 57.

68 http://www.kansascity.com/living/religion/article18756585.html.

69 http://www.gospeloutreach.net/613laws.html.

⁷⁰ https://www.becomingminimalist.com/8-essentials-for-a-successful-marriage/.

⁷¹ Storm, *My Descent into Death*, 33,35.

⁷² Long, *Evidence of the Afterlife*, 176.

⁷³ Ring, *Lessons from the Light*, 213.

⁷⁴ Ring, *Lessons from the Light*, 124-125.

⁷⁵ Ring, *Lessons from the Light*, 157.

⁷⁶ Long, *Evidence from the Afterlife*, 177.

⁷⁷ http://www.independent.co.uk/arts-entertainment/books/news/maos-great-leap-forward-killed-45-million-in-four-years- 2081630.html.

⁷⁸ Mary Neal, *To Heaven and Back* (Colorado Springs: WaterBrook, 2012).

⁷⁹ Long, *Evidence of the Afterlife*, 104.

⁸⁰ https://www.dailykos.com/stories/2015/1/12/1357344/-Empty-Churches-Go-On-Sale-in-Europe-as-Christian-Faith-Declines.

⁸¹ https://www.theatlantic.com/science/archive/2017/03/this-article-wont-change-your-Mind/519093/.

⁸² https://www.youtube.com/watch?v=VWvS1UfXl8k&t=16s.

⁸³ Storm, *My Descent into Death*, 27.

⁸⁴ Ring, *Lessons from the Light*, 50-51.

⁸⁵ https://www.desiringgod.org/messages/the-sum-of-your-word-is-truth.

⁸⁶ Ravi Zacharias, in his introduction to the updated edition of Walter Martin's *The Kingdom of the Cults* (Bloomington, MN: Bethany, 2003), 10.

⁸⁷ https://www.huffingtonpost.com/kathy-caprino/the-top-10-thingspeopl_2_b_9564982.html.

⁸⁸ Ed Diener and Robert Biswas-Diener, *Happiness* (Malden, MA: Blackwell, 2008), from chapter 6, "Can Money Buy Happiness?"

⁸⁹ Vicki Robin and Joe Dominguez, *Your Money or Your Life,* revised edition (New York: Penguin, 2008).

⁹⁰ J. D. Roth, *Your Money: The Missing Manual* (Sebastopol, CA: O'Reilly Media, 2011), 11.

⁹¹ Roth, *Your Money*, 11.

⁹² *Journal of Personality and Social Psychology* (vol. 35, no. 8), 917-927.

⁹³ *Social Indicators Research,* (vol. 97, issue 1, May 2010), 7-21.

[94] *Review of General Psychology* (vol. 9, no. 2, 2005), 111–131.

[95]

storage.cloversites.com/wakarusamissionarychurch/…/59one_another_s criptures.pdf.

[96] Steven Stosney, PhD, "One Thing That Will Ruin a Perfectly Good Relationship," *Psychology Today,* https://www.psychologytoday.com/ca/blog/anger-in-the-age-entitlement/201212/one-thing-will-ruin-perfectly-good-relationship.

[97] S. B. Algoe, S. L. Gable, and N. C. Maisel, "It's the little things: Everyday gratitude as a booster shot for romantic relationships," *Personal Relationships,* (2010), vol 17:217-233.

[98] David Niven, *One Hundred Simple Secrets of the Best Half of Life* (San Francisco: HarperOne, 2005), 176.

[99] J. F. Helliwell and H. Huang, "Comparing the Happiness Effects of Real and On-Line Friends," PLOS ONE, September 3, 2013 (8(9): e72754); https://doi.org/10.1371/journal.pone.0072754.

[100] https://www.anxiety.org/antianxiety-medication-use-soars-in-past-decade.

Made in the USA
Columbia, SC
08 November 2019